The Exceptional Teacher

Transforming Traditional Teaching Through Thoughtful Practice

Elizabeth Aaronsohn

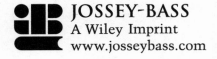

JOSSEY-BASS
A Wiley Imprint
www.josseybass.com

Published by Jossey-Bass
A Wiley Imprint
989 Market Street, San Francisco, CA 94103-1741   www.josseybass.com

Jossey-Bass books and products are available through most bookstores. To contact Jossey-Bass directly
call our Customer Care Department within the U.S. at 800-956-7739, outside the U.S. at 317-572-3986
or fax 317-572-4002.

Jossey-Bass also publishes its books in a variety of electronic formats. Some content that appears in
print may not be available in electronic books.

Library of Congress Cataloging-in-Publication Data
Aaronsohn, Elizabeth.
  The exceptional teacher : transforming traditional teaching through
thoughtful practice / by Elizabeth Aaronsohn.— 1st ed.
      p. cm.
Includes bibliographical references and index.
  ISBN 0-7879-6576-6 (alk. paper)
  1. Teachers—Training of—Curricula—United States. 2. Effective
teaching—United States. I. Title.
  LB1715.A26   2002
  370'.71—dc21   2003011732

Printed in the United States of America
FIRST EDITION
HB Printing   10 9 8 7 6 5 4 3 2 1

Contents

Preface

Balancing the Tension Between Contradictory Roles

This book is about the work of preparing people to become teachers. Its central themes have been shaped primarily by my own experiences as a public school teacher and as a public university teacher educator. It starts with the understanding that the process of teaching, at any level—pre-school through teacher education—is not nearly as simple or effortless as preservice and beginning teachers often assume, given their years of learning about teaching as if by osmosis—by watching their own teachers. Some fundamental complexities are not immediately obvious, and must be carefully exposed and examined.

As challenging as teaching is on every level and for every subject matter, the teaching of teachers involves some extra dimensions. Because the task of teacher educators is not just to help students grasp certain content and skills, but also to consider the youngsters that, as graduates, they will teach, teacher educators must model, and present as an on-going theme for reflection, the kind of teaching they hope their students will consciously choose to employ in their own teaching. And even more vital in the teacher education process than in other kinds of teaching is the need to balance the natural tension all teachers experience between two contradictory roles: *gatekeeping*, and its opposite, *non-judgmental nurturing*.

In the nurturing role, a teacher's responsibility is to treat each student as a whole person: to start with each student wherever he or she is, and support his or her growth over time, respectful of the student's intelligences, interests, cultures, and ways of seeing. On the other hand, as conflicting it may be for our nurturing side, teachers must decide, ultimately, whether a student is ready to move on in his or her schooling. As agonizing as that task is each year for all caring teachers, teacher educators must be especially attentive gatekeepers. We have the obligation to do our best to make sure the incoming generations of teachers are not only the most knowledgeable, skillful practitioners, but also the most reflective, imaginative, courageous, multidimensional, flexible, and fully actualized adults, worthy of having children's minds, bodies, and spirits entrusted to them.

Although the varied methods I have come up with for balancing the tension between the two seemingly contradictory goals—1) non-judgmental nurturing and 2) gatekeeping—do not always work, they often do. When they do, along with a growing repertoire of practical skills, preservice and inservice teachers achieve a greater self-awareness, which they incorporate as a habit of honest reflection on their own attitudes, thinking and practice. And when the efforts that this book describes are most successful, students achieve a more informed, generous worldview through the regular practice of assuming the perspective of another person.

Student writing has been central to reflection about a range of carefully designed activities and readings. The intersection between my two goals as a teacher educator—1) helping students in my classes grow from within as they confront the complex functions and contexts of teaching, and 2) my commitment to the generation-or-so of children they will teach—seems to be located primarily (though by no means exclusively) in that student writing. When the method works, students, reflecting on their own experiences in terms of alternatives they had not previously considered, can begin to see and decide for themselves what they need to do, in order to become the kinds of teachers they often wish they themselves had had. And although I insist on never giving up on anyone, this body of writing enables me, at the end, to form essential gatekeeping decisions, but always with an important caveat: I have learned never to presume to predict for sure how a person would perform as a teacher solely from how he or she operates in a university classroom.

For example, straight A university students—even those who read and write perceptively, and who reflect deeply and honestly on their own schooling—may turn out not to have (or at least not yet to have) the basic ability to see the world through another's eyes. That ability, I believe, is absolutely necessary, since they will have to deal with the full range of learners in their classrooms. Or a student who performs well in a teacher education class may submit without question to the "institutional realities" of traditional school cultures. One semester as a student of teacher education is not enough for a student to undo a lifetime of habits, and to gather the courage and maturity required to focus on the children rather than on his or her own performance.

On the other hand, I have also worked with university students who couldn't manage to do all the homework for a teacher education class, but who then showed up the next semester at a public school every day at 7 A.M., full of purpose and energy, and taught with incredible knowledge, skill, inventiveness, joyfulness, responsibility, and caring. Given that unpredictabilty, I have to trust what I know from my own experience: teaching is a relationship with students. Only the persons engaged in it can create and maintain that relationship. That is why it is so important that teachers know themselves.

When I interviewed in 1991 for the job I now hold at Central Connecticut State University, a member of the search committee asked me what I considered to be the knowledge base for an elementary school teacher. What did I think they need to know? My reply included the beliefs I had come to champion regarding both constructivist teaching and the contexts of schooling. But most important, I said, "they need to know themselves." I continue to believe that, but not just for elementary school teachers: I believe all teachers, including teacher educators, need regularly to examine and reflect on their own early formative and therefore deeply embedded experiences, in order to make conscious, thoughtful, unencumbered choices.

Although we can have students read about, practice, and consider certain research-based theories, and although we can try to expose them to and guide them through worlds outside of the ones they have always known, what teachers ultimately become involves a life-long growth process that is only begun in teacher education classes. Certainly, the path from excellent teacher education to excellent teaching is not linear, nor guaranteed; induction-year teachers rapidly become socialized into the often traditional cultures of schools, especially since the pressures to teach in these traditional ways are as much internal as external (Aaronsohn, 1996).

In this book I contend, therefore, that if teacher education students do not get an opportunity, within their certification courses, to unearth, examine, and reflect on certain assumptions embedded within themselves, and if we don't help them understand the power of school as a social context, there is a high probability that they will be swallowed up by environments which they will easily recognize from their own schooling. Then they might assume that all sorts of familiar but damaging circumstances are the natural "givens" of teaching and learning. Our task as teacher educators is to help our students discover positive alternatives for what it means to teach, and to nurture the development of their insight, and their courage, to choose for themselves.

Introduction

What's to Learn?

As a teacher/educator whose teaching career has now spanned more than forty years, I have often heard practicing teachers say, "Why bother with teacher education courses at all? Why not just send preteachers to us and let us train them here, in the trenches? After all, the university is fantasyland. *This* is the real world." A compelling argument. What *can* prospective teachers learn from books and class discussions that they cannot learn better on the job, in the company of a school full of veteran teachers?

My response to that challenge is complex. First, learning to teach is not all or nothing in either place—the university or the communities in which preteachers will be working. Teacher preparation needs to occur in both places. Preteachers must spend plenty of time and energy observing, reflecting, and then practicing on-site in schools. In fact, their teachers, too—the teacher educators themselves—need to continue to spend a great deal of time in K–12 classrooms, observing and reflecting, learning and teaching. But even that is not enough.

Frequently, preteachers looking at those early field experiences—as well as at the coursework, student teaching, and standardized qualifying exams—consider them to be a set of hurdles to jump over in a race to certification. Another way to look at the process of becoming a teacher, however, is the one this book presents, which is: How shall we prepare prospective teachers not just for obtaining a teaching job but for teaching well, day by day, so that children learn well and joyfully, for many satisfying years?

As the Preface suggests, many studies, disturbing to those of us who hope for significant change in teaching and schools, have indicated that, in general, the effect of teacher education courses is washed away within the first two weeks of a new teacher's teaching in a traditional school situation.[1] Regardless of teacher educators' efforts, most new teachers conform with astonishing rapidity to a K–12 school's "institutional realities." What they observe, are told, and are praised for in such settings tends to reinforce their own deeply socialized inclinations, the result of their years as students within structures, roles, expectations, and routines that replicate those of the traditional schools most preteachers attended (Aaronsohn, 1996; Zeichner, 1980; Koskoff, personal conversation, July 2001). Unless something dramatically transformative happens to challenge all our assumptions about teaching and learning, we tend to teach as we were taught.

For people who believe in traditional schooling, that may be fine. They would say, "Traditional teaching worked for us; it is what children need. Let's train new teachers to be excellent at it, and if that's all we want, let's do away with teacher education. All we really need is apprenticeship in schools." But I am assuming that people interested in the title of this book have already decided that something is not just fine about what Paulo Freire (1968) called "banking education," what one of my secondary education students called "plug and chug," and what a colleague of mine describes as "here's my brain, just fill it up and let me know when you're done" (LeGrow, personal communication, September 2001).

Goal: Examining Assumptions for a New Consciousness

If people who become teachers are to operate in their classrooms in ways that are significantly different from how they remember their own teachers doing it, they also need a frame of reference beyond the automatic one of memories of their own schooling. The overwhelming reality about teaching is that those internalized memories seem to be the primary resource upon which most teachers and professors draw for their own teaching (Zeichner, 1980).

One of the most obvious effects of the *plug and chug* method is that the facts students think they have learned are not really available for them to apply to real situations. One small experiment that I have conducted as part of my own teaching at the university illustrates this. All of my students in a first course in our elementary teacher education program have had to pass and even do well in a developmental or child psychology course as a prerequisite to being admitted to the program. Early in my semester with them, I assign a two-minute in-class freewrite on the following question, which we then discuss: imagine that Piaget walks into a second grade classroom. He sees the children sitting quietly in rows, with pencils and worksheets, doing math problems. What would he say? If even half or a third of the students can apply to this question their memorized "knowledge" about Piaget's stages of development, I feel elated, though troubled, because even those who don't have a clue about Piaget's view of that situation claim to have gotten A's in their psychology courses. So what is—or is not—going on in those courses—and in *our* courses? What *should* we teach, and how, so that people about to be teachers can have a real *working understanding* of developmentally appropriate practice, and can, in each unique situation they face, try to think their way through the connections between theory and application?

My experiences have allowed me to understand the extent to which teachers are inclined to replicate their own schooling. Accordingly, my goal has been to develop some methods for helping them overcome the "instincts" embedded in them by their sixteen years or more of schooling. Preteachers need the perspective of a larger, deeper context if they are to look honestly and critically at those previous experiences, and understand what it means that they have been shaped by them.

Why Does It Matter?

This book attempts to show that habits developed within the structures and assumptions of traditional schooling result in certain long-range outcomes that affect everyday adult thinking and operating. From my perspective, the result is troubling not only for our daily lives and relationships but also for our democracy. I have basically identified those outcomes in the following categories:

- Orientation toward dualistic (all or nothing, right or wrong, good or bad, one-right-answer thinking, with no real capacity for problem solving
- The assumption that text equals truth and that learning equals memorizing

- The inability to connect fragments of information into meaningful concepts
- No habit of searching for or understanding context
- No capacity for distinguishing what is important from what is minor
- The tendency to operate in terms of the lowest levels of moral development: fear of punishment or expectation of reward
- Difficulty in collaborating, turning all peer relationships into rivalries or conquests
- Dependency and powerlessness

If these are outcomes that we would not choose to create, as I strongly believe they are, what can bring about a shift in assumptions about what teaching and learning can be, and need to be? And what can sustain that shift, even within prevailing cultures of schooling? First, the school people's argument makes sense in this regard: the shift cannot happen if theory is taught in a way that is totally separate from practice. If university courses are only abstract theory, it is not at all surprising that the coursework part of the preparation might feel unrelated to the "real world" of actual children and teachers involved in the dailiness of classrooms in public schools.

Still, a crucial component can get lost, even when a thoughtful series of early field experiences is built into a teacher education program. What needs to be uncovered in teacher education courses is a whole range of unexamined assumptions that even we ourselves, as university professors, seem to accept uncritically.

Manageable Intent and Methodology

This book does not presume to provide a comprehensive look at all that has been written and all that is known about teaching and teacher education. It does not try to say all there is to say about traditional teaching or about why traditional teaching persists, despite over a century of research and action for change. Instead, this book is my own reasoned but also passionate reflection on what I have been learning over the span of a long career in the classroom (both K–12 and postsecondary) and in community activism, and what I continue to learn as I continue to teach. In approaching the material, I have used some of the procedures commonly used in qualitative investigation and documentation, such as systematically analyzing themes and patterns that emerge from student writings and from my own field notes from several years of teaching and giving workshops.[2] Although I do not presume to offer a comprehensive view of all aspects of teacher education, this book addresses a range of issues that recur in my own classes, in my consulting in schools and in the larger community, and in the most recent literature on teaching that is effective for all students. My approach is more practical than scholarly.

From trying to teach in a nontraditional manner, I myself have faced the persistence of traditional teaching in K–12 schools and in universities, even through the 1990s and into the new century, despite the large, consistent body of research recommending otherwise. But beyond my own direct experience of teaching, my primary sources of information have been my students. It is essentially from their struggles, and their voices, that I have done my learning. The material of this book consists primarily of those voices, gathered from their own writings, over at least ten years of teaching preservice and in-service teachers, both secondary and elementary. In the process of hearing their reflections, I have learned more than I had thought possible about traditional schooling.[3]

A limitation in my investigation is that there has been little opportunity to follow up on former students into their own classrooms. The study I consider necessary would be a longitudinal one, to observe the extent to which students were ultimately able to put into actual practice the insights they gained in my classes, and to what extent they were able to sustain the commitments they made then to themselves and to the children they hoped to teach. Even such an investigation, however, would be limited in terms of what it might discover about my teaching. Too many variables come into play for me to presume that a course or two with me caused a preteacher's success in overcoming both internal and external pressures to teach in traditional ways.[4]

What I have come to know is not much different from what many other teachers have learned from both their own experiences as students and their reflection on their own teaching. What I have tried to do here is say, "This is what I know right now, this is how I know it, this is the meaning I make of it, this is some of what

I have decided to do about it, and this is how it has worked so far." Because what I describe about student behavior and thinking is so ordinary and familiar, my hope is that other teachers and teacher educators will find my interpretation of and thinking beyond *what's going on here* useful in extending their own thinking and practice.

In the August Company of Other Researchers

As I have indicated, the full, complex story I have to tell is primarily contained in the words of the students themselves. Their voices are rich and compelling. They force us, as teachers and teacher educators, to rethink our practices. At least, they have forced me to do so.

However, f I had listened only to my own experiences and to student voices, however, I might have much more often fallen into despair. For my own clarity of direction and hope, I have found it necessary, and encouraging, to keep reminding myself that the struggle to address paralyzing student habits acquired within their prior traditional schooling is shared by all progressive educators. Reaching out to my colleagues through professional conferences and through their writings has been a crucial, steadying factor in my continuing to work for the kind of deep transformative change in education that I have believed in for much of my career, even if I did not always have ideas about how to work for it. I tell my students, "No one should have to do anything hard alone." People have been there before me, and they are there alongside me. Staying connected to them has reminded me that not only do I not have to do it alone, but I cannot, and neither am I expected to. I can and must do my share. This book in part represents that commitment.

Because this is a struggle that I do not engage in alone, I consider this book to be a companion piece to several other books, written by scholars/teachers whom I greatly admire. I recommend that the reader of this book move on to these writers' excellent works that have been most thought-provoking, accessible, and energizing for me in terms of what I have tried to write here.

First, for ongoing inspiration, I recommend a subscription to *Rethinking Schools* and all of its recent compilations of new and previous articles.[5]

Then, for rethinking almost all our assumptions about the teaching and learning processes, I refer the reader to the writings of Alfie Kohn, in particular his books *The Schools Our Children Deserve* (1999), *Beyond Discipline* (1996), *Punished by Rewards* (1993), and *No Contest* (1986). Though I now use each of these books in my various teacher education classes, I had not been aware of any of Kohn's work when I did my own initial research on either what I call *teacher-pleasing*, or the persistence of competitive structures in teaching. His thinking matches mine—or mine his. Fortunately, since he has done most of the writing about that thinking, and has done it brilliantly, I don't have to. Do read him.

There are two other scholars/teachers whose works I particularly recommend, for themselves but also as companion pieces to this book. One is my mentor and friend Sonia Nieto. I find particular resonance in the insights expressed in her book *The Light in Their Eyes* (1999), which draws its richness from the voices of a small but articulate number of preteachers as they struggle to come to terms with their own emerging multicultural consciousness. As is her previous book, *Affirming Diversity* (1992), *The Light in Their Eyes* is a pivotal resource for all teachers and teacher educators. Her clear, exquisitely, carefully considered, and warmly humane analyses are also represented in her many articles, all of which I recommend.

The most salient companion piece to this book is Gloria Ladson-Billings's *Crossing Over to Canaan* (2001). The philosophical framework of her book is congruent with my own philosophy of teaching. I share her passionate recognition of the need for bold, fully self-actualized, thoughtful, excellent teachers—especially for urban schools. Her book describes a carefully designed program to prepare such teachers, a program that I wish all teacher education departments would imitate. *Crossing Over to Canaan* follows one cohort of those excellent preteachers through their student teaching experiences, illuminating from a different angle what it takes to become what she calls a "culturally relevant"[6] teacher, as first described in terms of practicing teachers in her equally important and deeply inspiring book for teachers and teacher educators, *The Dreamkeepers* (1994). These are particularly hopeful and beautifully written books.

Though *Crossing Over to Canaan* (Ladson-Billings, 2001) is the closest in nature to mine, our books differ, although our pieces are companions rather than competitors. *Crossing Over to Canaan* describes and follows certain students through an innovative and exciting program of courses and field experiences geared directly toward preteachers who have chosen inner-city placement. However, mine is not about a program but about a few classrooms, and what some of my colleagues and I have learned in our teaching. It explicates the attitudes, assumptions, and skills of perhaps two thousand incoming students over the years, and it describes in step-by-step detail the way I work within my own courses to help students stretch beyond their real or perceived limitations. My goal, like Ladson-Billings's, is that the preteachers we work with will become culturally relevant teachers. If we had a program like hers . . . but maybe as a result of our combined books, more universities will!

In addition, I recommend my own first book, *Going Against the Grain* (1996), for a close look at what student-centered teaching and teacher-centered mentoring can look like in a high school. It concludes that it is a misuse of teacher education faculty members for us not to be working on-site in schools as part of our teaching load. Graduates as teachers need to be mentored in their induction years. The need is for nonjudgmental, noninvested feedback that is strongly grounded in the most up-to-date research on how children learn, as a new teacher struggles against the grain of traditional teaching that is both embedded within most of us as teachers and modeled in most K–12 school settings.

Importance of the Topic at This Time

This topic is especially important now, as national policy seems determined to impose more standardized testing on students and to rank—and even fund—schools and districts solely on the basis of those tests' scores. It troubles me that much of the present national focus on how to achieve and measure success in K–12 public schools in the United States is based on such surface evidence and on political or economic assumptions rather than grounded in thoughtful research or regular involvement with children in schools. "Good" schools have come to be defined in very narrow terms.[7]

It generally seems not to be educators who are pushing for high-stakes "standards" and that kind of arbitrary "accountability," but much more often it is businessmen, politicians, and the partially informed public they influence. The effect on teaching has already been drastic and in some cases devastating. We face an urgent situation in light of those pressures to keep our focus on what we know about how children learn, and what we in our most sane moments know they should and can learn. We also face an opportunity to link together in resistance with others who have a solid understanding of what learning and teaching really can be.

I hope this book contributes to a more research-based dialogue about education, and, in response to what seems to have long been a general contempt for schools of education, I hope it shows the crucial nature of a solid, clear, progressive, and practical teacher education program.

Achieving the Vision

My previous book represents what I learned as a teacher educator about the acculturation of young teachers within schools. For two years, I followed, as participant researcher, the professional development of one high school English teacher. My findings argued for the mentoring of new, idealistic teachers by university teacher educators, to help them maintain their ideals as they struggle with certain traditional structures, which some teachers call "institutional realities."[8] Since the completion of that research, I have realized that, as important and successful as that intensive individualized mentoring was revealed to be, presently existing systems require teacher education faculty to find less labor-intensive ways to be involved with the full development of teachers over time. Sadly, the traditional configuration of our primary workload at universities across the country renders essentially impossible the regular, personalized, sustained, and intensive availability of the teacher education faculty on-site at public schools.

Because the funding of that role does not appear likely, I am suggesting that if we can help university schools of education rethink the role of teacher educators, we can also do that crucial work on-site at schools—not just through occasional staff development workshops but also through sustained recurring workshops, and especially through regular individualized interactions with teachers and their aides or paraprofessionals in the classrooms in which they work. It seems to me that this kind of relationship is most important if we are to find placements for our preservice teachers that represent and allow them to try out the constructivist and equitable kind of teaching that we advocate in our courses. Basically, however, until we win that battle over how our time as teacher educators is used, our influence with practicing teachers is essentially limited to graduate courses at the university. Given that reality, our obligation is to rethink our own teaching, as we ask our students to rethink theirs.

The insights that emerge from this book should offer concrete ways in which teacher educators might engage preservice and in-service teachers in activities that encourage them to examine their incoming assumptions, and to entertain other possible perspectives. Over the long range, the book suggests coherent and collaborative teacher education programs that focus as much on preteachers' dispositions and attitudes as on knowledge acquisition. In such programs, undergraduate and graduate students will be consistently and deliberately encouraged and supported as they develop not just marketable skills but, more important, habits of critical thinking, of seeing from multiple perspectives, of coming to believe in their own capacities for growth, and, especially, believing in the growth capacities of all their students.

The goal is a new consciousness about what teachers are doing. Ultimately, as a result, instead of being swallowed up by the traditional structures and agendas of most schools, the teachers with whom we are involved will be able and eager to help redirect the transformation of schools, making them both excellent and equitable for all children.

Structure of the Book

My intent is to have the book represent what I have found from in-depth reflection upon most teachers' traditional schooling, spread out over many years of my own and my students' examination of memories, feelings, and, especially, assumptions. I reflected on what I have learned, not to "bash" anyone's schooling or even to say that traditional teaching cannot ever be good teaching, but to invite students, teachers, and teacher educators to be open to considering alternatives to the only style they may have ever witnessed.

I begin by showing how the game of reading the teacher rather than the text—a game I call *teacher-pleasing*—interferes with authentic learning.[9] Having established that teacher-pleasing is the learned behavior of most preteachers, I suggest an alternative paradigm and give concrete examples of some methods I have developed for breaking that conditioning. Then I address the work I do to have students examine how certain alternatives to traditional "discipline" and "classroom management" practices might create a healthier environment for learning than the ones in which the students themselves were socialized. Following the analysis of healthy community building in a classroom, in large part by overcoming certain assumptions and practices that might impede it, I suggest a natural extension of my model of justice and caring into how teachers think of the larger social community. Focusing on cooperative learning as a key strategy for rethinking relationships in a classroom, I address a complex range of factors that seem to keep many teachers from stepping back from center stage in their classrooms. In the chapters that follow, I discuss concrete, interactive ways to help teachers overcome their reluctance to *color outside the lines*. Finally, I define my own success in the qualitative ways all teachers do: the small and beautiful moments of student insight, which might, over time, if there are enough of them, transform whole systems.

Notes

1. I define *traditional teaching* as teaching in which the focus is on the content, about which the teacher is understood to be an expert, and which must be "covered" in such a way that students will be able to show that they have acquired a certain body of knowledge, which is characteristically Eurocentric. Student activity is that of watching and listening to the teacher. Students speak when called on, in response to teacher questions. Student conversation with other students is generally unauthorized. Absorption of product, not engagement in process, is the focus of this form of instruction.

2. The term that fits most precisely might be *practitioner research,* as defined in Anderson and Herr's article "The New Paradigm Wars" (1999), in which they define the term: "By practitioner research we refer to a broad-based movement among school professionals to legitimate knowledge produced out of their own lived experience as professionals. This includes an ongoing struggle to articulate an epistemology of practice" (p. 20).

3. I employed two methods of collection as I taught my classes. One was to ask students for copies of papers I regarded as compelling, for whatever reason, and to photocopy for myself certain other handwritten "conversations" (described as *writebacks* in this book) before I handed papers back to students. My intent overall was to gather copies of papers that represented the rich variety of ways of thinking that I was witnessing, as well as the evolution of the thinking of some students over time. My only attempt to be systematic was in occasionally photocopying a full class's freewrites in response to some specially designed activities, in order to capture the full range of responses. The student writing I gathered also included many final papers of synthesis and self-evaluation, in which students reflected on and put together for themselves the meaning of the course.

4. The great value of such a follow-up study, of course, would be that the on-site participant nature of the research I advocate would involve noninvested mentoring and support of new teachers. That is exactly the expanded role I conceptualize for teacher educators.

5. *Rethinking Schools,* 1001 East Keefe Ave., Milwaukee, Wisconsin 53212 (http://www.rethinkingschools.org).

6. Very simply, a culturally relevant teacher is one who genuinely believes that all children can learn, and who is deeply immersed in the cultures of the children he or she teaches.

7. Goals 2000: Educate America Act (http://www.ed.gov.legislation/GOALS2000/TheAct/) spends much of its focus on the presumed need to "make our schools competitive." Most recent examples of popular assumptions about what is a "good" school and how to make schools better appear in the September 1999 issue of *Life* magazine (Hirshberg, C. "How Good Are Our Schools?" pp. 40–42) and a National Public Radio poll conducted in September 1999. Alternatively, the spring 1999 issue of *Rethinking Schools* is devoted to an analysis of the "craze" of standardized testing, and most earlier issues deal at least in part with complex alternative views of what makes for "good" schooling, as does Jonathan Kozol's *Savage Inequalities* (1991).

8. My operational definition of *idealistic* is in opposition to *cynical,* and it assumes goals beyond "having a good job" or "keeping our nation competitive."
9. I define *authentic learning* as a disposition to free exploration of ideas, leaps of thought, and a wide range of perspectives.

This book is dedicated to the memory of Rosita, the children's crossing guard at the corner of East St. and Sunrise Ave., and to my teachers, my colleagues, my students, and their students for generations to come.

The Author

Elizabeth Aaronsohn, Ed.D., is an associate professor of teacher education at Central Connecticut State University in New Britain. She considers herself to be in her second thirty-year teaching career, having taught eight years each at three levels: high school English, college English and women's studies, and early elementary school.

Her teaching and research agendas are extensions of her two years as a civil rights worker in Mississippi (1964–1966) and more than four decades of antiwar and social justice activism. Since her book *Going Against the Grain: Supporting the Student-Centered Teacher* (1996), she has published several articles on preparing monocultural teachers for a multicultural world. Her daughter, Rachel, lives in Colorado.

The Exceptional Teacher

Chapter One

The Grading Game: Reading the Teacher Instead of the Text

I define *traditional teaching* as teaching in which the focus is on the content, about which the teacher is understood to be an expert, and which must be "covered" in such a way that students will be able to show that they have acquired a certain body of knowledge. Student activity is that of watching and listening to the teacher. Students speak when called on in response to teacher questions. Student conversation with other students is generally unauthorized. Product, not process, is the focus of this form of instruction. For me, the most heartbreaking problem with traditional teaching is that it interferes with authentic learning, even while students are socialized to believe that they are learning. Over the long term, I maintain, the habits of dependency and submission to authority that students develop in traditional classrooms undermine the chance for genuine democracy in our society.

I call this set of habits *teacher-pleasing,* and I begin with an analysis of teacher-pleasing as my theoretical framework. The chapters that follow examine the step-by-step processes I have developed over time for encouraging teacher education students to become

---

Note: Much of the material from this chapter (and the next) comes from an unpublished study, "Teacher-Pleasing, Traditional Grading—and Learning?" that three colleagues—Treva Foley, Judy H. Holmes, and Jeffrey Wallowitz—and I have presented at several scholarly conferences.

aware of the effects of teacher-pleasing and for helping them overcome it, at least for the time that they are with me. My hope, of course, is that once they realize what has gone on for them, they will decide to transform their own practice, as university students, as citizens, and as teachers.

> "I wasn't really taught or expected to think or analyze—
> just memorize."

Children in school learn well, and very early, that grades are the teachers' ultimate power over them. So they do what they have to do to get what they need. That orientation is very different from, and I believe inferior to, an orientation toward authentic learning, which I define as an intense desire to follow leads, discover connections, and explore how something works—all activities that characterize the way very young children naturally learn when they are on their own, or before that natural creative process gets reduced to school learning.

Because the work they do in traditional classrooms is usually not of their own choosing, either in content or in process, it is easy for students to disengage from it and learn (against their nature) to be satisfied—because the teacher usually is—with skimming the surface of any topic, as the textbooks do. Traditional teachers are (or at least seem to students to be) concerned with right answers, proper grammar, and correct form rather than full development of original ideas, both in classroom "discussion" and in student writing. Even by the time they are in graduate classes, students have rarely had the chance to be heard talking through their ideas, perceptions, or misperceptions. As a result, they stop trying and just give the teacher what they think she or he wants.

That kind of manipulation is a basically dishonest occupation. But I think it is ultimately what we encourage children to do, for their own survival in school. At least, that is what most of the students I encounter in my teacher education courses indicate in their writing that they learned to do:

- I saw school as something to be survived and I did whatever was necessary to ensure that I got out of school with a diploma ASAP.

- In high school, I rarely read the entire book, and I tended to listen carefully to what the teacher commented on and then studied only that for the tests. (It worked pretty well.)
- I always played the system. . . . I didn't have to do the reading, because the teacher "spoon-fed" it.

The extent to which that behavior becomes a habit into adulthood has grave ramifications for learning, for teaching, and for democracy:

- I found that the only way I could get the attention and the respect of older people, or express any sort of opinion at all, was if I took the consensus adult opinion as my own, whether I agreed with it or not, . . . to massage their egos.
- I learned to change my opinions to suit others, to avoid the humiliation of being left out. Today I find myself giving in to the majority opinion rather than concentrating on divergent thinking.

When I taught English composition at state and community colleges in the early and mid-1980s, I first realized that a number of students saw divergent ideas as un-American. My encouraging them to try out possible ways of seeing that didn't match the "right answers" they had been given seemed to threaten their entire worldview. The same was true of writing. It has been very hard for students to feel right about using "I" in their writing, or to talk about their own life experiences in an academic setting.

Carefully maintaining an academic distance and saying everything right can cause a student to forget what he or she meant to say in the first place:

Writing a sentence was like assembling something on the production line, entitled "what the teacher wants to see." It didn't matter what I wrote; it only mattered how I wrote it. Thus, writing was a very cold, logical, distant activity.

The sanctions against speaking in one's own voice, and the rewards for learning "proper" ways, are clear, but the person disappears, and so does meaningful learning:

- I hate academic writing, though I have spent countless hours in the past two years cultivating just that. And what for? I don't know. . . . I do know that it has not been without sacrifice that I can now knock out a dry and colorless execution of ivory-tower points without a tremendous effort. And people will read it and be very impressed.
- I know that experience of trying to explain something while having my grammar adjusted several times along the way. Knocks the wind out of what you have to say, doesn't it?

But what happens if teachers try, in their high school classes particularly, not to do that to students? For one thing, a cooperating teacher politely tells a university supervisor of student teachers, "We have to train them to write this way; it's what they'll get in college." And when I say, "No! It's not so! I teach college writing, and that's not what I've been looking for!" I am told, "Well, that's just you." But I know that not many—or any—college professors want to be reading defensive, distancing, safe, self-protectively obfuscating papers that essentially say nothing, as long as they are grammatically correct.

Teacher-Pleasing and Student Dependency

In order to go to the core of what learning could be, instead of what most of my postsecondary students over many years have reported it to have been for them, it seems to me that teachers and teacher educators have to begin by clarifying our goals. For several years I have done an activity in teacher education classes and staff development workshops.[1] I ask participants to freewrite and then brainstorm. I ask them, "What do we want the children we teach to be like when they're adults?" Each time, when they report, we cover the board or several pieces of chart paper with some thirty to fifty words that they have generated. The list always includes "independent," "honest," "caring," "being problem solvers," "compassionate," "lifelong learners," and "responsible." In some sessions, a student will offer "courageous," but usually not, so I suggest it. When everyone's thoughts are on the board, I ask, "So how does schooling help them get there?"

That question often puts them into conflict with their own schooling and their own teaching. When they're stumped, I ask them to back up: "Well, then, how did you yourselves acquire these characteristics?" Some reflect that they acquired almost all of them after their schooling was completed. Most say, essentially, "I'm not there yet." Even practicing teachers are stunned by the realization that although they have successfully reached their undergraduate goal of having finished college and obtained a job, there are undeveloped parts of themselves that they have not yet worked on, or thought about, and which were never addressed in their own schooling.

Then I ask them to notice the list. I ask, "Where's being able to recite random bits of factual information?" Sometimes "knowledgeable" makes it to the list. When I ask for what that means, groups quickly offer their insight as to how useless merely acquiring and reciting are, compared with being able to use, connect, and apply understanding of relevant pieces of information.

And then I ask, "Where's 'obedient?'" They're surprised. It's never there. Some insist that it is implied in the others. Some want to add it; they say, "Even as adults you have to obey—your boss, the rules, laws." So a conversation begins about moral development and about what freedom and citizenship involve in a democracy. We look at the difference between those socialized behaviors with citizens in a community allowed to function together, on the one hand, and citizen's blind obedience, on the other hand.

The impulse of some teachers and preteachers, every semester, to protect their right to demand the absolute obedience of children—as was required of them as children—frightens me, because these are teachers, or people beginning a program to become teachers. How is it that we call ourselves preparing students to live in a democracy, if so many teachers and preteachers accept the inevitability of their own essential powerlessness within their careers and within the larger society? Is democracy not about having a genuine voice? In fact, it has to a great extent been my own fear for the demise of democracy in America that has led me to begin our sessions together by generating this list of long-range goals.

Most conscientious teachers will say we want our students to be responsible, eager, self-directed young people. When we think about their social behaviors, we want them to be considerate of each other as well as of us—what we generally call *respect*. Most basically, however, teachers seem satisfied if students "do their work," "learn the material," and "do not interfere" with the learning of others or with the teacher's agenda.

But to what end? We might even go so far as to say that we want them to think for themselves: to consider, imagine, connect, reflect, consult, explore, create, and actively engage in constructing their own knowledge, even to take intellectual risks. So we are frustrated to find ourselves year after year involved with students, even "the best" students, who, although hardworking, quick, and eager to give right answers, are often not active, original, or complex thinkers. And how do they treat each other, even as they may be fawning to us? In part of our minds, teachers wonder, Is he or she saying what I want to hear? Am I being manipulated?

That's "the best." What about the others? "Unmotivated"? Is it, in fact, something innate in the children themselves, or is it something inherent in what we've always called "teaching"? In teacher education students' reactions to my classes, they reveal, and reflect on, their own deep socialization to dependency:

> At first I could only think about what *you* expected. It's what I'm used to.

And this, from a successful student in her thirties:

> This was so hard for me at first, trying to . . . stop trying to figure out what it was that the teacher *wanted* me to learn, to know. . . . The concept of pleasing the teacher, the parent, or whatever authority figure you choose is deeply ingrained in me.

Habits That Interfere with Genuine Learning

The premise of this book is that the structures that characterize traditional teaching, from elementary school through graduate school, undermine the very characteristics we wish our students to develop. The full development of our students, therefore, has to begin with teachers' and professors' rethinking of our own practices. And that has to begin with personal reflection on our own schooling.

For the most part, we were the successful ones. Most of us consider ourselves to be the model for what we want our students to be like. We want them to be as excited about learning as we remember ourselves to have been. We may even be inclined to say, "I made it through traditional schooling. Those who didn't make it were the ones who just didn't want to learn, and that's the case for our students who aren't making it now."

The outcomes of traditional schooling experiences are especially apparent to me as I work with undergraduate and graduate students in teacher education courses at a university. Though most of the students say they went to "good" schools, when I invite them to read for meaning most have no idea of what that is about. Few have the habit of reading in any way other than the collecting of "tidbits" of information. Most have always waited for the teacher to tell them what it all means.

Within traditional structures, students are not expected to be risk takers intellectually; they're expected to "learn" what we have defined as "important" to know. That learning consists of committing fragments of "right answers" to short-term memory. Students overwhelmingly report that such information is soon lost, making room for the next batch of facts to memorize for the next test. It is not available for later connecting or reinterpreting thought. This definition of learning lasts through college, even graduate school, unless a course taught nontraditionally interrupts and causes them to call into question that whole arrangement. But the work of uncovering is not easy, because there is first so much embedded habit and expectancy to undo:

> This was probably one of the hardest courses I have ever taken.
> It was such an *internal* type of learning. I have never taken a class
> where my thought patterns were changed, or where I actually grew
> as a person. It would have been easier to me if I were given tests
> and quizzes.

In traditionally structured classrooms such as the ones in which the task is to locate right answers and be ready to recite them verbatim, the real task is to produce a product, not to engage in a meaningful process. The result is that students have not developed—or have lost those they had in very early childhood—the skills and habits of figuring out, exploring, wondering, and asking. Even in adulthood, but certainly in the late adolescence of conventional undergraduate years, many students remain reluctant to speak in class, made fearful from years of experience of saying the wrong thing and being humiliated by the teacher, or by fellow students, or seeing that happen to others:

> Many students do know the answer to many of the questions posed by the teacher in class, but it comes down to the idea . . . that children/students tend to be afraid to answer a question for fear of being wrong and looking stupid. I still am.

Fear of Judgment Can Paralyze

Ultimately, the goal of schooling for most students seems to be to get through it—to survive the experience with the least amount of humiliation and failure and the greatest amount of acceptance and praise. That is what students report as "success." Hardly ever do they speak of achieving the joy of accomplishment that comes with genuine intellectual understanding. Even the most successful students hardly question that their survival depends on their becoming excellent at the game of teacher-pleasing. That, in fact, is what they have learned to be good at.

I know this deeply because, for one reason, my daughter, now having finished college but still hating school, has, since most of her early elementary years, felt both pressured and insulted by what schooling expected of her. A good memorizer, she consistently achieved high grades throughout her schooling. Paradoxically, this was at great cost to her sense of self and her respect for what is to be learned from most written text and from most teachers. Her considerable authentic learning came through whatever active field experiences and internships she was allowed, especially from a stretch of several years in actual work between her first and second tries at college. Though the format when she returned to college continued to be memorizing and test taking, she had finally developed for herself a framework into which some of the memorized material could fit. Still, she felt insulted and trapped, as she had felt as early as fifth grade, because even though her teacher that year gave exciting multidimensional projects, the pressure of teacher judgment took away my daughter's pleasure and sense of adequacy. With sad solemnity she told me, "Even the fun stuff, we get graded on it."

So powerful was her early socialization that even in that lively, caring, innovative teacher's classroom, my daughter's expectation of teacher judgment impeded and distorted her learning process and dampened her motivation. By then, and thereafter, she had become used to experiencing what teacher education students later described (in 1993):

> In high school I always felt that I wasn't learning anything. What I was doing was memorizing all the information for a test (swallowing all the information the teachers fed me), knowing the information for the test and forgetting it again thereafter ([after] regurgitating it back to the teacher).

Maybe that is why my daughter developed severe stomach problems in association with school. No chance to digest? For how many is schooling about the simplistic process of what one preteacher called the process of *plug and chug*? As another student wrote,

> In my experience, I found that things that I would have liked to learn and remember, I did not have the chance to because I was too busy memorizing the facts and worrying about what was going to be on the test and how I was going to do on the test.

While my daughter was in elementary school, I was seeing from the other side the same phenomenon in my freshman composition classes at a community college. My goal was to have students find their voices on paper. At first, most papers were careful, correct, and empty. When I realized that their fear of my judgment was getting in their way, I removed that in the most dramatic way I could: I removed grades and just gave conversational feedback as a stimulus for rewriting. Two things happened. One, the students who had not been successful with writing in their former schooling appreciated the freedom just to talk on paper, as I urged everyone to do. Their papers were full of life and energy. One fireman in his forties, finding for the first time that he in fact had a voice that could emerge on paper, said, with relief and joy, "The pressure is off." For them, the work of the class was no longer about the game of proving themselves to a teacher so that they could "do well." No longer a game at which they would surely lose, writing became no game at all, but a way to work out what they were thinking.

However, many students felt lost at first, especially those whose success in their former schooling had come from performing their perfect grammar and perfect five-paragraph theme formula. The rules had changed; in fact, there was no longer a game. It was hard for them to figure out that *what the teacher wanted* was whatever they were thinking (see Figure 1.1). Their habitual goal, of course, was the grade. With that gone, what was there to aim for?

Figure 1.1. Guidelines for Reader Response

You are asked to respond to each of the assigned readings with one of two kinds of reader response. A *reader response paper* is one to three pages typed double-spaced, with two photocopies to share in class and a list of questions, as described in the following. A *reader response journal entry* can be in very clear handwriting, and it can be somewhat shorter. Both, however, must follow the guidelines that follow.

What a Reader Response Isn't

It is not (1) the traditional summary or "book report" of the reading. The only functions of a summary are (a) to inform or to refresh the teacher's memory of the book, or (b) to prove to the teacher that you have done the assignment. But (a) I will have read all the texts, and (b) I fully expect and trust that you will have done the assignments.

It is not (2) the traditional judgment of the reading, or arguing a position. Agree/disagree statements are inappropriate here, because, having not had the experiences that the authors have had, you cannot judge whether they're describing those experiences accurately. All you can say is (a) whether what they describe speaks to experiences you have had or not had, (b) how you relate to what they describe, (c) whether their conclusions make sense to you, given the evidence they provide, and (d) what questions and feelings they raise for you.

But this is not about censoring your reactions. If the writer's viewpoint makes you uncomfortable, *say that, and say exactly why!* You're not in debate with the writer, not out to win or defend your position; you are in the process of figuring out why you think what you think. Being in collision over ways of seeing is a good way to examine that. Be open—not to swallowing whole whatever you read, but to rethinking assumptions.

What Is It, Then?

It is the written record of a personal engagement with the text—of having really listened to both someone else and oneself. A reader response starts from thinking about what you already know about what the writer is talking about, from your own personal, direct experiences with learning and teaching, in and out of school. But it does not stop or get stuck there. It's multidimensional seeing, active reading.

Step-by-Step Process for Reader Response

Active Reading

(1) Even as you're reading, *start right away talking back on paper!* As long as it is your own book, you will have to get used to writing in the book—another taboo. Jot down notes on your own thinking in the margins, or on separate paper if it's not your own book. Underline. Your job is to engage with the book or the article or story. Allow yourself to have a conversation, a mutually respectful dialogue, with the writer, to whom you're listening carefully. See what she or he is saying, trace interesting patterns, and find connections with what you already know or think you know.

Don't rush to finish the text. Listen carefully to your own reactions as you read. Don't brush them aside; take time to hear them and record them, and especially take time to sort out and record where they might be coming from. This is the stuff that will be uniquely *your* response to the text, because no one else has lived your exact life. Go back and forth between the text and your own remembering, reflecting, wondering, and so forth, including whatever else you are reading and directly experiencing in this course and any other. Making connections is the key. You may have to get used to reading this way, but the struggle itself may give you some useful information about how you've been taught to read and what that might mean for *your* teaching.

(2) While you're doing all of that, keep an ongoing list of all the questions you hope the text will have answered by the time you

finish it. What are you not getting? What confuses you? What do you need more information about?

(3) Keep some sort of record of compelling passages from the text that you think you will want to return to.

When You Finish Reading

(4) Now go back and skim your own marginal notes and your underlining, trying to be sure you really understood what the writer meant, and that you can differentiate the writer's voice from your own.

(5) Next, capture your notes of dialogue on paper, in no particular form. At the same time, revise your list of questions to take account of those the text answered for you, and then think through and ask more completely about those things that you are still puzzling over. These questions will form a substantial part of the group conversation when we discuss the text in the next class session. Questions may come in separate from the paper itself, or they may be included in it, but they should not be all that the paper does.

(6) Do a freewrite that shapes and develops the notes you've taken. *Your* thinking is what we're after here, with lots of specifics from both the text and your own experience. Let yourself discover, as you write, where the new ideas have taken you. Remember, this may be a new way of writing from what you're used to—not to prove anything or sum anything up, but to figure out what you think about some possibly new ideas and why.

(7) You may want to revise, based on what you find—or not. But at the end, do proofread—and fix! I do not want to have to wade through a heavily corrected draft, but I appreciate seeing penned-in changes in spelling and punctuation on a typed sheet. They indicate that you have read the final copy you want me to read. This stage is like dusting just before company comes, after you've constructed or remodeled your house.

Involving the Self While Being True to the Text

To do these writings, it is necessary that you feel free to use the word *I*. At the beginning of the semester, you may have to struggle to give yourself permission to do that. I do not want you to distance yourself from these readings. You don't need to worry about "saying something intelligent" in these papers; you do need to let yourself be passionate, reflective, thoughtful, and careful of the text (which means that skimming is not enough), so that what comes through in the paper is your personal experience of reading the text.

There are no right answers. We need everyone's responses.

Note
1. I began this practice even before I read in his book *Beyond Discipline* (1996) that Alfie Kohn also does this in his workshop sessions with teachers. Each of his writings confirms and extends my own thinking.

Chapter Two

Breaking the Conditioning

*This new learning style makes me nervous. I am used
to receiving test scores and paper grades to monitor my
progress. I think this gives me a feeling of comfort because
I know where I stand academically, and I know what
must be done in order to earn or maintain a desired grade.*

Recognizing and then working to overcome the paralyzing effects
of such habits as teacher-pleasing seems to me to be the necessary
starting place for a teacher education program. Otherwise, inevitably, the ingrained beliefs and assumptions from teachers' own
years as students compel them to perpetuate the traditional techniques. As is shown in later chapters, such dispositions as fear of
judgment have been observed to be characteristic of traditional
teachers in their own practice. If, as I believe, teachers need to be
courageous for the sake of their students, they need to have developed courage well before they find themselves in charge of a classroom. If they have not had the freedom to *color outside the lines*
before entering a teacher education program, I believe it is possible, though not easy, for them to begin to do it there. However difficult it is by then, the struggle is necessary if the cycle is to be
broken.

Most teacher educators are also products of traditional schooling. As a team investigating the pervasiveness of teacher-pleasing
in the early 1990s realized, all four of us—one high school teacher,
one teacher educator, and two preteachers—already well knew and
had been expert at "the game" from our own schooling. All of us
were troubled by it. Starting from that personal collective experience, we were interested in understanding and documenting sys-

tematically the extent to which traditional grading posed a deterrent to genuine learning in other students' experiences of schooling. The team interviewed and gathered written reflections from a wide range of students, mostly at the high school and university levels.

Our process of learning about our respondents' socialization to teacher-pleasing became simultaneous with the respondents' recognition of and struggle to come to terms with those very habits, since the two of us on the team who were already teaching had implemented changes in our structures. Having hypothesized that grading might be a pivotal factor, the high school teacher experimented with removing grades from her teaching in one of her classes for one semester. For my part, by then, I had already completely removed ongoing grades from all of mine and had begun to collect student reactions to the new structures. (See Appendix, "Grading Rubric.")

Our investigative team gathered sobering data from student interviews and writings about their experiences of traditional schooling. The word *game* kept appearing in what they said. Most students indicated that their preoccupying focus in school had been—and for many, it still was—figuring out the right answers and the correct behaviors each teacher required of them in order for them to get top grades or, at best, merely survive each class session. It turned out that instead of focusing their energy on making meaning from text, experience, and discussion, all through their schooling, students had been focused solely on getting the teacher's approval. Many students spoke of this reality, which they had never before thought to challenge. It was just a matter of "the way things are." One realized:

> All my life I have been so conditioned to come up with answers that sounded good or were to impress the teacher, [to get] the grade you wanted.

Even more disturbing was this well-developed defense:

> I was too busy trying to let everyone else know that I was smart, rather than being able to accept my abilities and acknowledge others' abilities. I used to make up answers when I did not know the answers.

Recalling their personal reactions to my removal of structures to which they had become so accustomed over at least twelve years of schooling, many university students' self-evaluations at the end of their course with me included such comments as these:

- I guess this idea of taking a course for meaning, and not for the purpose of just absorbing information and competing for a good grade, was one of the first obstacles in my way of thinking that I had to overcome in this course.
- I was still into the habit of reporting what I had read. This was me, trying to show that I had read the assignment and was getting the work done as [I was] told. . . . I was in that traditional mind-set of producing a paper because it was due on a certain day.

The steady reflection on their own experiences caused many to rethink notions they had never before had occasion to call into question:

- I always scanned quickly for facts and slowed down when I found one. I had even taken a speed-reading course in high school. It teaches to skip over the "fluff" and focus on the facts. This is all learning facts for the purpose of regurgitating on a test.
- I think that was a big problem I had in this class: I would read a chapter or a handout and try to find any little argument I could make.
- It was nice to read a book without having to memorize the information.
- I can say with certainty that my previous teachers have done a number on me. Give me a list of dates and people and a half hour and I can have them all memorized. If you talk to me about anything else, I will forget those names and dates. I am so good at that [memorizing] and I thought that that made me smart. . . . I'm not even sure if I know what the true definition of "smart" is anymore. Maybe that's a good thing.

They began to use reader response to explore aspects of their own schooling, most of them reflecting in complex ways for the first time on never having had a teacher who operated on Piaget's recognition that a wrong answer is a clue to how a child is thinking:

- I have always been a "good student." I can get good grades on tests because I know what information to look for when I study. . . . I memorize and forget. . . . Now when I look back at the schools I went to, I can see how I got into the habit of memorizing information.
- When I was in elementary school . . . I can remember teachers praising me for quick, thoughtless answers. I can also remember times when my teachers would make me feel bad when I would give a well-thought-out wrong answer. If I am praised for quick (memorized) right answers and condemned for well-thought-out wrong answers, do I choose to get good grades and make my teachers proud of me? At the time, I didn't find anything wrong with it.

As a result of their socialization to the expectation of judgment, of course, some students initially became defensive in reaction to my probing questions on their papers:

> In our class, I used to get nervous when I would see all the questions that you wrote on my papers. My first reaction was that my responses were not what you were looking for. I am trained to think that when a teacher questions what I say, I did not say the right thing.

Others recognized themselves and their friends in Frank Smith's description (1986) of students he invited at the beginning of his course to read a book of their own choosing and then write a paper of whatever length they felt necessary, for which there would be no grade:

> When I told my roommates about this first assignment of reading a chapter in a book and writing a paper on it, they said, "Well, then you don't have to do it if there is no grade." We are brainwashed into believing that the only things in this world that we need to do are the things we get grades for.

Students report having learned to censor their own intellectual instincts. Carefully staying within the safe boundaries of right answers, they avoid the free exploration, leaps of ideas, and perspectives that characterize authentic learning. Seeing themselves as performers under scrutiny, they come to think of that as learning.

What became clear to the four investigators and, more important, to many of the students themselves over time is that traditional forms of judgment interfere with the development of personal responsibility by making students dependent on outside verification of their abilities and thoughts. Conditioned within traditional structures, even successful students are insecure until a teacher tells them that their work is right. In fact, reports from elementary, high school, and university students confirm what I discovered in my work at the community college: the higher the achievement, the greater the reliance on teacher approval of the work and the greater the initial anxiety when that approval/ disapproval arrangement is withdrawn.

By no means am I suggesting, however, that all an individual teacher has to do to erase student dependency is to withdraw grades. Much more fundamental change needs to take place as part of that shift. But expect resistance, because the habits of traditional schooling have become deeply embedded in students' expectations by their years of prior school experience. As Haberman (1996) indicates in "The Pedagogy of Poverty," and as I discovered in my teaching at all levels, students themselves will be inclined to resist change from the process with which they are familiar and to which they have adapted, even if the change is for their benefit. Some children already "know" and have adapted to what "real school" and "real work" is by second grade.

Even if young students have not yet locked into the idea that school is what can be recognized as traditional schooling, many of their parents surely have. In one family I know about, a father, himself a teacher, showed appreciation for his toddler's drawing in the only way he knew how: he wrote a big "A" on it. One parent of a first grade class I taught in the early 1970s was confused to the point of outrage at the difference between her own schooling and what she had observed of mine as she glanced into the room: "How can my son be learning if you're not standing up there teaching?" Unfortunately, that parent was never convinced by the workshops I conducted, by invitations to visit and observe, or by personal reassurance. And her son, pretty inevitably reflecting his mother's contempt, resisted in multiple ways within the classroom.

However, during those eight years in which I was teaching kindergarten and first and second grades, many parents other than that one parent noticed with pleasure in their surprise that their children were not yet bored or dreading school as they remembered themselves having been. Their children came home excited about reading and writing, curious about their world, being active, and becoming independent learners, though they were not bringing home the expected worksheets. Through visits and workshops, the parents began to recognize the legitimacy of a situation and a process that looked and sounded so different from their own schooling. Eventually, most learned to delight in seeing children deeply, productively, and happily involved with each other and with materials in small clusters and all kinds of postures all around the room, and the teacher somewhere in the room, aware and accessible but not obviously "in charge" or the center of full-time attention.

With the support of my principal, after the first year, the report cards I wrote for those classes were narratives, not numbers or letters. Most parents adjusted to that change as well. They appreciated being told *what* their child was doing in certain subjects (and between subjects) rather than *how* their child ranked in comparison with others in the class. Considering how divergently my daughter's fifth grade teacher dared to operate, despite her own traditional schooling, it is possible that if she had also initiated authentic assessment instead of grading as a natural part of her courageous, groundbreaking, nontraditional, and project-oriented approach, she could have caught the children early enough to help them overcome their already learned need for concrete external validation. But the idea of authentic assessment had not yet caught hold, even in Vermont, where she was breaking new ground in teaching, by the time my daughter was in her class (in 1985).

Withdrawing Grades Exposes Problems in Traditional Schooling and Testing

As I have suggested, the level of student anxiety tends to increase, at least initially, when the foundation upon which their prior schooling had previously been built disappears. This is especially true with students who have been successful in "the game" of traditional school structures. Some such students might not recognize that a teacher is serious about assignments being done as scheduled if points are not taken off for late papers. In a very few cases, a student has assumed that he or she can just turn all the work in at the end of the semester and get credit, in spite of the student not having had papers to share with peers in our weekly three-reader groups, and in spite of his or her not having gone back and forth with me in intensive *writebacks* (as I will describe), a significant part of "the work" in my classes.

What I have noticed over time is a very strong correlation between students' external locus orientation toward the assigned work of the course and the rigidly authoritarian nature of their upbringing, as they disclose it over time in their writings, in terms of their own experiences of being disciplined.[1] Fascinating and frightening connections have emerged, considering that these students hope to be teachers or, more troubling, already are teachers. The high school English teacher member of our team had anticipated this, wondering to what extent the withdrawal of traditional forms of approval/disapproval would seem to give license to students who have never experienced being trusted with their own learning, or who have been oriented toward reward or punishment in strict traditional families as well as in school. To some extent, the high school English teacher found that, without surprise, this withdrawal did give license, but not for many of the students. Most rose to her new expectations, appreciating her trust—as one graduate student had the distance from her childhood to recognize:

> When I was young, it never occurred to me that I had any control over my life. Other people and circumstances controlled me. . . . Everything seemed to happen apart from me.

Generally, students want to translate the nonjudgmental feedback into what they can recognize as grades. A few counted the times I had written "Yes" in their margins, assuming that it meant "doing great," which to them translated to an A. Once I realized that, I had to reconsider whether I wanted to stop using "Yes" or "OK," and for a while I started writing instead, "I hear this." Like the high school students we studied for a semester, and coming from essentially the same expectations and "rules," undergraduate and even graduate students were uncomfortable about not knowing "where they stood" at all times. Thinking of evaluation basically as a function of comparison with others is, of course, still an external orientation. Our structures raised the question for them: Can the process and product of work bring satisfaction if there are no others with whom to compare?

Like some of the high school students, a few of the university students resented not being reminded about obligations. And like some of the high school students, several at the university perceived themselves to be enrolled in a different curriculum from that in which other students were enrolled, particularly in courses that had several sections and professors. They felt that they were being deprived. They preferred having the traditional textbooks, from which I should lecture, and quizzes and tests, on which the feedback would be either "right" or "wrong". That would provide "proof" to themselves and others that they were indeed "accomplishing something"—or "learning."

Resistance to Transforming Their Locus of Control

In both the high school English experimental classroom and my own courses, an occasional student refused to go through the self-evaluation process at the end of the semester, saying that giving grades and actually doing all the evaluating is the teacher's job. All the others spoke about never before having been given the opportunity—or obligation—to evaluate their own growth over time. Most say that it is the hardest thing they have ever done.

> My locus of control was never my own. I was a pawn to my surroundings. If someone else said I was good, then I was. My perception of self was based on what everyone else wanted rather than what I thought of myself.

The people saying such things are teachers—and people planning to be teachers! I worry greatly about their locus of control within their own classrooms, where, for the most part, they are accountable only to the children they face every day.

Presented with the idea of eliminating ongoing grades, teachers ask, If there are no grades, how will I know who in my class is understanding the material and who isn't? How will I motivate my students to do the work if they aren't being graded? Parents ask, How will I know where my child stands if there are no grades? How will I know how well they are learning? Students ask, If I don't get grades, how do I know if I'm learning? How do I know how well I'm doing? And if I'm not being graded, if it doesn't "count," why do the work? All of these are legitimate questions, each of which can begin to be addressed by inviting a questioning of assumptions about what learning is, and what about it should and can reasonably be measured. After that conversation, we address how.

In our three-year study, the preteacher members of the team conducted interviews that in most cases allowed the speakers to find their own answers to these questions, or at least new questions to consider. In my teaching, the questions arise in class, in conferences, and especially on their papers. In each case, there is a chance for dialogue and reflection. Given the chance to think it all through, teachers admit that, as was done to them, they use grades as threats, "motivating" students by relying on their fear of failing. Most people who are parents soon understand, with reflection, that grades can show a comparison with others but fail to prove that learning has occurred, or even record that a substantial amount of effort was put forth, or that there has been personal growth. The grades certainly don't convey *what* a student is doing or learning; they just show *how well*, compared with other students. Students come to realize and agree that, ultimately, no matter what grade the teacher records, they themselves know what they learned or didn't learn from an academic project, unit, or experience. Nevertheless, they are used to having the teacher collect and evaluate and grade whatever they produce. In fact, that product is not even for them; it is for the teacher.

Despite our removal of ongoing grading, the high school teacher and I were still required by our institutions to turn in final grades. So we, and a like-minded fifth grade teacher who was interested in our study, asked students to self-evaluate—and include in their self-evaluation a suggested grade. We found that, often, the

younger students seemed capable of more honest, realistic attention to the body of work they had accumulated for self-evaluation
than were some of the university students. Accounting for this difference raises more interesting considerations. One possibility is
that the university students had become, cynically, so deeply invested in "doing well" that honesty about themselves was not a consideration, or a habit. Any source of pride in achievement other
than a high GPA (grade point average) may have been effectively
extinguished by then. So much seems to be at stake, especially
their "marketability," first for college entrance and then for jobs.
Another possibility is that in spite of my efforts to help them
stretch beyond what they already thought they knew, and beyond
oversimplifications and right answers, because I did not scold or
punish, they honestly didn't realize their own inadequacies. So
dependent on external evaluation and being told what to think
and know, such a person who doesn't "get it" doesn't even realize
that he or she doesn't get it.

What *Is* Accountability?

These are possible explanations for why even some university students whose work met merely minimum requirements for thoughtfulness claimed a top grade for themselves, but another possibility
is that they had learned to equate grades with output. Certainly
they had produced a huge amount of writing on paper and had
spent a great number of hours producing it. That should be worth
something; it always had been so in their previous schooling. For
me, it was worth *something:* it was bottom line for passing. In terms
of students' socialization to expect a reward for the time spent or
the number of pages produced, reward-oriented college students
were not significantly different from their high school counterparts
in that regard. In fact, they may perhaps therefore be, as Haberman (1992) argues, not yet developmentally ready to become
teachers. But here they are, at most, a few years away from being
the sole authority in their own classrooms. Accountable to whom?

> I remember [that] when I heard about the lack of grades in this
> course, I was scared. How would I know that I was good enough
> to be here, how would I judge myself?

Equally important, accountable for what? What do they represent, even our high grades? Even in a graduate teacher certification course, preteachers report about their K–12 and even their college experiences:

- I was expected to read well enough to pass a test on the information, so I was not motivated to really understand what I was reading.
- I don't think I learned much from high school except how to find loopholes to get good grades. By finding all the loopholes, I was on the High Honor Roll. But I never learned to read for meaning.

Given all of these complex realities, the issue of grading at the end of a semester is always agonizing for me, as I understand it is for many of my colleagues. It was so even before I stopped giving ongoing grades. How does one evaluate any individual representation of a student's work? What is it that we're after? Just right answers? I have seen other teachers' and professors' complicated point systems and rubrics. These are painstaking attempts to be both clear and fair. However, I have frankly heard from some students of such faculty members, and these students have felt so closely directed by the rubrics that very little of what they really wanted to learn or explore or do has shown up in the heavily monitored document they've produced. They consider it to have been composed/written for the faculty member rather than for their own learning, or for that of their own K–12 students. They cannot see the relevance of what they consider the professors' "picky" demands as they struggle to figure out, say, how to construct a unit lesson plan that will engage all their students.

I have also experienced reading stiff, distracted, even empty teacher education comprehensive examination papers, or sections of papers, at the end of graduate programs, from students whose earlier work in my course I knew to have been rich, lively, knowledgeable, original, and passionate. What happened? When I asked, I was told, "I thought I had to follow the format exactly."

This commentary is not meant as a critique of my colleagues' teaching. I myself, for example, have carefully designed a lesson plan format that I expect student teachers I supervise will use (see Appendix). Some student teachers find that my format helps them do plenty of prethinking before they rush to decide what they will do. But others are as put off by mine as they are by the one in the student teaching handbook, which requires them to say verbatim what they will say and what the children will say, whereas mine rejects such scripting, asking student teachers instead to be open to the unpredictable things children will say and to be prepared to follow lines of error to probe for how a child may be thinking. But some student teachers' reactions suggest that mine, too, may have become, for some, just a fill-in-the-blank form.

Despite my convictions, with full understanding of how subjective grades in most subjects inevitably are, and how even professionals often disagree in their assessments of the same piece of work, I have been drawn on occasion to consider something like rubrics, to try to be as clear as possible about what is expected of students in my classes. The closest I could allow myself to come, and still stay true to my long-range goals for students, became a list of standards (see Figure 2.1). In reaction to incidences of students' choosing wildly unrealistic grades, for the one or two in each class who might need that reality check, I include in the self-evaluation guidelines this statement: "Simply surviving the course does not constitute an A."

Figure 2.1. Assessment Standards

Expectations: as I try to help you "get" the complexity of the content of the course, I monitor and try to nurture your growth over time toward:

- A clear understanding of the complex material of the course
- Overcoming reading for performing, remembering, or arguing; instead, reading for meaning
- Responsibility to group, however configured
- Examination of assumptions
- Original construction of knowledge
- Seeing patterns, making connections
- Practicing of strategies taught in the course
- Developing habit of multiple perspectives
- Depth below surface of *all* reading, writing, observing, and reflecting

---

It is not surprising that, given the years of conditioning, university students might at least initially find it extremely difficult to break through the walls that keep them from accepting my feedback and from seeing all the writing and rethinking as a process, valuable for its own sake. In the reader responses, as well as in the rest of the writing, lesson planning, and long-term projects, a few students still operate by trying to give me, as professor, what they assume I want, rather than allowing themselves to follow their own hunches (Holt, 1967). These students remain uncomfortable with uncertainty, and frequently resent not having quick closure or definite right answers. My colleagues and I have reason to worry about what kind of teachers such students will become; we especially worry if they are already practicing teachers. But we have to hope that even if such a student ends the semester without having stretched his or her boundaries about learning and teaching, we will have planted a seed that may take root someday.

To be sure, one semester is a very brief time to expect students who have spent twelve to sixteen years in teacher-pleasing to have given it up completely. Part of my own struggle at the end of a semester, at grading time, is recognizing and accepting, as an inevitable result of their socialization, to what extent some students try to turn the work of our class, using my guidelines, into a new teacher-pleasing game, with a variation on the rules. In fact, they don't even need to "psych out" what I strongly believe in; I let them know quite clearly by (1) the readings I assign, (2) the activities I have them engage in in class, (3) my requirement that in choosing and engaging in their projects they must stretch beyond what they already know—or think they know, and (4) the classrooms to which I bring them on field trips.

I give the option of "I'm in struggle on this one" as they examine their end-of-semester position regarding each of the assumptions they find in their accumulated portfolio of writings. For a very few students, though the quality of their work was in their hands from the beginning, their grade at the end suddenly means everything to them. Those few students are willing to compromise what they really think by claiming to have been transformed in all their thinking, in order to say what they think will please the teacher, even when the rest of their semester has made that transformation unlikely. But who can say for sure? Maybe the work of synthesizing has made a great difference. Giving that possibility the benefit of the doubt, if there is solid supporting evidence, I figure that being able to put it all together convincingly would at least have gotten them a high grade in a traditional classroom, so I usually turn in at least a B. In fact, I sometimes even turn in the A- or A they request, if the evidence over the whole portfolio and semester has indicated plenty of original thinking going on and plenty of honest struggle. For me, it is the willingness to stretch and struggle that matters.

Though each situation is an individual one, anyone's attempt to con me provides yet more information about the negative effects of traditional schooling. When so much is at stake for them, as seems to be the case in the grading game, it's quite understandable that some students might revert to strategies that have "worked" in the past. I have found that among these particular students, those whose internal locus of control has not developed at all during the course of the semester, tend to select themselves out, deciding that teaching is too much work. The gratifying thing for me is that, overwhelmingly, students have grown enough during the course that, like most reader responses, their self-evaluations read honestly and powerfully.

Inevitably, however, no matter what the grading procedure, some students are dissatisfied. Colleagues, all of whom give regular ongoing grades, as I used to, widely report the same experience, regardless of how they approached the grading process. In my case, a few students each semester become furious when I reply to their suggested grade of A that I feel more comfortable with a lower grade. So we negotiate. My role is to listen, as well as cite specifics based on the general standards (see Figure 2.1). Nevertheless, stuck in the teacher-pleasing paradigm, such students, whether they come to complain or not, blame the professor for not "giving" them the grade they feel they rightfully deserve. Inevitably, they say that I do not like them; they feel that they have failed at pleasing me, and that is all that matters. None of this is easy or comfortable to deal with, most especially because it all misses the point of what I had been trying to get at in my classes. Clearly, students have an intense investment in doing well, regardless of whatever we as instructors think is going on in our classes. My hope, buttressed by considerable data, is that most students who come in with that focus ultimately find themselves able to broaden their perspective and let themselves just learn, once they redefine *learning* as being vastly more complex than short-term memorizing of decontextualized information.

I do not wish to give the impression that most of the students in my classes resist or sabotage the nontraditional processes of my courses. The vast majority of those who have been reading conscientiously and writing thoughtfully approach the task of self-evaluating with apprehension, to be sure, but they also enjoy the opportunity to put the course together in their own terms. Often the paper of self-evaluation they write is rich in connection and meaning making, based on a process of reflection that they have ultimately found rewarding. Several students each semester come to class the last day, saying how proud they are of how they have grown and how proud they are of the portfolio and self-evaluation paper which represent that growth.

Note

1. *Locus of control* describes whether action is internally or externally motivated. See Levin and Shanken-Kaye, (1996) for useful further definitions and applications (beginning on p. 55).

Chapter Three

Seeing the Possibilities of a Different Paradigm

Students seem to understand my reason for removing grades when I tell them, "I can't teach you and judge you at the same time." That statement itself challenges deeply held assumptions. But adjustment to self-direction takes time. Those whose sole focus throughout their schooling has been "doing well" by pleasing the teacher can feel confused and set adrift by the projects I assign, most of which ask them to create their own paths within the readings and activities. Students have reflected on what that shift forced them to realize:

- It's so obvious now, paying attention in class, how brainwashed my classmates and I are. We want specific directions, strict guidelines, [and] complete instructions, and we ask many, many questions (about what you want us to find).
- It's aggravating to me now, because I realize how I've been conditioned. I never chose to be this way. Because if the choice [were] mine, I wouldn't be so "tight."

My fear, and that of many teacher educators, is that if preservice teachers do not develop a fully internal locus of control well before they enter classrooms as teachers, their ability to help their own students grow will be seriously compromised (Haberman, 1992).

Nevertheless, young people still pretty much habituated to external locus of control, at least in the context of school, are the ones who are "in the pipeline" as preteachers. That's a given. If we as educators understand that transformation is a long-term process, we have to believe that what we do can make a difference, if not before people become teachers, then perhaps when they come back to us for graduate classes. We have to remember that they are the way they are because of what they experienced in school—until now. We have to trust that what was learned can be unlearned, if enough of us are committed to that process. First, we have to imagine, What if their own teachers had invited them to participate in their own learning and self-assessment as early as elementary school? So, as all teachers must do, we start with where they are and support them as they stretch, little by little.

How to Get Them to Read, Without Quizzes and Tests?

For the first time in my life I am actually enjoying reading.

One of my colleagues has for several years invited her graduate class in early childhood education to construct their own syllabus. She comes to the first class with a very bare outline of a syllabus, accounting for certain skills she feels they must develop and certain issues she feels they must address. From there, she makes it their task collectively to flesh out the work of the course. What particular areas interest them? What do they want their focus to be? For most of her students, as is almost always the case with mine, this is the first classroom situation in which they have had a say in any aspect of what they would be learning. Some are suspicious and uneasy: Is the teacher disorganized? Will I get what I paid for in this course? But within a few weeks, my colleague finds, as I do, that all students have risen to the level of responsibility inherent in the freedom of making choices. Many make the transfer to the constructivist project-oriented approach that the course is about, and they realize that it is possible—and much more energizing!—to teach and learn in this more collaborative and interest-driven way, even in early childhood.

Looking for ways to make the experience of my own teacher education courses one through which students might undergo a more fundamental process than just memorizing and reproducing information, I believe that I have, over many years, discovered bold

ways to ensure that in the process of becoming self-directed learners, most students will do their homework in depth, and will come
to class ready to participate fully in discussion.[1] The procedures I
outline here offer colleagues in both secondary and postsecondary
courses one rather labor-intensive but extremely effective and satisfying way to address familiar and persistent problems of student
passivity, as well as of shallow student reading and thinking. It at
least interrupts students' expectation that once they've turned in
a paper, they're done with it and with the ideas it purports to represent. The total process I have evolved replaces the need for
quizzes and tests; it replaces, as well, traditional book reports, term
papers, and other traditional representations of student reading.

Reader Response

Though I had been fumbling toward a kind of reader response format in my years of teaching English in high schools and then in
colleges, I did not experience it as a student until my first doctoral
course, at age fifty. Several years later, I witnessed its effectiveness
in two years of intensive biweekly observation and conversation
with a high school English teacher who used it with her students.
Learning from her especially, I have used it ever since with my
teacher education students, and I have found it to be enormously
helpful in getting students to read for meaning, to reflect on their
own lives in terms of the text, and to write honestly, even eagerly,
and compellingly.

Before I was exposed to reader response, I had deliberately
avoided using any text at all in my freshman composition classes,
because I wanted students to write from their own experiences,
and I did not know then how to have them do that and still be
responding to textual material. Until then, I had taught high
school and college English the way I had been taught about how
to read and write from text—distancing academic literary criticism.
Reader response allowed me to integrate the reading of provocative text with personal writing.

As the guidelines I offer suggest, reader response is not easy. It
is not possible to do a reader response without complete and careful reading of the text, for example. Some students may initially try,
especially those stuck in external locus of control and adept at the

essential game of traditional schooling—figuring out the quickest, *easiest* way to produce something that looks like what the teacher wants. It is even hard for conscientious students, who, for the most part from the same traditional schooling, are unaccustomed to making their own meaning from text without the teacher's lecture or "answer pulling" (Holt, 1967). They come to their first three-reader groups very tentatively, afraid that they haven't done it right or gotten the right answers. It takes several weeks to get used to reading not to "know" (by which they mean to "remember all the minute details") and to trust their own thinking:

> It has been very hard to erase all these years of spitting out answers like a robot. No teacher ever asked me how I felt about something or what does it mean to me.

Although students are invited to feel free to say that the text confused them, angered them, made them uncomfortable, and so forth, the constraint against any type of judging of or arguing with the author is a strict one, within whose boundaries anything is open for exploration. At first, most students don't know what to write if they are not allowed to either summarize or judge. The effect of those boundaries is that most students come to realize how tied they have been either to unquestioning absorption of whatever they read, or to considering themselves to have done some thinking when they judged a piece of text as good or bad, or right or wrong, in terms of what they already know—or think they know. Some examples of this behavior, more fully discussed in a later chapter, are especially startling in students' oversimplification of historical or sociological "facts."

While some see the structure of reader response as just another constraint, others find enormous freedom within it, like a poet composing a tight haiku or sonnet: they need to pare away, be clear, figure out what they really mean. For such students, this challenge to their mode of reading and responding is their first recognition that the distancing habits they've formed from their previous schooling have kept them from full rich exploration of ideas *they* choose to find important. They begin to take the risk of naming and letting go of the traditional assumptions whose effect, they now see, had

Figure 3.1. Venn Diagram for Reader Response

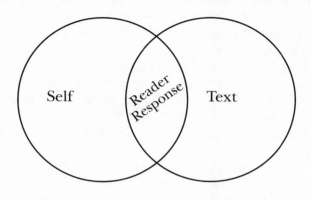

been to silence them. They are freed from teacher judgment (and also from peer judgment). When I ask at the end of the semester, "Who in here are the smartest students?", no one has an answer. Learning to trust their own voices, most students let go of the inflated, labored, "impressive" language they had developed as their academic writing style through many years of schooling, and allow their writing to be a way to discover what they *think* (Lorde, lecture at Williams College, 1984; Elbow, 1981). As a result, the voice of their writing inevitably becomes more clear, more powerful, and even much more grammatical.

Initially uncomfortable with letting go of habits of writing to prove what they know, students learn to engage at the intersection of text and self in their writings, thus reading to understand and apply rather than know or critique. In that complex process of reader response, and the ongoing dialogue which I describe later in this chapter, students identify, confront, and examine their own previously unconscious assumptions about children, about teaching and learning, and about the sociopolitical contexts in which schooling takes place.

Step-by-step, the process is this. Students bring to class what they wrote, with two extra copies. They share papers and insights with only two or, at most, three others for a generous chunk of time. Each person has about seven minutes to be the center of that small group's attention, in a listener response session, again with no judging or arguing. Each person's voice, on paper and then in dialogue, gets heard. During that time I stand or sit somewhere in the room, but always at a respectful distance from the groups. My task is to eavesdrop intensively, simultaneously on as many groups as I can from one position. Then I station myself somewhere else and listen and watch. But I rarely intervene. At the end of the twenty-one or so minutes, I invite the students to freewrite about what perspectives they got from that interaction that they hadn't considered before.

Students enjoy the safe intimacy of the small groups, being genuinely heard without being judged. The level of responsibility to the group is high: hardly anyone comes without a paper—or at least some thoughtful notes—to share, even though I do not take off points for late papers.

Teacher Feedback and Talking Back: A Tutorial Conversation on Paper

The internalized constraints on the freedom to discover what they think by writing are a direct result of socialization to writing whose purpose is to impress a teacher. Many students confess early in a semester to a set of paralyzing assumptions about themselves and about writing that I have also heard from doctoral candidates: if one is a "good writer," the work is easy, fast, and correct in a first draft:

> I don't like to write. It takes me too long. I am not the type
> of person who can easily grab a pen and a pad of paper and
> put my ideas down and have them express exactly how I feel.
> I search for the right phrase, wording, etc. It is very time-
> consuming. I do enjoy letter writing, though. Perhaps I am
> not being judged or evaluated (for a grade or for how and
> what I think and feel).

Beyond reader response, the complex strategy is to further evoke in-depth reflection by means of sustained dialogue stimulated by problem-posing questions in the margins of student writings. For example, one ongoing conversation probes a student's stated reluctance to write, exposing a common but deeply hidden underlying fear:

> Student: I've always been very reflective about what I put down on paper. I like a lot of time to think things over and let my ideas ferment.
>
> Professor: So "on paper" feels permanent?
>
> Student: Yeah, I guess so. If it's not going to come out like Pulitzer Prize material (which it never does), then don't write it.
>
> Professor: I anticipated this fear. It will be important for you as a prospective teacher to recognize *how* this gets internalized.

Such one-on-one conversation between student and professor over time is what allows the examination of assumptions to occur. Each of their papers becomes my text; I write marginal notes to the writer, and the writer in turn replies, for a round or two of conversation. A colleague described it as my having a tutorial session with each of my students, as, week by week, the student and I talk to each other on paper in a dialogue initiated by each piece of the student's own writing. At the end of the semester, in their final papers of synthesis and self-evaluation, reflecting on their experience of the course, students often mention how much time and energy—and thought—the writebacks took, but also how valuable they were. Though many students, at least on some level, have found having to do them tedious, some of those same students were among the ones who reported appreciating my taking the time really to *listen* to what they had to say, as well as appreciating my urging them to consider their own ideas more deeply, even when that process was not at all comfortable:

> You interacted with our thoughts. The questions you asked made me see . . . differently.

Figure 3.2. The Process of Writebacks

Becca Fournier
September 18, 2002
Dialogue #3

Jamie - 19, Becca -19

[handwritten: OK-I'll stop by office during hours   Let's confer a role play about this process, ok? In class, or in my office? You decide, ok?]

I was helping Jamie do her math homework when this conversation arose...

Jamie: Why can't I understand this stuff? It seems so easy in class.
Becca: Yeah, it's always easier when the teacher is giving you the answers. *[handwritten: ok?]*
Jamie: How am I supposed to learn this stuff for the test? I'm going to definitely fail!
Becca: I have been horrible in math all of my life. It was always so hard to learn
a new formula or equation to use. *[handwritten: ① Jamie, what do you really feel here?]*
Jamie: Tell me about it, I'm going to have to do a million homework problems to get this
right! *[handwritten: what's your goal, Becca? ②]*
Becca: Don't worry, it's happened to me before too. If you keep up with everything and
practice everything over and over, it will come to you.

Well, I'm not sure how well this one worked. Jamie was <u>still a little</u> upset after

this conversation, even though she was a little more calm and ready to move on.

However, I noticed that I didn't identify any feeling. *[handwritten: aha!!]* Instead, I just kind of let her know

that I have been in the same situation that she has been in and I know how she feels. Is

that the same thing as identifying a feeling?

[handwritten: ③ not really. Let's see what the book has to say about the difference, in Chap. 1, ok? But before + as you re-read, think: "what was she feeling? If I felt it too, I must have a name for it."?]

(Just work)

Becca Fournier
10/2/02

Re-write to Dialogues from 9/18/02

① I was trying to let Jamie know that I understand her, yet I am supposed to be helping her cope with her feelings by identifying those feelings. By saying this, I am somewhat justifying her thoughts, but I guess I'm denying her feelings by telling her what's happened to me.

② My goal is supposed to be to get Jamie to identify and cope with her feelings, but instead, I'm just giving her advice!

③ After re-reading, I couldn't really find anything about the difference. But, she was feeling frustration because she couldn't understand the math. Maybe if I said, "That must be really frustrating", she would have had her feelings acknowledged, rather than me just letting her know how I feel.

④ I'm denying her feelings (w/out even realizing it back then!)

⑤ I identified her feelings - frustration?

⑥ Didn't occur to me one bit!

⑦ Under that anger was sadness and disappointment for me ignoring him. He wasn't so mad, but more upset.

Figure 3.2. The Process of Writebacks, continued

8. Yes definitely with good reason. I felt terrible!

9. I would have tried to stop the fight before it started, by trying to get Jimmy to cope with his feelings. I'm beginning to realize that it's the best way to deal with a situation!

Dialogue Attempts - "How To Talk"   9/19/02
                                      Laura Petraitto
                                      EDTE 210

① Thursday after school, I am at my
daycare. The 3 year olds I am in charge of
are playing outside. "Eddie" is using his
walkie talkie as a gun, which is not
allowed. ① *toys- watching lots of TV?*

Laura: Edward, walkie talkies are for talking. *OK!!!*
They are not guns.
Eddie: OK (continues playing) *but please a gun?*

This, my first attempt! went pretty well!! *Yes!*
Eddie was not upset, and took my
"information" and used it to change his
behavior.

② The same day. I am still at the daycare.
Now I am in charge of the after-school
children. I am watching 5 year-old
Austin in the sandbox. He is frantically
digging up a hole and flinging sand all *Good!*
over the sandbox, hitting the other children.

Laura: Austin, *or "what you are doing," or "flinging sand"* you are getting sand all over *the*
the other children. *them,*
Austin: (ignores me)   *or worried?* ④
Laura: Austin, I get angry when you ignore me.
Austin: (continues digging)
Laura: AUSTIN! the sand!! *ok!*

Figure 3.3. The Process of Writebacks

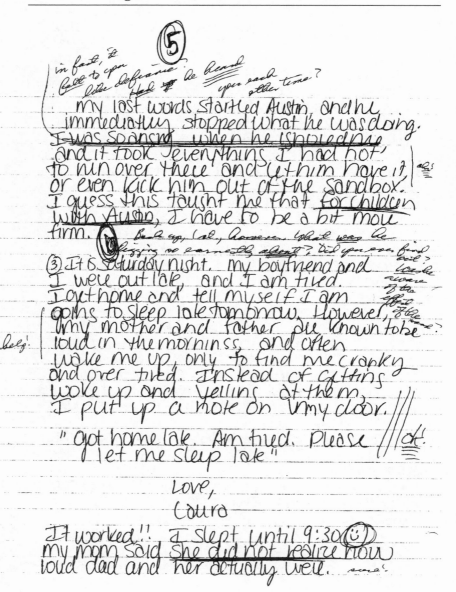

Figure 3.3. The Process of Writebacks, continued

Just work,
then file

Laura E. Petrolito
October 8, 2002
EDTE 210

Writeback To:
Dialogue Attempts – "How To Talk"

certainly possible!

1.) I think that Eddie may have picked up on some of the other violent behavior from some of the older kids at the daycare. Violent behavior is definetley discouraged at my daycare, but some of it goes unseen.

2.) When Eddie continued playing, he took his walkie-talkie and used it to summon his friend, Nicole. He did not use it as a gun for the rest of the afternoon.

3.) The way I addressed Austin's issue was probably not as appropriate as it could have been. I indirectly placed the problem on him, saying YOU are getting sand all over everyone. I was putting all of my disappointment and blame on him alone. This may have not been the right thing to say. I should have said, "Austin, when you dig like that, sand gets all over the sandbox".

4.) The reason I said that I get angry was because I was under the assumption that we should tell the children how we felt about their behavior. I truly was angry at the fact that Austin was ignoring my attempt at getting him to stop flinging sand.

5.) It is possible that he may have not heard me, or he could have been sort of tuning me out. Either way, it got me very frustrated and angry. I suppose I should have tried to find out if he had truly heard me. Maybe next time instead of yelling across the playground I should go over there and look him directly in the eye.

6.) I did find out later why Austin was digging so frantically. He was pretending he was a dog, digging up his bone. I don't think he meant to fling sand all over the sandbox, but I did inform him later that the sandbox was for building castles and making small hills, not digging. I will observe Austin's behavior in the sandbox in the next couple days and see if he has remembered what he should not be doing.

Figure 3.3. The Process of Writebacks, continued

Laura E. Petrolito
October 23, 2002
EDTE 210

Last Word To:
Dialogue Attempts – "How To Talk"

1.) Unfortunately, the sandbox is closed for the fall, so I will not get a chance to see Austin's behavior in the sandbox. However, if there is another situation like that one, I will first try to find out why Austin is behaving that way. I will then try to guide him in the right direction and give him fair choices.

2.) I would not say that the majority of my staff uses "violent" tones with the children. The owner of my daycare and all of her adult staff members all have as many as 20 years of experience with children, and from what I see, they do not use "violent" methods the majority of the time. I have seen my employer and her staff use methods such as (genuine) choices, using feelings, and giving information. I am trying my best to model their methods, but myself and one of the younger (college-aged, teachers to be) employees are still learning. However, my employer does make an effort of having mandatory staff meetings that discuss methods of engaging cooperation from the children and making them happy as well at the center. It will take a lot more time and experience for me to get to their level.

3.) Underneath my anger, there was a sense of frustration because I felt that I was not in control of the situation, and Austin was ignoring my "authority" over him. "I'm angry" can be heard as a threat, because usually when an adult gets angry, that means the child is going to be either punished or yelled at. This is a natural association, that comes even from our early years from our parents.

Although the workload on both sides—students and teacher—is enormous, it is never a mindless or repetitive chore for me to sit down with a set of student papers. Each paper is a new, engaging, often exciting, and always stimulating conversation. Isn't it for that feeling that we become teachers?

By the end of a semester, most students achieve some degree of useful reflectiveness, even about their own anxieties:

> Unfortunately, I still find myself thinking about grades and papers and projects and how I measure up to everyone else. It think it is very hard to overcome twelve years of product orientation.

The hope, sometimes realized, is that seeing these habits in themselves will allow preteachers to notice teacher-pleasing behaviors in the elementary and secondary classrooms they visit. Ultimately, those who have arrived at a very sophisticated level of consciousness report—or at least can consider when I probe—for example, that seeing children wildly waving their hands for teacher attention means something other than that these children are "excited about learning," which is the conclusion most observers draw from such a scene. The most reflective preteachers recognize in the enthusiastic handwaving and "Oooo!" the possibility that what they are witnessing is students trying their hardest to be the first to impress the teachers with their answers. "Right answers," after all, are the currency of the game of teacher-pleasing. Another way of interpreting such a scene, however, could be that children are eager to process the topic at hand aloud, eager to have a say and be heard. In that case, I ask this: Why not instead let them all talk to each other in very small groups, even twos, for two minutes, before calling on anyone? Then everyone gets to have a say.

What emerges overwhelmingly from student reflections is that the dominant mode of teaching, K–12 and through most college courses, continues to be the teacher-centered, content-centered kind of situation most of us experienced in our own schooling. Students report experiencing agony in apprehension that the teacher will ask them to read aloud, or expose them in any way in front of their peers. It is helpful not to let ourselves forget, as teachers and teacher educators, that this is how we felt as students:

> I can remember [that] in elementary school my teachers would always walk around the room looking over our shoulders. I felt like they were spying on me. I was afraid to put down a wrong answer because they would see it and correct me in front of everyone.

John Holt (1967) observes, "Teachers not only like right answers, they like them right away" (p. 100). Preteachers, like many practicing teachers, identify the "quick" student as the "bright" one, rewarding impulsive surface thinking more consistently than reflectiveness—maybe to keep their own tight agendas moving along:

> My schooling programmed me into believing that the faster you could find an answer the smarter and better a student you were.

Both high school and university students report that, to them, regardless of—or perhaps because of—the insulting generic "comprehension questions" at the end of a textbook chapter (which often served as both their homework and the next day's class "discussion"—usually meaning "checking for recall") reading is a task for finishing as fast as they can—and not for contemplating, especially not in terms of their own lives. Whatever they don't "get," the teacher will "go over it" in class. The struggle to learn, therefore, is not associated with deep satisfaction but with a well-internalized habit, based on the assumption that they are not capable if they don't "get it" right away. That assumption usually comes from a teacher's well-intentioned but often devastating habit of quickly going on to someone else for the answer:

> I've found that whenever I find myself encountering something . . . too difficult for me, my mind seems to automatically shut off. I will try for a while, and if I cannot come to a correct solution soon, I will stop.

What Do You Do When You Don't Understand What You Read?

As I indicated earlier, the reader response guidelines and the ongoing dialogues on their papers, designed to encourage students to explore their own experiences in terms of a text, were new and awkward for most students. I was after their thinking, not some right answers I already had in my head. Some early, fumbling reader response papers produced direct, honest descriptions of their own socialization, revealing feelings that are crucial for teachers to consider:

> I associate (identify) with the child [in Holt's *How Children Learn* (1967)] who knows the right answer but because he does not feel sure enough [about his] answer, [he] will remain silent because he fears that a trap has been set for him. I did not want to get hooked into answering a question, because what if I got it right and she asked another, even harder, comprehension question? I just stayed quiet.

The resistance to being probed for even deeper thinking expressed by this student sabotages what we as teachers know our task to be, if we desire to help students become more complex thinkers. The defensiveness and suspicion expressed in this student's statement persists for many teacher education students, undergraduate and graduate, even though the probing I do is mostly not public but on their papers, individualized and private. I never intentionally or consciously attack, and though I do my best to keep my tone and my questions positive, some students are inclined to perceive my comments as attacks. In fact, the conditioning has caused them to expect that any teacher who marks on their papers is saying, "You are wrong!"—no matter what the actual words say. The struggle to think things through is not one that most students have developed, and to do so is not something that all welcome or enjoy, which we as teachers, with all good intentions, have discouraged by playing our traditional roles in their earlier years. But we can change our practice and help them learn to read for meaning for themselves.

What I have discovered to be increasingly true, in at least the last decade, is that, to a frightening extent, many students are not accustomed to expecting of themselves that they will understand what they read. Many reveal that they have been socialized to pass their eyes over the words of a text—any text—and by taking notes or highlighting, they commit to short-term memory what looks like something that *might* be important (that is, it may appear on a quiz or test), and then wait for the teacher to "go over it" (that is, *tell* the students what the reading meant). One sobering comment can stand for the many that I have heard:

> I never read for content; I just memorized it for a test result.

Some students, finding certain readings beyond their own schema, have never developed the habit of taking their confusion as an opportunity to explore how different their own schooling was from what was being described. For example, a number of students in one undergraduate class, early in my teacher education career, had great difficulty understanding Sylvia Ashton-Warner's book *Teacher* (1963), then one of my anchor books (and a source of my own inspiration as I had shifted suddenly, without new preparation, from high school teacher to first grade teacher). When I stopped the class and conducted a meeting to examine their feelings, I discovered that they were accustomed to having been given only dry textbooks; they were accustomed to reading for facts rather than for nuance, feeling, or meaning. Instead of trying to imagine what Ashton-Warner was describing, they were reading literally, without hearing any shift in tone or voice. They were not backing up to reread passages that seemed strange to them, and they thought they were required to "know" the English or Maori idioms, names, and places! Of course, they had translated their anxiety into a dislike of the book. One student explained her feelings on paper, in a freewrite before our class discussion, and this dialogue followed:

> Student: I get all jumpy and aggravated when I don't understand.

> Professor: I want you to say lots more about this, if you will.

> Student: I don't like feeling like the one who doesn't understand. I guess I'm trying to build up my patience. I blame the other person when I don't "get" (understand) something. If others understand, I should too.

What helped this student feel less "jumpy"—and greatly helped me understand his socialization—was our open in-class discussion of the widely shared misunderstanding of Ashton-Warner's context and perspective. The impromptu class conversation revealed that many had become stuck in what they could not recognize as relatively unimportant details. Several students, preoccupied with their own failure to "know," and having no experience of any other way to read, gave up in frustration. This class was the first to state outright to me that even in their college classes, students were used to being told what was important, and were used to being drilled and tested on those small things. Through that dialogue, which continued within their papers, most saw that their habitual focus and dependency—not any personal inadequacy—caused them to miss the meaning of the whole, and they were unable to trust themselves—or to even bother to try—to figure it out.

One unfortunate consequence of this experience, however, is that although I have recommended Ashton-Warner's *Teacher* (1963) to many individual students, I have not used it as a class text again since that semester. Instead, I changed aspects of my guidelines for reader response. In addition, I began inviting students to come for conferences with me, to offer an alternative venue in which they could begin to develop the habit of really reading what is really there, and making meaning of it. The reasons for that at first eluded me, but now it seems clearly to have to do, at least in part, with years of passivity in traditional classrooms. In fact, as I soon discovered, it was not just Ashton-Warner's book but almost everything they're given to read that initially stumps certain teacher education students.[2]

I have changed something else, as well, as a result of what I learned from my students' paralysis with Ashton-Warner's simple journal. Whenever I've been invited to engage in individual teacher observations as part of in-service staff development, or whenever I've supervised student teachers, I have become more assertive about pointing out the dependencies I see a teacher enabling, though never with that intent. In one third grade class, for example, I watched as a teacher led the children through a vocabulary exercise, using a story in their basal reader. For homework, the children had already picked out words that they didn't know the meanings of as they had "gone through" the story. As she called on children around the room, each child had a chance to offer a word from his or her paper, which the child either sounded out or, more frequently, spelled aloud. The teacher nicely validated each offering, writing it on the chart, to be defined. Then the teacher had each of the children, as individuals, locate each word in the text, one by one, along with the sentence that contained it. She had that sentence read aloud by a child. She asked for a definition. No one had one for any of the words—although a few guessed. They waited. Then the teacher gave her definitions, which were very carefully and thoughtfully geared to the students' level of understanding. She said each, and then she wrote it on the chart paper. At the end of the exercise, the children copied the words and definitions into their notebooks.

When the teacher and I had a postobservation conference, I found out that her goal was to have them know the vocabulary so that they could read the story eventually. A worthy goal, and a very gentle, validating, and helpful manner of achieving it, especially since the story she chose seemed to have been beyond the reading ability of most of the children. But the teacher was doing all the work. No wonder her first comment when we sat down to process the lesson had to do with her disappointment about their not having paid full attention. Essentially, I observed, they were bored with the passive position she had placed them in, though with all good intentions.

I offered a few suggestions about how she might have engaged them in constructing some of their own meanings. She might have jigsawed the list of words, having the kids work in pairs, assigning them to struggle for a few minutes to get the meanings of one or two of the words from the context. She might have let them use the pictures and ask each other lots of their own questions beforehand about what might be going on in the story. Even if she wanted to keep the lesson teacher-centered, she might have invited lots more discussion about each word, probing for some of their own prior experience that might help them associate meaning with each word. In full class, too, she might have contextualized the words by briefly and perhaps dramatically telling the story herself, and then having pairs of children work together for two or three minutes to figure out what a strange word might mean in that context. All of those methods are strategies researchers have written about, and they are ones that, I trust, are taught in university reading courses. Each of my suggestions, of course, would have taken more time than that one third grade teacher seemed willing to give, which seems to be the case for most teachers, if most of my students' underdeveloped abilities to read for meaning are any measure. If the long-range goal, however, is for students to become readers instead of memorizers of lists of words and definitions, that kind of time needs to be taken.

Internalized Pressure

Quizzes and tests, the ultimate performance measures, seem to be an especially serious and universal source of anxiety, and even anger, for students. The very word *quiz* triggers considerable stress in my "gradeless" class, and students cannot relax until we actually do my only "quiz." In the fourth or fifth class meeting, as I had announced on the first day, I quiz the students on each other's names. They expect individual writing or reciting, and many are very nervous. They come with many strategies. Some, of course, seem resigned to failing. I quickly conduct the quiz in my usual collaborative manner, having them in pairs or threes associate names with people as they go around the circle, calling the names one by one, helping each other remember. That is my way of showing them what I strongly believe: no one should have to do anything hard alone. We naturally learn people's names not by memorizing frantically but in the process of actually working directly with people. In the same way, we can learn whatever facts we have reason to *use.*

The tension that preceded the quiz, however, becomes a common and effective vehicle for reflection about their own schooling. Focusing on getting right answers in individual tests of performance seems to produce a high level of fear, but also a high level of guilt for anything less than perfection in students of whom perfection had come to be expected:

> Although I was guilty of being "lazy" as an adolescent, I have spent the past few years of my life killing myself to get A's. When I don't get an A I tend to kick myself, thinking, "I was careless, I knew that." A little neurotic, but maybe if there wasn't such an emphasis on my "abilities" as a child I wouldn't have such a compulsive NEED TO DO WELL FOR THE SAKE OF GRADES.

The pressure to get and stay at the top seems to produce a completely distorted view of the learning process. It is not surprising that university students in elementary education courses—especially those who have themselves experienced low levels of success in terms of grades in certain subjects (usually math, science, and social studies)—tend to avoid teaching those subjects, once they are employed as teachers, without realizing that neither the subject matter nor their own abilities was the necessary factor in their nonsuccess. The language in this student's statement is quite revealing:

> I have always had a hard time in math. From the first grade until high school, I was always in the low-level class. I did not have a disability, nor was I put in a special class, but feelings of inferiority were always present. I knew I was behind. I knew I needed to get good grades. I felt that I just had to pass, but I confused myself even more. I started to become closed-minded and started having an attitude toward understanding math.

Guilt over failure to meet internalized teachers' demands of meeting absolute standards of neatness, correctness, and promptness continues to influence university students in their teacher education classes, and continues to take on disproportionate importance. One might say that they learned their early lessons well—too well. Sometimes those feelings paralyze the students' freewriting until they learn to trust that there will be no teacher judgment. In many students' experiences, I have learned that promptness and perfection of form had not just been about effective communication, time management, responsibility, and courtesy, but had seemed to be all that had mattered to their teachers. One student submitted a stunningly thoughtful two-and-a-half-page paper early in the semester, with three minor penciled-in editing corrections. The sad revelation is that the student felt compelled to attach this note to it. In her experience, perfection of form had mattered tremendously:

> Student: I apologize about the lateness and you will never see a messy paper like this again. I had problems with my word processor.
>
> Professor: What are you talking about? I *love* it that you proofread! Look at where your terror of teacher judgment and expectation

of perfection comes from, J! No wonder there's so much fear of teachers! This paper looks *fine* to me, and what's more important, it says something *real!*

Another brought in a doctor's note to explain her absence from class. Reminded that the teacher trusted her responsibility and did not need to see it, she attached it anyway to her next paper, but she learned something important from the interaction:

> I know you said that I did not have to turn this in, but I still felt more comfortable doing so. I just have to break the old patterns about the student-teacher relationship from the past. Thank you for your trust.

In the margin next to her word "trust," I responded:

> It's the condition that makes teaching/learning possible. I feel sad that your experience has been not to expect it.

Notes

1. The material from this section comes in large part from a paper I presented in January 1996 at the annual conference of the International Society for Exploring Teaching Alternatives.
2. I am not sure why the number of preteachers—and even graduate students—who cannot read for meaning seems to be increasing, but I notice with alarm that it has done so over the past decade. I am also not sure what it will mean for the quality of their own teaching—if they make it through the program—that they have successfully relied on memorizing, teacher lectures, or other compensatory skills to get through all their years of schooling. My sense is that it must make them insecure as teachers.

Chapter Four

Falling into the Role of Traditional Teaching, and Climbing Out of It

As Alfie Kohn (1996) indicates, "right behaviors" seem to be the social side of traditional academic "right answers"(p. xv). The readings, response papers, writebacks, and conversations in my teacher education classes urge students to stand back from and gain perspective on the traditional conditions they had taken for granted as being intrinsic to schooling. Without honest and courageous examination, they might unconsciously reproduce those conditions in their own teaching:

- I always knew that I didn't like the stiff environment that I was taught in but I just assumed it was normal like every other school. Everything had to be just so: straight desks, straight lines. I *know* this is why I think the way I do about teachers' expectations.
- I think that kind of teaching made me less independent in some cases. My teachers always told me what to do and exactly how they wanted it done, so that's what I did.

Am I Part of the Problem? How a Personal Journey Led Me to This Research

The origins of this chapter can probably be traced far back to my earliest teaching at a high school whose exterior reminded me of a factory. I myself taught quite traditionally in that first high school job, starting in 1959. The role I easily slipped into found me controlling all the conversation by "pulling answers" (Holt, 1967) from the front of the room, especially with my freshmen and sophomores. I saw myself grooming the students in my English classes—as I had been groomed—to be literary critics. But several factors drew me away from that role, especially with my seniors. One was that I was only about five years older than they were, and I was still (as I understood much, much later) in late adolescence myself. To a great extent, I identified more with my seventeen- and eighteen-year-old students than with the other teachers, who, to me, were "old"—over thirty. Another was that I had just come from graduate school seminars set up in a circle, which I reproduced in my senior "advanced" classes, in which I began to do a little more listening than in the other classes, though I was still essentially preaching and pulling answers. Another was that our vehicle for discussion in those courses was very wonderful personal literature, such as Joyce's *Portrait of the Artist as a Young Man,* Fitzgerald's *The Great Gatsby,* and the poetry of e. e. cummings. I was sometimes finding myself as interested in the students' ideas, feelings, and lives as I was in their grammar, paragraph structure, and "right answers."

Though I had not yet learned to ask them to talk on paper, some of my students were doing that in our conferences outside of class, coming up with some original ideas and connections. In contradiction to the traditional role, I was being real with them as a person, excited about what we were reading. I was getting to know them as people, learning along with them and from them. But, basically, I still did most of the talking, and, basically, they did their best to please me.

Then, as a result of two years as a civil rights worker in Mississippi, from 1964 to 1966, my ideas about teaching and learning profoundly changed.[1] As a volunteer "teacher" in the Mississippi Freedom Schools, I realized, for the first time in the summer of 1964, that schooling can be an agent of a people's oppression. I saw then that where freedom has to begin is in how children are educated. Paulo Freire (1968) was wise to understand that teachers are not deliberate agents of oppression. Most teachers, I think, went into teaching at least partially thinking that they were helping to fulfill Thomas Jefferson's expectation: for real democracy to occur, the citizens need to be literate and to practice decision making.

Since I left Mississippi in 1966, I have spent my teaching career, from K–12 to graduate school, trying to act on what I learned in the Civil Rights Movement. Even when I operate with a "curriculum," I consciously ground my teaching in the social, political, economic, and personal realities of students' lives, and I encourage students to do the thinking rather than parrot mine.

Once I began supervising student teachers as part of my doctoral program in teacher education in the late 1980s, I had the opportunity never available to me when I was a teacher myself: to observe other teachers in their classrooms. However, even in the early 1980s, I already knew something about what must have been going on in high school classrooms, at least in those attended by the students who thereafter attended community and state colleges. The writing voices of my college freshman composition students were cautious, empty, and lifeless, even if completely correct. So I knew that high school English was still being taught by formula, at least to working-class and lower-middle-class students. From my community and state college students' narrowly defined views of the world, especially regarding history and current events, I could tell that their high school social studies classes had not invited them to question or even understand the way things are in the world. All that they had obediently "learned" had long been lost from short-term memory. Little of the information they collected and "knew" was available to them for application to present situations. Furthermore, I knew from their postures and silences that many of them were accustomed to being scared or bored, but in either case, passive. The reality under those impressions has been directly confirmed by the writings that students have since done in my teacher education courses.

Much of what I actually saw as I watched teachers and students in K–12 classrooms in the late 1980s disturbed me. What I witnessed helped me understand and extend my doctoral readings, especially Sennett and Cobb's *The Hidden Injuries of Class* (1972) and Lillian Rubin's *Worlds of Pain* (1976). Those books describe working-class and just-above-poverty-class silence, humiliation, sense of personal inadequacy, desperate but largely unfulfilled desire for autonomy in work, all-or-nothing thinking, and failure of community. Behind all these characteristics I saw American public schools, even those whose students are middle class. It became my goal to bring this reality to light.

How Do Teachers Read Kids' Behaviors?

When they first begin to visit classrooms, most preteachers tend just to watch—and identify with—the teacher, and they block most feelings except for whether or not they themselves feel warmly welcomed and accepted. The result of such a focus is that until we have had plenty of conversation in teacher education classes, whenever a new observer sees a child act out of feelings of inadequacy, boredom, or frustration, that visitor is likely to join the teacher in assuming that the child is a problem.

Unless preteachers develop the habit of closely observing children and tuning in to them, they are likely to be teachers who believe that a child who does not behave in a perfectly teacher-pleasing way is deliberately trying to sabotage the teacher's lesson. I have watched some of my student teachers not see, or at least not respond to, the discomfort, anxiety, boredom, and even anger on kids' faces and in their bodies. I have asked those student teachers afterwards what they were thinking about when they went on with the lesson that was part lecture, part answer pulling. Some were troubled. Others blamed the kids for not being "prepared." Clearly, such a teacher becomes frustrated when the lesson does not go well. Who would not?

How the teacher deals with his or her own frustration is the key issue. The ones who blame the children are the ones I worry about. When the teacher who does this is one of my students or student teachers, I have an obligation and an opportunity to ask that student to reflect. Furthermore, I must help guide that reflection toward the preteacher's developing a habit of tuning into children, and of looking first at his or her own pedagogical choices whenever a lesson or situation does not go well. However, what if that teacher is a veteran teacher in a school that has not invited me or another teacher educator to do staff development? If he or she should happen to become a cooperating teacher, we are looking at a potential role model of practices that are not respectful of children, and the familiar but oppressive cycle continues. The challenge for teacher education programs, then, is to locate the teachers who are effective role models of the kind of teaching that respects children. There are many out there, but not yet enough.

I had occasion to interview a cooperating teacher I will call "Ralph," as part of a semester-long investigation into practicing teachers' attitudes about their work. Ralph was eager to talk, pleased to be asked. He said, "Nobody ever asks teachers what they think!" Although honest, gracious with his time, and forthright, this successful department chair and veteran of twenty-five years as a high school English teacher did not call into question certain of his own underlying assumptions about students. Nor did he question his role in regard to them, or certain school practices, such as tracking, that directly affect them:

> I will tell you this: I do a lot more quizzing in the noncollege classes, because there's a tremendous tendency to not do the homework. So I use my quizzes to fight that off, and they're very thorough quizzes.

Although he recognized his students' passivity, his diagnosis of what that required of him is one I have heard from many K–12 teachers, and also (especially) from college professors:

> But you find yourself constantly fighting that attitude of indifference, because it's just crazy indifference, you know. You have to . . . I have to provide the spark in that class, far more than I do in the other class. I have to be the inspiration, totally, in that class, because there's nothing that's coming, almost nothing that comes from them. They want me to give it all.

Though he had not visited any of their homes, he spoke with conviction about what he presumed the family lives of his "noncollege" students to be like. In spite of his assertion of sympathy for what he assumed they did not have in their lives, he had decided that being tough with them in class was the way to motivate them:

> So what you have to do is battle. You're battling all the time in that class. You waste more energy battling than you do anything else, you know? "Aaron! Aaron! Did you read it last night?" You

know. "What do you mean, you didn't read it? Why didn't you read it? What did you do last night? Tell me what was so important that you did last night. Please, I want to know. Did I give you too many pages?" And you do it that way, you know.

Playing the Role

Without examination or conscious struggle, the cycle of low self-esteem and fear of judgment that many teachers experienced in their own schooling becomes the unconscious mode out of which they operate. The role they expect to fill has a well-defined script for them to follow. It "worked" for them, so they replicate it. But even if they see it not working for the children in their classroom, it takes courage to dare to deviate. Change is difficult for anyone, but it's particularly difficult for people whose self-esteem may still be tied to being approved of by those in authority. It is especially difficult for those who are accustomed to one right answer in a zero-sum situation to even imagine stepping outside the role—or dare to color outside the lines.

Many researchers have made the observation that, unlike people undertaking study for any other profession, preteachers already know intimately what the role is like before they begin their coursework. Characteristically, many preteachers at least vaguely feel—and some insist—that they really don't need any coursework, except perhaps for some hints and tricks about what to do with a particularly badly behaved child, or where to find neat activities. I myself was that kind of impatient education student and new teacher; I thought I was born knowing how to teach high school—just let me get in there and do my stuff!

Of course, "my stuff," predictably, was the kind of thing I had seen and experienced all my life, since kindergarten, where I, too, had been made to sit in rows and stop "chattering" with my neighbor. At best, as a new teacher, as I began this chapter by admitting, I tried to turn my thirty-student senior literature class into an elite and sophisticated graduate seminar in "lit. crit.," but I pulled answers, interpreted and delivered meaning, and required formulaic five-paragraph themes from my ninth graders. I was the sole expert resource, owning the process of filling students up with knowledge.

In addition, I was probably as authoritarian in my own classroom management as my own teachers had been. I cannot forget how I behaved in a role play as a student in the required educational psychology class. I shocked myself, and the professor and the other students, by yelling at "my class," shaking my finger, and threatening dire consequences if they didn't "behave." I wish that instead of just giving me a lower grade for that revelation of my deeply embedded reaction, the professor had used it as an opportunity to address and help the whole class address and come to terms with the origins and persistence of authoritarian styles. He did not provide that reflection, and it took me many years to figure it all out for myself. I confess this with extraordinary humility because it would otherwise be very easy to scapegoat the individual personality of Ralph, the English department chair, whose interview reveals what I have found to be the thinking of a prototypical traditional teacher. What I see in Ralph is in all of us (including myself) who were trained to be—and who for a while, or forever, enjoyed being perceived as—expert, brilliant, in control, and at center stage, because we knew instinctively how to play that role.

How instinctive this role playing is was demonstrated to me by how my daughter took on the teacher's role when she invited me to play school with her when she was in second grade. It took a while before I understood the frustration I was feeling at her tight, formal, almost pompous speech, her yelling at her student—me— and her blocking of my initiatives, my slightest movement, my divergent answers. Almost all her language was in the form of commands. Certainly she was playing out what she herself was then experiencing in her second grade classroom and had experienced in first grade. It wasn't until she was in the third grade that I was able to say to her, "I won't play school with you if you're Mrs. B; only if you're Ms. P." Immediately she was able to shift personalities and "be" the nurturing, creative, open third grade teacher who was then redeeming school for her—for a while. My "quitting school" on her, and talking to her about why, forced my daughter to think about how she wanted to be in the classroom and how she wanted her teachers to be—though very few teachers thereafter ever were. What I am finding with most preservice teachers, however, is that they have done very little examining of themselves and their own schooling in terms of the role they are about to take on. One secondary education student acknowledged:

> I had not considered that the teacher, speaking the most, domi-nated the classroom in a negative fashion. . . . I never questioned that method . . . that whole thing of, "If I'm not in front of the classroom, am I still the teacher?"

Another student, examining the model, decided that it is that way by right:

> The teachers are the teachers not just because of training and a formal education, but because they have been around longer. They have experienced life, . . . and they should be looked up to. . . . They must do most of the talking so that the students will take in the life experience of the teacher. . . . The attention span of most students is short.

Without ever examining *why* children lose their incredible pre-schooling ability to concentrate for long periods of time on tasks they have chosen or invented, preteachers and practicing teachers at all levels tend to assume that young students will have "short attention spans." Teachers generally also see only two extreme options: if the teacher cannot control the kids, they will run all over him or her.

I worry about people planning to be teachers who think of chil-dren the way this secondary education student did. He was among the most reluctant in my class to think of teachers letting go of con-trol enough to allow students to work in cooperative groups. Not surprisingly, he also was one who remembered having been "made to feel stupid or unimportant" in school and then having retaliated by sabotaging the teachers' agendas whenever he could. Thus, he expected his own resistance, without understanding it as such, from the students who, incidentally, would be there in the class-room with him:

> I have not had much exposure to adolescents in the past few years, but I find that when I do run into kids today, I find my toleration level dropping and I am sometimes quick to anger. Now I realize

that kids are going to be an integral part of my profession in
a few months, so I will have to learn how best to deal with them . . .
not [to see them] as a bunch of snotty-nosed, bratty kids.

Is this the person you want teaching your children? Unfortunately, I have heard similar statements from other preteachers,
practicing teachers, and paraprofessionals over the past decade.
Very frightening. It offers insight into why so many children feel
so alienated from school.

Even people who go into teaching feeling that they do not
want to be yelling at children find themselves doing it as part of
their socialization into schools. The schools in which they find
themselves teaching turn out to be mostly like the ones in which
they grew up. In both, silent kids are "good" kids. One first-year
teacher at a parochial high school wrote to me of her experiences:

Lots of discipline problems. I never yelled . . . but the yelling
I've done this year! But I learned early that yelling doesn't make
any difference. But I still have to yell. Those old nuns have totally
silent classrooms. The control they have!

The tangible signs of control become that part of the role in
which new teachers and student teachers such as this one feel they
have to prove themselves to other faculty members:

That came as just a basic way of being, for me, to think that
screaming at the kids just doesn't seem like a good thing . . . but
he [her cooperating teacher] felt like I had to be stronger, and
sort of change my voice tone, and change the way I stood, and
things like that.[2] . . . So I dealt with it, and I did what he wanted
me to do.

The power position of a traditional teacher causes surprising
and disturbing reactions. I was able to generate amazed reflections
on that power-over stance in a quick role play in a secondary education class, just by having the desks returned from our usual circle to rows. I let each student experience one minute of being up
in front of that arrangement, while the rest of us overplayed being
high school students. Most of them reported in their freewriting

afterwards that they felt uncomfortable in that kind of in-charge position, in a variety of ways:

- I felt naked, exposed, on display, vulnerable.
- They seem to *dare* you to teach them. You'll have to work hard to motivate them.
- It was definitely you against them. I was self-conscious . . . nowhere else for them to look and awfully expectant. They expect stuff from you. . . . Isolating.
- Power. Everything rests on you. You're expected to perform.

   But also, unfortunately:

- But I'm getting used to it from microteaching and subbing.
- I started wanting to cheer up everyone, but then I got over-whelmed and angry.
- To ease my discomfort at being looked at (which I hate), I became authoritarian.

Metaphors for the Role of a Teacher

That is how easy it is to fall into the role. Not a single aspect of traditional teaching is, by itself, oppressive to students, nor do teachers ever consciously decide to be oppressors. What is important is to consider the range of ways teachers describe what they are doing, and where that sense of themselves leaves the children.

   It seems to me that the language of combat, which I have heard astonishingly often, especially but not exclusively from high school teachers, comes from the almost inevitably adversarial posture of teacher-centeredness, as described by the previous student voices. High school teachers talk about their work as being "in the trenches," "on the battlefields," or "out there." They ask, Who's going to win? But what do the children feel? "Under the gun" when called on? The effect, as always, is that they learn what they are taught. A 1986 dissertation reported that 72 percent of high school students felt that obedience and respect for authority should be the primary requirement for a good citizen (Johnson, 1986). No wonder many students in teacher certification courses think the same.

Given the widespread nature of their assumptions about what children are like and what the teacher's role in reaction to that must be, it is not surprising that in my classes and in staff development sessions within schools, K–12 teachers and preteachers react strongly to my asking them to consider alternative approaches as they work with children whose behavior they cannot allow. Almost all at first insist that unless the teacher is authoritarian, the child will get away with something. Indeed, this seems to be the predominant view in our dualistic culture: either we punish or we are doing nothing, letting them get away with everything. There's no continuum of possibilities. Because this issue is one of the most difficult ones I deal with, I have learned to come at it in a number of ways.

Common Definitions

Getting preteachers to reflect on their role, and to see where that sense of themselves leaves children, is a complex task that I undertake from many different directions. One approach is to problematize words and concepts that they may not have examined. For example, how students seem to define certain frequently used terms, such as *listen, cooperate,* and *good,* reveals levels of understanding that have nothing real to do with the intellectual development that should characterize learning. Instead, their common usage, at least among most of the students I have encountered in teacher education courses, suggests that the goal of these students' own schooling was nothing deeper than teacher-pleasing. Because those goals had already become most preteachers' expectations of the children they would teach, I spend time in class interrogating and redefining those key words.

The list that one class generated—which subsequent classes essentially affirmed—in brainstorming meanings for the terms *good* and *bad,* in terms of students, is quite disturbing (see Appendix). It is almost entirely about not disturbing the teacher in any way. The frightening prospect—for me, at least—is that such a "good" student having become a teacher will not only require the same of her or his students, but she or he will continue to do as she or he is told, even as a faculty member and citizen.

Figure 4.1. The Classroom Management Continuum

Authoritarian	Mutually Respectful	Permissive
rigid structure	clear, flexible structure	no structure
teacher's absolute control	everyone's real needs get met	chaos

Nontraditional teaching is not "unstructured." Seeing the possibilities as a broad continuum rather than as the traditional either/or, control-or-chaos, or structure/no structure trap is helpful for teachers in making their choices—and knowing that they have real choices. Teachers' authority is in their experience and wisdom, not in their position.

This continuum also provides a useful framework for evaluating frequently advocated classroom management strategies. I place all behavior modification programs only a little to the right of the edge on the authoritarian side: manipulation by reward rather than by punishment is still manipulation.

Being *good* in terms of teacher-pleasing had constituted many preteachers' success through school, especially elementary preteachers. The inappropriate association of *good student* with *being good* is highlighted by a study Ladson-Billings (2001, p. 75) refers to—one revealing that kindergarten and first grade children in school had already gotten the distorted but clearly delivered message that "*good readers* were people who sat up straight, listened to the teacher, and didn't talk". Considering that the distortion of meaning starts that early, it is no surprise that university students could not imagine themselves stepping over the lines that would cause them to be defined as "bad." *Bad,* of course, includes *outspoken.*

How deeply internalized that was! Academic errors seemed to be evidence that the student is a bad person, requiring contrition. Many times, "I'm sorry" appeared in response to my marginal comments that pointed toward a clearer view of the text or asked them to clarify sentence structure. They had learned to apologize for mistakes as if student error was an affront to the teacher rather than a vehicle for learning. One student's response in an undergraduate class was especially vivid in her description of young, silenced "good girls":

> I was never a troublemaker. I always tried to please my teachers and was very flattered by the least little compliment.

Thus cowed into silence, most students seemed to wait for someone else to speak in full-class sessions, though the safer small groups pleasantly and sometimes passionately buzzed.

Accordingly, the word *cooperation,* as most students and perhaps teachers, parents, administrators, and politicians tend to use it, seems to mean compliance with the desires of the person in authority rather than working together in mutual give-and-take, or operating together. In addition, though many teachers and pre-teachers resist hearing this about themselves, a similar misuse of the word *listen* is deeply embedded. To most university students, and their friends, parents, and teachers, the word *listen* is interchangeable with *do as I say,* or *obey,* especially when they're referring to an adult-child or other unequal power dynamic. Trying to redefine it so that we all mean *pay close attention, not only with your ears but also with your understanding* is imperative if teachers are to begin to use my favorite "discipline" text, *How to Talk So Kids Will Listen, and Listen So Kids Will Talk* (Faber and Mazlish, 1980).

Really Learning to Listen

How to Talk So Kids Will Listen . . . is the most transformative reading of all the courses in which I use it, and I use it in almost all in courses I teach. It is not just another "how-to" book; instead, it is a guide for learning how to take the perspective of another person—in Piaget's words, to "decenter." Learning to decenter is perhaps the most significant task in teachers' reflecting on their role and on where that sense of themselves leaves children. Faber's and Mazlish's book is also as relevant for students' work with diversity—demographic studies, community service, and visits to schools—and the rest of their reading and thinking—as it is for "classroom management." I consider its philosophy—that everyone deserves respect—to be the core of my teaching, no matter what the particular subject matter.

Although the book is written for parents, teacher education students easily translate the philosophy into the teacher-child relationship. I choose to use it instead of the one Faber and Mazlish published later with two teachers, *How to Talk So Kids Can Learn at Home and in School* (1995), because the newer book, while geared directly toward teachers, does not require reader interaction. It does all the work for the reader and therefore turns out not to stimulate the depth of individual reflection, personal memory, and struggle that the first book does. Faber and Mazlish's book (1980) is the one vehicle I have located that seems to help teachers effectively achieve the most important knowledge base of teacher education: a teacher's genuine consciousness of him- or herself.

The evidence of students' writing makes it clear to me that the use I make of Faber and Mazlish's book makes a difference in its impact on students. Though it is helpful to read under any circumstances, it seems not to have the same powerful effect on people who read it on their own during their student teaching, on teachers in occasional staff development sessions, or on people who read it straight through sometime before they took my course. It is the reflective writing stimulated by the book that seems to make the difference. I spread out the reading and writing over the entire semester to guard against students reading the book too fast, because it can be a deceptively easy read. I require reader responses to each of the first seven chapters of the book, followed by feedback and then ongoing writebacks, for at least one "round" of conversation between us.

In addition, I assign regular, frequent, genuine attempts to use what the students read. At best, the reader responses, writebacks, and reflections after recorded actual dialogues tackle students' own sometimes painful early experiences as children. They recall incidences and feelings associated with (1) having had their own feelings heard and acknowledged or, more usually, not having had them heard or acknowledged; (2) of being treated with respect by adults, or of being accustomed to being disregarded; (3) of being encouraged in developmentally appropriate ways to develop autonomy or not, or of overdependency; and (4) of being included in the decisions that affected their lives, or of having most decisions made for them. It is not easy work, but many students feel ultimately empowered by it, and by the regular practice of the strategies with people in their own daily lives. One undergraduate spoke of the struggle:

> It is very difficult to unlearn something that you've been doing for twenty years of your life. Something that your parents have taught you was okay, like . . . denying someone his or her feelings, placing labels on people, etc. All of these "methods" . . . have been drilled into my subconscious all my life and will be difficult to get rid of.

Late in a semester, another student reflected on her changing relationship with the child whom she baby-sat:

> It is amazing to me that by changing the way I listen and talk to him, he has also changed. There is less frustration on my part, less defiance on his. I had always thought in the past that it was his responsibility to change and that he eventually would. It never occurred to me that I would need to change first.

A second-year teacher says that *How to Talk* . . . (Faber and Mazlish, 1980) was the book that made the most difference to her in the course, because it provided her with "another perspective, that of the child." After months of practicing it in her classroom, and noticing a difference in the classroom climate, she found herself further validated by an administrator:

> I felt so proud when at the end of the observation she stopped me to tell me how she was amazed at the climate of my classroom. She said, "You and your students all seem so calm and comfortable together in this classroom. I can tell you have worked hard to make it feel that way for all of you." I felt like shouting from the rooftops and handing her a copy of *How to Talk* . . . right then and there!

To be sure, not every student was sold on the book's approaches, especially at the beginning of the semester. Many become defensive and resistant: "I'm already very good with children," or "My friends all say I'm a good listener." In addition, some initially assume that accepting all feelings strongly advocated in the book's first chapter means accepting all behaviors. It takes plenty of discussion and a second reading of that chapter ("Helping Children Deal with Their Feelings") for some to recognize that accepting all feelings does not mean accepting all behaviors. Most students work through their fears and misreadings after stating their surface reactions in the reader responses, and having the write-backs as a place to rethink.

A very few exceptionally thoughtful students do, however, perform the hard work of challenging their own first thoughts all on their own, even from the beginning—as did one student, who, as early as September, already used the reader response process as it was intended to be used. In her response to Chapter One of *How to Talk . . .* , she has reflected on paper, ". . . and I'm realizing this only as I write" and "And, again, as I'm writing, I'm seeing . . ." She concluded:

> It seems that the key here is to take children's feelings seriously. My feelings while I was reading indicate to me that not only do I not do this now, but neither does society. The "wrong" responses were what seemed normal.

Needless to say, this student's presence was very helpful in her small groups. Others stretched as a result of her explanations and perspectives, well beyond her own and their initial gut reactions about what they thought they read. Her careful reading brought her to understand what quite a few did not, at least at first:

> Chapter Three ["Alternatives to Punishment"] clarified a lot of things for me. Not punishing a child does not mean allowing him to get away with whatever he likes. Instead it teaches him to deal with the natural consequences of his actions.

Others arrived at insights that were uniquely their own, as a result of their genuine attempts to apply the book in actual live interactions. In reflecting on their interactions and language, recorded in dialogues, they processed the theory on their own terms, constructing their own knowledge:

> I came to the conclusion that when dealing with my brother, what I may interpret as "caring about him," he may see as me being domineering. So, because of that, I've attempted to change the way I talk to people, especially my brother.

As a result of the work with *How to Talk* . . . (Faber and Mazlish, 1980), in the context of other readings and activities, many students had looked very hard and honestly at themselves. I quote at length from this graduate student's final paper, for both the telling quality of his introspection and for the distance he has traveled from the role he had thought he had to play as a teacher. What he conveys, however personal and specific, is not unusual in any significant aspect. Since most teachers' own schooling has embedded in them certain assumptions about children and about the teacher's role, behaviors based on those assumptions almost inevitably result. Here he courageously acknowledges, has examined, and has begun to transform all of that:

> When I started this course, I felt I knew everything I needed to know about teaching, children, and, most important, myself. . . . I felt that children had some thought processes, but they needed somebody to guide them in everything they did. To me, children needed strict guidance. I was that guidance.
>
> The minute I walked into a classroom, my instincts told me that I needed to get control of the class and make sure that nobody deviated from what I wanted them to do. If they dared disobey me then it was their fault and they needed to be punished and be used as an example for others to see.
>
> I never thought about how the students felt, nor did I go out of my way to try and understand why they were acting the way they were.
>
> I was so busy trying to teach them that I wasn't letting them *learn*. . . . I would get frustrated when they didn't do as I asked. Just as I would do with my own children. . . . I desired the best for them but didn't see what they desired for themselves.
>
> Before I took this course, I didn't know why I did the things I did. When I yelled at a student or *demanded* that [he or she] pay attention, it didn't dawn on me why I needed to do that. The confrontations between myself and the students were commonplace, but I never stopped to ask why.
>
> Not until I started reading *How to Talk* . . . did I realize that the problem wasn't the student. The problem was me. I needed to correct myself—in a sense heal myself and come to my senses. Although I shouldn't be so hard on myself because I really didn't know that I was doing anything wrong. I was working with the

experiences I had accumulated through my personal and educational life.

How to Talk . . . gave me my first insight into how to let a child learn. Chapter by chapter, the authors started putting together the building blocks to seeing the world from the child's perspective. It felt strange and out of place at first because it was so foreign to me. But as the book kept feeding me new ideas, the better I felt about myself as a teacher. . . .

Another one of my biggest satisfactions is my communication with Sherina. We've managed to become very good friends. This is especially important to me, considering [that] Sherina had been expelled last year because of her behavior and attitude. I believe that she was misunderstood by the people [who] dealt with her, myself included. Her change in my class has in large part come because of my change in how I treat her.

I came into this class believing that I was going to learn how to make my students behave and listen to me. I realize that this class has nothing to do with *making* a student behave and listen. This course has taught me that in order for the student to change, I have to be the one to change. . . . I am glad to say [that] I am happy with the new me.

The Power and Challenge of Working with *How to Talk So Kids Will Listen, and Listen So Kids Will Talk*

In my regular visits to schools, particularly but not exclusively in inner-city schools, I have witnessed too many teachers, paraprofessionals, and administrators dealing with children in the way this graduate student recognizes he had been in the habit of doing: yelling, commanding, imposing. As he describes, his behavior came from his conceptualization of his role: to "make the children behave." As other teachers will openly admit, once I probe, the need to make children "behave" is really their need to "look like a good teacher in case a parent or administrator walks by." The underlying need seems to be their own insecurity, their deeply embedded fear of judgment by someone in authority. For some teachers, it is something else as well: controlling the children in their classes has to do with bringing some order to their own internal chaos. So many students have written and talked about these sources of their assumptions that I have reason to believe that those pressures within teachers are not uncommon.[3] But how unhealthy for and unfair to children!

I consider it my job to encourage teachers and preteachers to engage in deep examination of their assumptions about their role, and at the same time to provide effective, mutually satisfying alternative ways of operating, so that everyone's legitimate need for respect gets met. This book has been for me the vehicle that combines those processes. It gently forces self-reflection.

One persistent challenge for me with the use of the book, however, as I engage in conversation with some students on their papers, is to help students balance loyalty to their parents and teachers with honest critique of their own histories. The hard work I am asking them to do is to bring to full consciousness, and thus make available for their own examination, any resonance between their early lives and the disrespectful traditional practices described in both word and cartoon drama in the book. When some students become defensive about disclosing, even to themselves, I do my best to remind them that this work is not about blaming their parents or teachers. In order to make the point that it is natural to parent in the ways that we were parented, and that their parents certainly did what they did with all good intentions, I lecture very briefly about the centuries-old cycle of authoritarian child rearing advocated in European treatises, as exposed by Alice Miller in *For Your Own Good* (1980). In my Approaches to Discipline course, the Miller book is one of the jigsaw choices, and it is consistently the one that turns its readers around.[4] In some semesters of that course, I have also used it as a full-class text, but it seems to work best as a jigsaw choice, because it is so heavy and depressing that having other more positive books being read at the same time by other students provides balance.

Mostly, change comes as students begin to practice for themselves. In the required twenty-five or more genuine attempts through the semester, almost all students begin to develop the self-discipline of taking a breath and thinking before reacting with "instinctive" or deeply embedded—and thus now automatic—patterns. The assignment is to record on paper each "dialogue" and then reflect on how it went. Reflecting on the ones that did not go well, especially at the beginning of a semester, is more instructive than reporting only the successes.

Taking the at-first awkward steps of responding in more respectful, thoughtful, and perspective-taking ways to children, peers, or even their parents, students are often stunned by the positive results. When that occurs, even those who started out defensive come to wish their parents and teachers had known of these approaches. As hard as it is throughout the semester, and sometimes even well before the end, many students resolve to continue to reread and practice in order to internalize the new approaches. Recognizing the oppressive cycle, they realize that they can break it, now that they see, and now that they have alternatives from which to choose. *How to Talk* . . . is a tool to help them create and maintain healthy relationships with their own children, their students, and others. At the very least, the practice—combined with the focused introspection, some class discussion, and some role play— seems to have made them more open to thinking from someone else's perspective, and not be so quick to react out of "instinct."

> After a few sessions, I began to realize that my objectives were related to short-term goals rather than long-term goals. . . . Change will take place only after I shift from How do I control children? toward How do I teach children to become caring and cooperative adults?

All Sides of the Chair

My intention and hope is that the mindfulness established by the ongoing reflection and practice will carry over into how preteachers and teachers think about people whose life experience is different from theirs. The first chapter of *How to Talk* . . . (Faber and Mazlish, 1980) requires the reader to put him- or herself into the shoes of the other person. That is the hardest task, of course. To provide another approach to the concept, I set up a kinesthetic/ spatial/interpersonal activity, based on the task that Piaget invented to test for a child's capacity to move past the egocentric stage. Piaget essentially asked the child, "What would this doll standing on the top of this mountain and facing the other side see?" If the child described only what he or she could see from his or her own side of the mountain, Piaget determined that the child had not yet learned to decenter.

In my adaptation, I put an empty chair or desk in the middle of our circle of desks. I give the students thirty seconds to draw or sketch the chair. Next, I ask students to make eye contact with any person across from them in the circle, and then, in thirty seconds, draw the chair again, this time from that person's perspective.

It is very interesting to see students at first sit still in their chairs and struggle to imagine, or try to flip the chair in their minds if they happen to have well-developed spatial intelligence. In each semester, only one or two at most will think of getting up to go to the other person's space, even when I say, and repeat, as I have begun to, "Do whatever you need to do to draw it as the other person sees it." Once someone dares to get up out of his or her own chair, the others are at first shocked, and look at me. I repeat, "Do whatever you need to do." Now feeling released to do it, most get up. Still, some do not go to see before they draw, not quite believing that permission has really been given. To be sure, their deep

Figure 4.2. All Sides of a Chair

socialization not to get up out of their seats unless they are specifically told to do so becomes one of the topics we discuss afterwards when we process the activity.

After the second quick sketching, the task is to check the accuracy of their second drawing. Most students quickly get the point of the chair activity: to see accurately from someone else's point of view, one has to put oneself (physically, in this case) in the other's shoes and not assume that one's own view is all there is, or that one can know without checking with the other as to what the other knows or feels or sees. When I ask which drawing is accurate, of course, the students realize both are, and that it takes every perspective around 360 degrees to represent this physical object. Stretching the activity beyond its literal physicality to its metaphorical possibilities, they usually see that there is no one right answer when different people have *points of view*, and certainly none to be accessed from a single stuck position.

That simple, quick, concrete, and even rather dramatic activity of looking at all sides of the chair is a useful one for practicing empathy. It emphasizes and helps students acquire the consciousness brought about by working with Chapter One of *How to Talk* . . . Even when students don't initiate the connections, the combination of experiences provides a shared frame of reference.

Seeing the chair from different points of view has been an especially effective metaphor for responding when some students are outraged to read the views of some of the parents quoted in the article "Why Some Parents Don't Come to School" (Finders and Lewis, 1994). The immediate assumption for most before they read the article is that parents who don't show up for conferences just don't care about their childrens'education—or about their children. Even after they have read, in fact, it is not uncommon for students to write, "Why don't they just get over it?" in reaction to some parents' descriptions of their reluctance to enter a building in which they themselves had felt failure and defeat as children. Our work with the chair exercise and with the first chapter of *How to Talk* . . . has provided a language through which I can ask students to begin to accept that the difference between their own life experiences and someone else's doesn't make one of them right and one of them wrong. This isn't easy, of course, but practicing teachers and preteachers often come to see that it might be teachers' feelings of frustration at play when they blame parents for not showing up for parent-teacher conferences. After teachers worked so hard to get the room and themselves ready—some even bringing cookies—they felt stood up.

Having their own natural, legitimate feelings acknowledged and accepted, teachers are more able to see that, separate from their own needs, feelings, and agendas, parents, too, have legitimate needs and points of view. Both are real. Because we now share a framework of the metaphor of the chair, I am able to ask them how the situation might look from that parent's perspective.

Very occasionally in the sides-of-the-chair activity, however, students have drawn both views of the chair facing the same way. It was only when they checked with the other person that they realized their mistake. Each said, "It never occurred to me that it would look different from her or his side of the room!" Two students in a particular graduate class, both of whom had drawn the chairs facing the same way both times, were people of middle age—bright and articulate students with fascinating life experiences. One of those students took the chair exercise as a stunning reality check, and he worked extremely hard on himself thereafter, to his and my great satisfaction. The other student fought decentering, especially in regard to Kozol's *Rachel and Her Children* (1988), insisting that Kozol must have deliberately left out important information about what the people in the book had done to cause their own homelessness. She could not—would not—get beyond her assumptions about how they must have originally become homeless to see what circumstances were like for them once there. Regardless of the thoughtful, complex discussions that went on in her jigsaw group on that book, and regardless of her own sensitive reading of other literature, she insisted that she would not be moved to care about them, or even accept the credibility of their stories. Stuck in her own life experience, or chair, it was necessary for her to believe that the situation in which they found themselves trapped was their own fault.

But by the end of that course, as Chapter Seven in this book suggests, the semester-long reading of Ann Petry's novel *The Street* (1946) had done the subtle work that none of the other readings (or this student's reading of the powerful details of *Rachel and Her Children,* or her classmates, or I) could do to get her to move even temporarily out of that position. She could not see *Rachel and Her Children* from the inside. This student had admired and cheered all along *The Street*'s strong, moral, heroic main character, Lutie Johnson, a proud African American single mother walled in by discrimination. After doing everything she possibly could to make a life for herself and her son, after playing by all the rules, Lutie fails at the very end of the book. The student who had resisted all the other efforts to get her to decenter could finally see that no matter how hard one works, our society does not make room for certain people. Lutie finally drew her over to the other side of the chair.

Moral Development

Our discussion of the "Alternatives to Punishment" chapter of *How to Talk* . . . provides me with a rich opportunity to get students to make their understanding of *morality* much more complex than they had considered. At first, most want to say that morality is "knowing right from wrong," "being good." They tend to say that one can learn to be a moral person only by being punished for doing wrong. The contradictions are obvious, however, from their own reader responses to the chapter. Whereas many students deeply internalized the punishments they witnessed others experience for daring to step out of line, and censored their own behaviors accordingly as young children and adolescents, others admitted that the punishments they received did not really "work," except to make them more determined not to get caught. In either case, their own insights make it easy for them to recognize Kohlberg's lowest level of moral development: doing right out of fear of punishment. They are less convinced that the next level is as low as where Kohlberg places it—expectation of reward—until we go through the entire list, redefining morality in much less narrow dimensions than the ones to which they are accustomed. When I add, with concrete real-life examples, those higher levels that the students may have memorized in psychology classes but never thought of in terms of their own or children's behaviors in school, some lights go on. It is particularly challenging when I ask them to look at justice in terms that have nothing to do with revenge, and then I add Gilligan's concept of caring (1982) to that consideration.

Figure 4.3.   Levels of Moral Development*

---

6. Sacrifice for others

5. Justice and caring

4. Consideration for others

3. The rules

2. Expectation of reward

1. Fear of punishment

It is my analysis that even well-meaning traditional teachers can lock children into the three lower levels, bound by external locus of control. I contend that it is possible—and necessary—to teach even elementary children to develop the empathy and reflection to operate at level 4, skipping the lower three.

*Based on a synthesis of Kohlberg's, Gilligan's, and my own thinking

---

What is most astonishing for most students, most of whose lives have been spent obeying the rules, is the highest level, which suggests that the highest level of moral development is engagement in civil disobedience, sacrificing oneself for the betterment of mankind. To be sure, to that one I add names that Kohlberg would not have included. To join Jesus, Gandhi, and Dr. Martin Luther King, I add Antigone and Huck Finn, and tell their stories dramatically. Then I invite students to think of other selfless, courageous, and utterly responsible people they know of, male or female. My intent—and I will admit that I do preach about this— is to get students to consider that it is possible, and necessary, to teach for a much higher level of moral development, skipping entirely those that depend on external locus of control. It takes a great leap to think of teaching even the youngest children to develop consideration for others. But unless that is the goal, it is quite possible that many young people, and even adults, perhaps even some teachers, will remain stuck in the lower levels for much of their lives. With what result for society? The society we have now, perhaps? The whole session on moral development is a recapitulation of the early exercise that asks students to think about the characteristics they want children to have when they are adults. At the very least, this exercise blurs the focus of what they came to the course to know, and that is my intent!

The combined cognitive and social skill development that I aim for is represented in part by this student's conclusion:

> I believe [that] in order for me to deal with situations, I need to see myself more clearly [as] to what triggers my emotional reaction. . . . I do see myself holding a certain image of what I believe is a "perfect" teacher. I am beginning to understand where many of my frustrations in the classroom may be stemming from.

Such consciousness is the first enormous step. The next steps are to replace the old instincts with healthier, more mutually respectful alternatives. That is a life's work, but it can be begun in one course.

Notes
1. Refer to Aaronsohn "Learning to Teach for Empowerment" (1990) for a fuller investigation of how the Freedom School philosophy and the experience in Mississippi informed my thinking and my teaching.
2. I discuss the gendered aspect of this situation in a later chapter.
3. Haberman (1992) makes a strong argument for not allowing people to become certified as teachers until they have reached enough maturity to be fully self-actualized adults.
4. Jigsawing is the process of dividing up a text or group of texts among students, so that each person or small group has responsibility for a manageable piece of the "puzzle," upon which they become "experts." The whole class then puts it all together for the "full picture" (Aronson, 1978).

Chapter Five

Justice, Mutual Respect, and Caring Instead of Control

Practicing teachers in both my graduate classes and staff development sessions indicate that one of the things that drive them crazy about kids in school is how careless, unkind, and even cruel they are to each other. These teachers are not alone in this concern, as the nation has seen dramatically in the last few years the highly publicized incidences of students going crazy on each other in school. I am not surprised to learn that nationwide research since Columbine has shown that the most effective violence prevention program is Second Step (Committee for Children). I know Second Step to be a carefully designed, comprehensive, systematic approach through which children can develop the exact skills I discussed in Chapter Four: empathy, impulse control, anger management, and problem solving.

Power Over, or Power Within?

As excellent as Second Step is for teaching children skills for healthy relationships, its message will be confusing if it is taught as an add-on or within a traditional authoritarian classroom. For the program to be fully successful, the classrooms in which it is taught must become fundamentally transformed. It is for this reason that I ask teachers to consider deeply how they themselves deal with children, and I ask them to develop, at least as options, the respectful approaches offered in *How to Talk So Kids Will Listen, and Listen So Kids Will Talk* (Faber and Mazlish, 1980).

The norm in traditional classrooms is a power imbalance between children and teachers. If that classroom is also authoritarian (such as the ones I must have been raised in, and such as the many that teacher education students remember theirs to have been), children learn through "the hidden curriculum" that they are powerless to negotiate their needs, ideas, or feelings. Quite unconsciously in most cases, teachers in these classrooms, feeling pressure themselves to perform to administrators' standards, force children to produce "work" and exhibit "behavior" within certain narrowly defined parameters. The norm is either to withhold rewards or mete out punishment if those expectations are not met. The result, as I suggested in Chapter Four, is that children remain stuck at a very low level of moral development.

Frustration and anger on both sides of that power arrangement are inevitable. Children may seethe but are powerless to express without sanction what they are feeling. How the teacher handles his or her own disappointment in these situations is key. When children experience the teacher (or any other adult) as a person who might attack them, if only in words or tone, they are learning that violence is the way adults deal with their own anger.

When teachers instead approach children from a basic philosophy of unconditional positive regard and with confidence that all children can learn, their developmentally appropriate methods and their own emotional balance and honesty will model active and conscious practice of empathy, impulse control, and anger management.

Within such an environment—including special education classes and even classes that have children who have been identified as socially and emotionally maladjusted (as graduate student writing has shown)—children can become empowered to develop frustration tolerance, internal locus of control, and a healthy, realistic sense of personal efficacy. This, it seems to me, is the real goal that every teacher strives for, in his or her own way—to create and maintain a healthy, positive, academically oriented, and effectively functioning classroom in which children feel safe to learn, and teachers feel satisfied and fulfilled.

The Transformation of Two Special Education (SEM) Teachers

Jen and Dawn came to my Approaches to Discipline graduate class in the same spring semester. From different towns and schools, they were both special education teachers in self-contained classrooms for children identified as having social and emotional maladjustments (SEM). Both were pleased to share with other members of our class that they were known in their schools for having excellent control over their students in their strict behavior modification and reward/punishment systems. As Jen said in her final paper:

> When I first began this course, I came in with the belief that it would be an easy one for me. With my vast training and knowledge of behavior, I thought that I would certainly have a lot to contribute and that I had very little to learn.
>
> My goal for my classroom at the start of the semester was to keep control and be as proactive as possible to prevent negative behavior from occurring, so that my students could learn. . . . Ignoring was a prominent technique in my strict, complex, consistent system. . . . I felt [that] most inappropriate behavior exhibited was attention-seeking or manipulative.
>
> I did try never to yell, and I discouraged yelling in my aides. I found other adults in the building quick to restrain students and scream in their faces to scare them into calming down. I did know that these were not methods to help a child relax. But I used time-out and tokens for every infraction. I used [learning] centers as a reward.
>
> For the past five years as a teacher of SEM students, I was taught many of these methods or acquired them on my own, because they were effective in keeping the children under control and getting them to do whatever I asked. However, deep down, I became a teacher because I wanted to help students build confidence and believe in themselves. However, I was asking them to feel and behave in a uniform manner.
>
> I realized [in the "Approaches to Discipline" graduate course] that I was doing all that I hated when I was in school. . . . Now, after all this reading, reflection, and discussion, my tolerance has improved tremendously. . . . We're making more time to talk, and I notice nice changes in their attitudes. I see setbacks to old instincts, but in myself as well. . . . I am experiencing a feeling of

relief . . . and confidence. . . . I'm still working and learning, but I like where I'm headed.

"You could teach that (graduate) course," Dawn had been told by a coworker. Both Jen and Dawn had been sure that the *How to Talk* . . . (Faber and Mazlish, 1980) methods of respect, acceptance of feeling, alternatives to punishment, and other nonauthoritarian approaches might be fine for "normal" students, but not theirs. Then they read Alice Miller's *For Your Own Good* (1980) and found themselves facing, in themselves and each other, the roots of their own "instinctive" need for absolute control. They both began to try the *How to Talk* . . . methods in earnest, describing and reflecting on breakthrough after breakthrough. By the end of the semester, both had significantly transformed their teaching. As Dawn wrote in her paper of self-evaluation:

> My style was very authoritarian, with strict rewards and conse-
> quences. . . . I wasn't looking at my behavior plan as manipulative,
> and was even surprised when I discovered that I was manipulating
> my students to behave in the ways that were most suitable to me.
>   I was keeping class rigid and "structured" for the students, or
> so I thought. I fell into a pattern of obeying people in authority
> around me who firmly believe that my class should be run in this
> tightly controlled manner, because our kids are "so sick" and "can't
> handle any freedom or unstructured situation." . . . [But], if any-
> thing, they require more delicate treatment and time to talk rather
> than strict behavior modification.
>   I'll never forget, in my first dialogue [practicing *How to Talk*],
> I acknowledged Josh's feelings about forgetting his gym sneakers,
> instead of acting on my impulse to threaten him with a conse-
> quence if he didn't complete his work. I looked at the situation
> later and was thrilled with not only avoiding the problem but also
> making Josh truly feel better. . . . I admit, this was extremely diffi-
> cult at first. It was quite a change and seemed funny to go against
> my impulses.
>   Fortunately, it has become like second nature to me, and
> what incredible benefits it has had! The greatest benefit is the
> change in the rapport that I have with my students. I no longer
> have to "force" them to temporarily comply. . . . They know that
> I am going to accept their feelings and work with them to solve
> their problems.

All of my students have changed and benefited from my new techniques, but I feel that one particular student has made the most growth. S. started off his year having an enormous amount of difficulty. He would fight or [take] flight in just about any situation. We often felt desperate and didn't know how to handle him. We resorted to power and control.

In early February, for the first time, I acknowledged S.'s feelings about a student and I didn't reprimand him. . . . This was the turning point in my relationship with S. . . . I found that he needed to let out his feelings to me every morning before he could join the class. This one-to-one time talking with me helped him to feel like he could get through his day.

It has now been about four weeks[, and] S. no longer needs this. He unpacks his bag, comes right to his desk, eats his breakfast with the class and willingly (and excitedly) participates in [our] morning meeting.

When I first started taking this course, I honestly thought that the idea of not using rewards and consequences was absurd. . . . Now, instead of punishing, I've been focusing on conflict resolution. I tell the kids not to think about consequences for their behavior but what we can do to help them solve the problem. This was surprising for the students at first, and [it] took them time to trust me. Unfortunately, they are used to getting punished, and many of the students are even comfortable with it. I've been teaching them ways to deal with freedom and expressing themselves. The kids even like helping each other solve problems. They give advice in kind and caring ways.

Jen and Dawn realized the extent to which much of the tension they had been experiencing in their classrooms had been a direct result of their own confrontational stances with the children.

I do not intend to oversimplify, or blame teachers for student violence in schools. But it does seem to me that our own behavior is not by any means irrelevant. We have to look seriously at our own agency in the classroom and see what we are teaching by example. People come to teacher education courses saying they want to make a difference in children's lives. Teachers do make a difference—in everything that they do in their interactions with children and in how they carry themselves. Children learn from us, no matter what we think we are teaching; it is not limited to the conscious curriculum. That is why the most important knowledge base of teacher education is the teacher. The next most important knowledge is that there are options other than the ones we may have been raised with. We have choices, and we have the obligation to use those choices responsibly for children.

The Effects of Competition

It startles teachers from all districts and schools when I suggest, in response to their discouragement about how children treat each other, that they might monitor *themselves* for the level of competition in their classroom structures. Although the terrible events of school violence are tragic, I am also not surprised that they are occurring in "good" schools, in "good" communities. As student reports suggest, it is in the most affluent schools that competition seems to be the most emphasized, and the most vicious. Competition is deeply ingrained in our society. Well-meaning teachers often use it to "motivate" children, pitting them against each other to raise the level of excitement over a lesson or activity. Research makes clear, however, that when children see each other as rivals for resources, position, or teacher approval, relationships suffer or atrophy (Kohn, 1986). As students discover when we play "Musical Chairs" in our teacher education classes, the more anxiety in a "game" in a classroom—especially if there is no team for support, no next game to come back and win, and no guarantee of teacher and peer approval no matter what—the closer children might come to aggression.

We can create, instead, collaborative classroom communities in which children learn to trust, enjoy, and care about each other. To begin with, I urge teachers to notice their own use of competition between children as motivation for students to engage in tasks they would otherwise, often quite legitimately, find tedious, even meaningless. The questions to ask about competition, it seems to me, are these: What do I notice on the faces of the losers? Why am I structuring this task competitively—for lack of an alternative I can think of? What might be the advantages? Disadvantages? To whom? and Whose needs are being met here? Then, How else might I construct the task? And, finally, or perhaps first, because it is the most important, What learning do I hope children will experience from this task? To what extent has winning become the children's focus—losing the academic learning in the process?[1]

Posing these questions causes preteachers to step outside of and look critically at institutionally structured competition, such as "ability group" tracking, which begins as early as first grade reading groups. Preteachers' writings and discussions from personal experience confirm the research. At its least insidious, tracking lets children know who the teacher thinks is smart and who the teacher thinks is not smart. Hierarchies develop that early, and they persist because the placements persist, as the research on tracking convincingly shows (Oakes, 1985).

Other competitive structures are less obvious. Teachers use them because they work. Many preservice and practicing teachers are surprised to realize that even when teachers use "I like the way [Jane] is sitting" to get the others to sit up quietly, there is another, certainly undesired result besides the instantly successful achievement of the other children's compliance. What happens, as well, is the setting up and reinforcing of hostilities between children, especially if one has become cast in the role of "teacher's pet" and others are habitually seen as "troublemakers." When some children feel like winners and some feel like losers, the possibilities for community building are seriously diminished. Most teachers do not see "I like the way . . ." in those terms. They use it because it works, much more positively than pointing out the children who are not complying. And those are usually the only two alternatives teachers believe they have. At the very least, however, on some level, even the youngest children feel manipulated, even by the praise.

Most university students and classroom teachers, as well as teacher educators, have generally come from traditionally structured schooling. Because we are so accustomed to the competitive structures that traditional teachers use to control their classes, we hardly pay attention to them. Then we blame the children, or their families, or their neighborhoods, for behaviors that may to a great extent stem from their having been cast as either winners or losers in our classrooms. Being able to look at oneself and one's own classroom choices for reasons why things may be happening is characteristic of a really mature, thoughtful, and culturally relevant teacher (Kohn, 1996; Ladson-Billings, 2001). That ability has to be developed.

Often, in fact, as is described in Chapter Four, most young people who choose to be elementary teachers, especially, have themselves been "good little boys and girls," some even perhaps teachers' pets, in their early schooling. Inevitably, they internalized a teacher's reaction to other children who were not "good"—children who were not as docile as they themselves had had to be, or as they remember themselves having chosen to be. The primary quality of *good,* as many preteachers (and some practicing teachers) define it, is *quiet;* the primary offense in a traditional classroom is *talking.* As a result, when I ask university students and practicing teachers to collaborate, to talk with each other, many are stunned and are fearful of the consequences of breaking such a strong taboo.

I keep learning how strong a taboo that is. In a recent staff development session of teachers and paraprofessionals at an elementary school, only my second session with that faculty and staff, I asked everyone to talk with each other in two's for two minutes (as I often do, either when no one seems to feel confident about speaking to a topic in a full-session discussion, or when, as in this case, everyone is excited enough so that all want to speak aloud and be heard at once. So I give them all that chance, and then we resume). One participant, who herself keeps the children within very tight boundaries of acceptable behavior, told me that she felt insulted by what she thought I was doing. Operating from the only frame of reference she knew, she felt that I was mocking and punishing them all for talking to each other so much. Such strict taboos against students talking to each other within a classroom must be examined if the development of collaboration and caring rather than hostility, fear, or unkindness is the goal, as most teachers agree it is.

Learning to Trust Themselves and Each Other

Despite the more than century-old theories of John Dewey and those nearly as old of Piaget and other proponents of learning as a social activity, every aspect of the process of interdependence with peers seems to be new and threatening for most university students I have encountered. Being "good" had made talking to each other taboo in traditional classrooms. More especially, arguing was absolutely taboo in traditional situations, where the norm about difference is, "If you're right, I must be wrong." More usually, the reaction to difference of opinion is either stony silence or capitulation. Not part of most incoming students' vocabularies is, "We have a problem here," or "Let me try to understand how what you're seeing is different from what I'm seeing." Unless teacher educators address this as an issue, how will new teachers operate as fully adult and healthy faculty members?

Students' experience of not trusting peers to hear one's emerging or incomplete thoughts—anything but a sure right answer—stifles a teacher's or professor's early attempts to have students explore, fumble, and create together. Terror of peer judgment, like terror of teacher judgment, makes K–12 and college/university students at first especially reluctant to expose their writing to each other's scrutiny. I have found that this is so initially, even when the guidelines are to listen for meaning rather than comparing, pouncing on, or correcting any errors in each other's writing.

As the research on cooperative learning suggests, it takes six weeks for students well socialized in traditional classrooms to begin to let go of their deeply internalized habits of individualism and competitiveness (Johnson and Johnson, 1975). Several factors contribute to student expectation that they dare not trust another person, and that they dare not be caught talking with him or her, but nothing contributes to this fear more than grading. At all levels of schooling, habits of rivalry for scarce good grades keep students from wanting to share ideas with each other or to spend time or effort helping someone else acquire concepts that they themselves already "have." Most have no experience of seeking each other's assistance in study groups; clearly, in our society, joining together is cheating, and asking for help is weak. Therefore, it is not surprising that instead of seeing each other as resources, university students, school faculties and staff, and even university professors may still see each other as impediments to their own success or as rivals against whom they measure themselves (Fischetti and Aaronsohn, 1990).

A tragic consequence is that large numbers of the students who enter teacher education programs, especially elementary education, report low self-esteem. Some report having learned to blame themselves in situations that so inappropriately become competitive:

> I feel like I am stupid because all the people around me are doing well and I wonder what's wrong with me. Why I can't do it?

Such students are afraid of being criticized or laughed at, from years of experiencing exactly that, often with the full, if unconscious, permission of and modeling by the teacher (Polakow, 1993). I have witnessed the process. Even in early small groups, passive students may perpetuate the cycle of letting the ideas and directions of one assertive person dominate in a group, rather than risk disagreement. Meanwhile, most of the rest of the group smolders in passive-aggressive silence, and some engage in out-of-class backstabbing. The special problem of having such feelings and behaviors last into teacher preparation is that a person becoming a teacher who feels that inadequate, who measures her- or himself against others, who does not dare speak up, but has not examined and contested the structures that formed those patterns, may continue the cycle with the children she or he teaches, and as a faculty member.

For teacher educators, it is necessary for our own sense of self-efficacy to recognize that supporting university students through their developing skills of interdependence is as much a sometimes lurching, slow, and long-term process as any "academic" or other cognitive teaching is, and as the development of social skills is for K–12 children. One cannot be in a hurry for recognizable results and stay in teaching. For example, early—and even midterm—group task orientation in some project groups in university classes focuses on What are we supposed to do? or What does she want?—which are variations on What's the right answer and What page is it on? It takes quite a while for most to be able to say, to themselves and to each other, What if we . . . ?

In some cases, individual members of project groups feel restrained by the others, fearful that what the others produce would not represent them in the same best light that doing the task alone would. And *that*—with its resentments—exists often with good reason, since occasionally some students, those still stuck in external locus of control, have learned to get by. That is, they try to "hitchhike," even in teacher education classes.

This is especially enraging to the conscientious members of a group if the teacher/professor gives group grades. So I do not. Instead, I try to maintain individual accountability by assigning regular journal entries of reflection on what each student is doing and learning as long-term projects unfold. My systematic noticing of who is, and who is not, doing his or her share seems to give the others confidence to move forward without the person in question, if all attempts to help him or her develop a new level of responsibility for the group fails. The very process of having to be assertive and clear, but caring—always with my support but usually without my intervention—can provide the rest of the group, many of whom grew up avoiding conflict at any level, with an opportunity to begin to develop important lifetime interpersonal skills.

Of course, the familiar process of doing the work alone is more comfortable for most students whose schooling has been traditional. More than one student reported preferring to be "in charge" of a group, because of his or her earlier experiences of essentially doing projects alone, unencumbered by but also enabling the other students' dependency. Except for the teacher, I'm sure, everyone's focus seemed to be on their only goal—the grade:

> Student: All throughout K–12, I was always the group leader and I did all the work. This way I could be sure to achieve the grade I wanted—an A or a B.
>
> Professor: So who did the learning?
>
> Student: Me.
>
> Professor: Was that just fine with you?
>
> Student: Yes.
>
> Professor: With them?
>
> Student: Yes.
>
> Professor: With the teacher?
>
> Student: No.

While the easy exploiting of one or more group members by all or some of the others is certainly a scenario that I have witnessed and heard reports of, especially when the group is larger than three or four, it is also possible that their willing complicity is a matter of the self-appointed "leader's" perspective. It could also be the case that, from their perspectives, all or some of the rest of the group members, during all those years of school, felt that the "leaders" would not let them participate, as I have also sometimes witnessed, as groups confer during class time.

Whatever the actual situation, the long-term effects depend on how the project work is monitored and what the expected outcomes are. I have discovered, from both my own experimenting and from others' experience and research, that unless a teacher/professor is consciously helping students develop the complex social skills of collaboration as well as the academic skills, information, and understanding that the project is designed to teach, the long-lasting result is that (1) some people learn that they can exploit others and get by, (2) some resent but feel powerless to interrupt intimidation, and (3) some learn that they can't ever count on anyone but themselves. All of these feelings/learnings undermine genuine democracy ultimately, in a faculty or in a society. At best, a student whose tendency has been to take over figures out, through a semester-long series of experiences, that his or her taking over will not work to achieve the goals of this class's collaborative project activities. At best, as well, the process of reflecting on her or his habit directs the student to a conscious choice:

> Generally speaking, I would say that group work is often difficult for me. I don't like to refer to it as a weakness, really, but because I am so assertive, I know I have to hold back in groups so as not to be overbearing.

In the courses I teach, the focus of the readings and collaborative activities, combined with the intensive reflection that is the primary content of the course, provides the context for such a person to step back and notice how she or he is operating. One student came to what I consider pivotal insights:

> To someone who has always listened this way, I'm sure this sounds shallow, but the truth is, I didn't always listen this way.

My preconceived ideas about who was smart and who wasn't, who
thought like me and who didn't, helped me tune in or tune out
people in class and in other settings.

Including Everyone

The most successful cooperative groups in my classrooms at all levels of schooling seem to be those whose members have previously
practiced successful cooperative learning. That has to start somewhere, of course. My investigations suggest that, although altruism
and caring are as much a part of human nature as competitiveness
and individualism (Kohn, 1986; Boulding, 2000), once students
have learned to see each other as rivals for teacher approval, those
positive instincts no longer feel natural to them. Empathy and trust
take time and effort to relearn. Even within one semester, however,
much of the resistance to working interdependently in cooperative groups can be overcome. In fact, many students comment,
especially in their self-evaluation papers at the end of a semester,
on how important the group interactions had been for them:

> It made things seem a little clearer to hear what others thought
> of what they had read, and maybe seeing it through their eyes in
> a way I hadn't thought of yet. I liked the group work, and although
> it didn't always run as smooth or quick as we would have liked,
> a lot came out of it.

For most, as well, it was empowering to be heard. Sadly, for
many, it was the first time they had felt truly heard:

> I understood what I had read a lot better after a group discussion
> and I enjoyed expressing my own view on it and having people
> actually take what I said into consideration.

The sharing seemed always to stretch people beyond their incoming perceptions, because although they were all reading the
same text, everyone brought something different to the reading
and therefore got something a little bit different from it. As the
guidelines for reader response indicated, the full picture of a text
could emerge only when everyone in the class had had his or her
say about it.

There were other advantages to the process as well. Some who came in with underdeveloped reading skills were able to get help from their peers, though, to be sure, they were accountable as individuals for doing what they could in reader response as well. Three-reader groups provided a safe opportunity for surface readers to see other, deeper ways of working with text; for the most part, once they got over their own defensiveness, they learned from their peers' processes and began to develop more competence as readers and writers without having to feel competitive or inadequate. More frequently, as was my goal, group sharing of papers offered opportunities to hear perspectives that not everyone had considered. Instead of getting stuck in feeling that since hers was the minority opinion she must be wrong or, alternatively, that the other people in her group were just not smart, and therefore not worth listening to, this student valued her own thinking enough not to be swayed. At the same time, she recognized that their life experiences must have led the others in her group to whatever blind spots kept them from reading the article as it had been written:

- Looking back on that situation, I can truly say that it is not about making someone else agree with you. It is about trying to hear all different sides of the issue and trying to stretch yourself to see something different from the way you always saw it.
- I usually am very opinionated and will close up when other people state their opinions, but reader responses helped me to listen to everything that the other people had to say because we were not allowed to interrupt the person reading their papers. It also helped me to see that everyone comes from different perspectives because we are all coming from different places in our lives.

Even those who came to class on a given day without having read the assignment were able to participate in a group by listening. The papers they turned in afterwards reflected the conversations they had heard, as well as their own thinking. Though in some courses that might have been considered cheating, in my view it was a way for everyone to be drawn in, no matter what they came in with, and to get them thinking. The expectation, of course, was that if they had already sat in on a discussion, the paper that followed it would have more depth than if there had not been the prior chance to share ideas. As I see it, the more chances to hear or read something that will make a student think, the better, no matter when it occurs.

It was especially valuable to the majority of students to have access to the life experiences and points of view of students of color, who are still drastically underrepresented in our teacher education programs. Although it is not fair to ask the students of color to educate white students about racism in the United States, my experience has been that once the format of the class creates a community, many students of color welcome the opportunity to tell their stories and be heard. One graduate student of color freewrote after a particularly profound disclosure that she had felt safe enough and moved enough to share. The freewrite surprised me in her focus on what *she* was learning—or at least on the receptivity she was feeling—from the others:

> I had a wonderful class. We are all growing as individuals and as a class. If we could stay in this course forever it would be great. . . . I sometimes think that, as a person of color, although educated, I am missing some pieces to the puzzle I call my mind. Often I need to speak to someone who is different to see a different perspective.

Ultimately, in addition to all the learning about text and about each other that I saw happening through the three-reader groups, the students were practicing—most of them for the first time in a classroom—the cooperative learning model that I hope they will use as teachers:

- We not only read about cooperation, we worked with it, and as a result, we can see firsthand that it works better than competitive settings. At least, I feel that it does. . . . Thanks for showing us a working example. Now it is up to us what we do with it.
- This technique you encouraged us to use just helped to remind me that we, as American teachers, are too isolated and that we need to support each other through support groups. . . . You have made this point over and over again in your responses to my responses. You have said such things as, "Why are you carrying this alone?"

Respectful Attention

The key to the success of the three-reader groups seems to be the discipline of respectful attention to each person's paper and time to talk. As part of the process of establishing freedom from the need for rivalry for the teacher's approval, I have found it useful to set clear guidelines regarding replacing language of judgment with language of active listening.[2] It is a self-discipline for me as well: I try to model that process by my weekly comments on their individual papers. In addition, first in their three-reader groups in class, and then in other small-group sessions, students practice the social skills of respectful attention.

The first step seems to be removing "correcting." The second seems to be replacing evaluative praise with descriptive encouragement (Faber and Mazlish, 1980) and genuine statements about one's own experience of the other's ideas—such as "When you said . . . , I was reminded . . ." or "What you said made me think about . . ." or "Wow, I never thought about that" or even "I'm confused by what you said—can you help me understand?" Within a few class sessions, conversations within those three-reader groups tend to be quite animated. I am always thrilled to notice that, physically, students lean in toward each other, intensely trying to hear, concentrate, and understand—very different postures from those of students sitting in rows when one student reads or speaks, always addressing his or her comments to the teacher in the front of the room. But here, instead, quite soon, students who had initially hesitated to expose their writing to others have relaxed and seem to enjoy and genuinely learn from the exchange.

Before the three-reader groups disband, after the sharing of each person's paper and interacting with its ideas, participants do two more things. First, as individuals now, each person freewrites about what she or he has learned from the group conversation, and (a new one I am beginning to try) what they might now emphasize or change in their own papers, as a result of that conversation, and why. It is all an exercise in rethinking. Then, a final task, back in the group: to *decide together* what issues their conversation about the text raised that they think the class as a whole should address.

Much learning comes from this half hour or so of class time, in which I am not at all involved, except, from a respectful distance, to observe and make note of what I may need to address as a result of what I see and hear. At its best (and this is often the case), the full activity extends the social skills of (1) listening with full attention, (2) respectfully hearing each other's perspective, and perhaps, but not necessarily, having to reconsider one's own in terms of it, (3) assertively and responsibly keeping strict time (a task each student gets the chance to perform) so that no one's paper is left unheard, (4) focusing, even within a free-ranging brief discussion, and (5) group decision making. At the same time, the complete activity involves students first as individuals in their active reading and writing of reader response, then in their sharing, then in their focused conversations, and, finally, in their deciding what's important or left unresolved. This engages students with the text and its ideas in a multidimensional way that is much richer than any lecture-and-test process I could provide.

Their group consensus questions and comments provide a next direction in which they are invested for each topic. In addition, of course, each person's paper, now enhanced by his or her new thoughts, comes in to me at the end of class, and the dialogue with me begins. Ideally, the engagement in thinking, constructing knowledge, and understanding deepens. I really love this whole process!

The three-reader groups in which students share perspectives on a text provide useful practice for the next stages of teacher education class work. They are "jigsawing"—a set of about five books within the class, group planning, and projects.

The jigsaw method allows a whole class to get the benefit of five or six different books (or chapters) without having to read all of them.[3] Each person chooses only one from a list I provide, and then reads in three or four chunks and writes reader responses for each chunk, sharing responsibility for that book with at least two others in what become "expert groups" on their particular books. They hear each other's reader responses, just as in the regular three-reader groups. Then they decide, as a group, how to represent to the rest of the class the key points that their book is making. This step requires them to move beyond their own experiences of the text to complete understanding of what the author is saying. It requires them to come to consensus about what is important—and about meaning. Very valuable conversations come from that process. Within it all, to be sure, I intervene by continuing to read and give extensive feedback on the individual reader responses, by checking in on the directions of the "expert groups," and by ensuring that they will accurately represent their books to the rest of the class.

Then they have to figure out, together, how they will present, without lecturing, what they want the class to understand. It's a lesson planning activity of the most complex kind. As I keep reminding students, "No one should have to do anything hard alone." Sometimes, at this stage, I myself meet with the group to hear their final planning, but for the most part I try to leave the decision making to them.

One of the most important advantages of the jigsaw process is expressed by this student:

> I have difficulty presenting information to a large group because of insecurity, . . . but with this jigsaw approach I found it easier to overcome my fear of speaking to a large group of people. Even though I spoke alone, my ideas about the book were represented by a small group and supported.

Finally, after each presentation, there are questions and comments, at which time I get to ask questions designed to add, if I feel it is absolutely needed, to what has been presented. Then, the "audience" members freewrite to give constructive feedback, with what *How to Talk* . . . (Faber and Mazlish, 1980) calls "descriptive praise" rather than "evaluative praise," to the group who presented. There is learning going on at every step. Although inevitably each person gets considerably more out of the book he or she worked on than any of the ones that others present, ideally everyone gets at least a taste of the others, and sometimes much more, if the presentations fully engage the audience:

> I was very moved by the skits—I could see Frank shutting down as Peter dictated the rules. They demonstrated clearly what the lack of understanding and compassion for a child's culture could mean in terms of what and how he learns, or is prevented from learning. Our job as teacher gets bigger and more complicated every day.

In reaction to another group's presentation, through skits, of some of the very complex aspects of Beverly Daniel Tatum's *"Why*

Are All the Black Kids Sitting Together in the Cafeteria?" and Other Conversations About Race (1997), one student seemed to have understood the most important idea, even from a book she had not read:

> I never understood just why African Americans separated themselves at certain times. I always looked at it as reverse discrimination, but now I have another perspective on the whole idea. . . .
> I definitely feel much more comfortable with the fact that it has nothing to do with me as to why they choose to sit together. It has more to do with [their] connecting and identifying with each other.

The dynamics of long-term project groups are more complex than the carefully timed and monitored in-class three-reader groups. Much of the project work is done outside of class, so students have to practice without my direct monitoring or support of what may still be very new social skills. Many of them forget—or, used to compartmentalizing, never make the transfer—that what they've been learning in *How to Talk* . . . (Faber and Mazlish, 1980) are exactly those skills that they need to use to deal with or avoid frustration in peer interactions.

Besides those social skills, the conditions for the success of cooperative learning groups seem to include these: (1) clear but not rigid guidelines, with plenty of choice (some students feel I give too much choice; they're so used to just doing as they're told), (2) reasonable expectations of what can be accomplished in the given amount of time, (3) the presence of at least some members who have fully developed internal locus of control, (4) just enough but not too much or too little time together in class, (5) frequent individual and group reflective writing on how the work is going, and (6) my accessibility, still from a respectful distance, unless they call me to consult, and then a very measured bit of direct strategic teacher intervention. Given these conditions, most groups work through their collective logistical, interpersonal, and directional frustrations, and they experience the thrill of learning both for themselves—not for me—and with each other. That thrill is itself the best motivator for successful collaboration on the next learning activity.

The other not incidental learning that students do is about themselves. One student freewrote:

Hmmm. I think I kind of attempted to blame other members of my group for not accomplishing things right away. I'm learning that blame is pretty useless. Ultimately, we were able to work as a group. I came to see that I had been trying to say [that] it's not my fault that we're not getting anywhere as a group. I sat back and crossed my arms—[and] shut down. In the future, I'll try to engage myself and others in group performance.

Given at least most of the carefully designed conditions previously described, many collaborative project groups, over time, develop strong connections with and liking for each other—an outcome found by researchers in cooperative learning at all levels of schooling (Aaronsohn, Foley, Holmes, and Wallowitz, 1994; Aronson, 1978; Johnson and Johnson, 1975; Sharan and Sharan, 1976). Students' sense of responsibility shifts, over time, from having to accomplish an assignment for the teacher to having to bring what they promised to their group. It's a much higher—and more innately satisfying—level of moral development:

Normally, I only talk with the people sitting next to me in my classes. I sit in the same seat all the time and talk with whoever is around me. You get to become pseudo-friends with those people. . . . But in here, I think that I have made a few good acquaintances that I trust my feelings with. . . . I think everybody in this class tries to help each other out.

Accountability and "Standards"

Teachers and professors are increasingly pressured to prove that our students are learning. Increasingly, as well, we are pressured to prove that they are learning not just the same skills but also the same content that others in the state and country are learning. Well-meaning teacher education professors, focused intently on preparing student teachers for the standardized tests they must pass to achieve certification, sometimes seem to me to take a narrow view of what and how to structure their courses. Their focus is on the big high-stakes test rather than on the deep conceptual understanding of that tested content and skills that students will need *as teachers* for the thirty-plus years *after* that single qualifying exam. I have spoken with colleagues who feel obliged to rush to cover a body of material that they expect will be on the test, regardless of whether the preteachers in their classes deeply understand and feel ready to try to teach each concept being "covered." What is our obligation to our students? And to their students? How far can we see?

Under the pressures of accountability and standards, it is tempting to revert to what we assume worked to make us learn when we were students: an emphasis on facts, performance, and grades. My premise is that that is exactly the opposite of what needs to happen—that genuine learning is inhibited, even crushed. For the focus on "knowing," on performance and grades, most of us need only to look for evidence in our own life stories, as well as in our careful observation of our students. We may remember that the threat of grading often causes fretting to replace thinking. Making a piece of work look right or sound right so that it will get a good grade replaces the desire to express, explore, connect, and communicate, and to keep a conversation going for the sake of more understanding, more pleasure.

Ultimately, if the pressure is too great and the pleasure of accomplishment too infrequent, the student simply gives up. Maybe that didn't happen to us; after all, we made it to college, graduate school, the teaching profession. Aware of the theories of multiple intelligences, however, most of us who became teachers have probably acknowledged to ourselves that at least part of the reason we "made it" was because we happened to have as our dominant intelligences the ones most valued in school and on standardized tests: verbal linguistic and mathematical logical. Those of us who teach or observe special education classes recognize how frequently children so labeled have, as well as certain definable problems, incredible musical, spatial, or kinesthetic intelligences. Often, in fact, children considered for special education placement are those who have often acted out in classrooms in frustration at their failure to operate within certain narrow structures and "standards" set by traditional expectations.

Many teachers and professors report believing that without ongoing grades or the threat of a test to pass, students will not work. Many students report believing that, as well, even about themselves. However, my own experience over at least the last twenty years urges me to believe that, for the most part, students work more rigorously, more diligently, and, most important, more thoughtfully when they know that their ideas will be heard with respectful attention, and that they will not be judged.

My experience of inviting students to engage in personal terms with a text through reader response (and of replacing grades with nonjudgmental constructive feedback) has suggested a positive and even astonishingly successful way to have students come up with frequent, honest, passionate, reflective, and ultimately satisfying writing—not merely as products that prove that they read a text competently but also as vehicles for their own exploration of self and the world. This is true even for students who had been in remedial, lower-tracked, or even special education classes during their elementary or high school years. In fact, in my experience of this process, when a reader or writer focuses entirely on the content of the writing rather than on mechanics, even the mechanical quality of the writing improves!

Too much is at stake when we subject students to the harsh glare of teacher judgment while they are still experimenting with their own identities and abilities. All that grading and testing is like continually pulling up by the roots a seed we have planted, to see how it is growing. When we role-play that exact scenario in class, even students who have never nurtured a garden understand: it dies. The connections become real:

> My brother's art teacher had constantly criticized his work. She
> rarely gave him a good grade on a drawing he worked hard on.
> It [had been] an enjoyable thing for him to do and she turned it
> into something serious. He had to have every single little detail
> done according to her standards. He got so frustrated, he just
> gave up on it.

Why *Does* It Matter?

I have been suggesting throughout the book that there are long-range effects on everyday adult thinking and operating that come from the habits developed within the structures and assumptions of traditional schooling. These effects, I am suggesting, have very troubling effects on our democracy.

Briefly recapitulating the list of outcomes that seem to result from the socialization within traditional schooling may have even more meaning at this point in the book than they did when I named them in Chapter One:

- Orientation toward dualistic (all-or-nothing, right-or-wrong) one-right-answer thinking
- Assuming that text equals truth
- Inability to connect or make meaning of fragments of information; no habit of searching for context
- Intolerance of uncertainty or difference
- No capacity for distinguishing what is important from what is minor
- Tendency to operate in terms of fear of punishment or expectation of reward—the lowest levels of moral development
- Difficulty in collaborating, turning all relationships into rivalries
- Underdeveloped capacity to enjoy or even know how to invent, create, play with other possibilities
- Dependency and powerlessness

A frightening list of characteristics, indeed, but all recognizable in our society. But not characteristics of ourselves? How did we escape? Because of our success in traditional school, or in spite of it? So what about people who are or soon will be teachers?

Weaning students from their sole focus on "what the teacher wants" seems to be harder in direct proportion to the number of years of socialization in traditional teacher-pleasing, and harder if the paradigm shifts in only one class. Nevertheless, one class is better than none. Most students of all ages demonstrate and report that they can at least begin to overcome the dependency and powerlessness imposed upon and embedded within them by traditional schooling (and frequently, as well, by authoritarian parenting, and often by our unjust society) if certain conditions are in place. Basically, the intense pressure of an authority figure who stands over them to criticize must be replaced by a fully self-actualized adult who believes in them and provides clear, supportive, knowledgeable, honest, and respectful feedback.

I am the first to acknowledge that this kind of nonjudgmental supportive feedback is not easy to give consistently, but without it the student feels criticized and defensive and shuts down. At the beginning of my giving feedback each semester, even though I never use red pen (and I ask the students to freewrite and discuss about why), many students see all that teacher writing on their nice clean paper and feel immediately defeated, even before they actually read what I wrote. Some try to justify, as if my questions are attacks. I have to tread very lightly, and hold honest conversations about their feelings and my own perceptions and intentions—on paper, in class, or in conference.

The other conditions within which students seem to overcome dependency include: (1) students having reason to feel invested in projects they have had a real opportunity to choose and (2) students feeling safe and valued within a community of their peers. Given these conditions, I have found that most students will put time, energy, will, intelligence, and thoughtfulness into the learning tasks that help them go in positive directions, even if the path is not direct (Kohn, 1996; Kozol, 2000; Ladson-Billings, 2001; Polakow, 1993; Ashton-Warner, 1963; Holt, 1967).

The alternative to this kind of relationship of child to adult, or student to teacher, is the kind of situation that frustrated teachers and professors usually attribute to students' purported "lack of motivation." But when we look instead at our own classroom structures, philosophies, and approaches, the possibility emerges of seeing that no children are necessarily "at risk"; instead, all children are "children at promise" (Polakow, 1993).

Given the deeply internalized pressures that most university students bring with them into teacher education classes from traditional earlier schooling, it seems that teacher educators in particular have an obligation to reconsider the processes by which we are inclined to conduct our classes. While deploring student silence, memorization, acceptance of surface right answers, careful avoidance of divergent thinking, and poverty of imagination—all aspects of dependency—teachers and professors might usefully wonder if our own, perhaps unconscious reinforcement of students' teacher-pleasing behaviors reproduce those very behaviors that we wish to eradicate. Who as teachers themselves will be able to use with full understanding such progressive methods as authentic assessment, for example, if they have never been authentically assessed themselves through a range of genuine learning experiences leading to self-evaluation? And how will they be prepared to engage in the complex self-assessment of teachers increasingly being used in some states, or even feel empowered within their own classrooms?

Teacher education classes can be the place to ask students to unlearn habits of (1) fiercely self-protective individualism and competitiveness, (2) orientation toward reward and punishment, (3) misdirected focus on getting through (rather than focusing on deep thinking about the rich theoretical content of teacher education research and its practical application), and (4) total dependency on teacher direction. Classrooms can be places where people about to become teachers can construct their own ways of seeing and thinking from wider perspectives as they practice, recognize, and internalize behaviors that are caring, creative, decentered, and responsible—that is, the behaviors that should characterize the kinds of teachers within whose classes children can achieve all our long-range hopes for their lives—and their own.

Notes
1. See Kohn (1996). Also, see Chapter Seven for more discussion of how I use "Musical Chairs."
2. As defined by Thomas Gordon in his book *T.E.T.: Teacher Effectveness Training* (1974). See also my first book, *Going Against the Grain* (1996), and my paper "Dialoguing for Student Reflectiveness," presented at an international conference in San Juan, Puerto Rico.
3. Like cooperative learning itself, this is a method I thought I had invented as a college teacher of literature and writing in the early 1980s. It was not until I began my doctoral program and began reading Slavin, Johnson and Johnson (1975), and Aronson (1978), among others, that I realized that there were books written about what I had been doing. See also Aronson (1978).

Chapter Six

Moving from Right Answers to Multiple Perspectives

The negative outcomes of traditional schooling listed at the end of Chapters One and Five are certainly not ones that teachers or parents would choose for our children. In fact, I anticipate that some readers might reject the conclusions I have drawn, preferring to conclude that inherent mental incapacity accounts for a store clerk's inability to make correct change, a bureaucrat's inability to think beyond "the rules," or a college student's docility or apparent dullness. Looking only at decontextualized situations, it is easy to blame the individual or class of people. But I have taught, observed, read, and researched about teaching for long enough, and I have observed, cared for, and worked with young children and adolescents outside of school for long enough, to believe that we err in thinking that the problem is in the person, or that person's particular family or community.

By the time a person becomes a teacher, he or she may no longer have conscious memory of all the adjustments and shutting down required by traditional schooling. Thus, the inclination is sometimes to forget or not consider the impact of our teaching on a bright, curious, creative, active, imaginative, eager, lively, confident, and beautiful young child—and which very young child is not all of these? The tragedy is how early in both a teacher's career and a student's young life this forgetting or lack of consideration happens, despite all the excellent research done by educators. Basically, it has been noticed: we do to children what we think we are expected to do, and that is usually the embedded memory of what was done to us.

A recent case in point reminded me of exactly that, during a staff development session at a K–6 school in an inner city. When I exclaimed about the child on the cover of Ladson-Billings's *Dream-keepers* (1994), saying, "Isn't he beautiful?" one teacher replied, and several others concurred: "I don't notice if he's beautiful; I just notice if he behaves."

Unintended but Predictable Outcomes of Traditional Schooling

From a teacher's perspective, having the children "behave" may be the precondition for the teacher's ability to teach what he or she feels required to teach. But what if we look from children's perspectives? Even from the outside, it is easy to notice the obvious restrictions that get imposed unnaturally in schools, even on five-year-olds, and perhaps even earlier, in increasingly academically oriented day-care settings. Sitting still for hours, limited or nonexistent free exploration of concrete materials, having to wait one's turn until twenty-five others have had their turns, having to "keep up" with some often developmentally impossible external standards or else being labeled "behind"—all of these insults have to have cognitive, physical, and emotional costs.

Beyond the obvious, it seems clear to me that many students schooled in traditional classrooms feel essentially powerless, at least in that portion of their lives. As much of the recent commentary on school violence suggests, that piece of the profile seems consistent. Even students who do not take such drastic measures as violence—those who give up and drop out, including those who are later incarcerated, having long felt themselves to be failures; or even those who go on and study to become teachers!—report feeling alienated within and from school. They talk of feeling disconnected from much of the academic material and process, from themselves, from the caring of adults in the building, and from each other. They feel devalued for their age and inexperience, and they feel especially devalued if their primary intelligences are ones other than the only two—verbal and mathematical—on which classroom tasks and standardized tests focus, and this that they honor, exclusive of all the other intelligences. Students are well aware that they have often been judged, as well, for their family structures, their socioeconomic status, and their race. Tracking as an institutional structure reinforces those judgments, easily persuading those accepted into "higher" tracks that at least they are better than somebody. Maybe being "better" makes them Somebody.

Teachers in many schools are troubled by what they consider to be children's "out of control" behaviors in unstructured situations such as hallways, the lunchroom, the playground, or the bus. Why do children have to disregard the needs and feelings of others, get even, be first, viciously protect turf, exclude others? Indeed, it is apparent that those same behaviors can last into adulthood, and become neighborhood, highway, workplace, and even more public behaviors, including national policy. Interestingly, these have come to be the behaviors rewarded by the TV shows that North Americans seem to find the most fascinating. Even if those behaviors also exist in places other than schools, they get a good shove forward in schools, in ways that prior chapters have attempted to analyze.

Moreover, although certainly not exclusively in schools, it is especially in schools where, by content and process, the dominant culture (which includes the assimilated cultures but hardly ever the rich original cultures of our immigrant pasts) is presented as the only valid culture. Even a cursory look at most U.S. textbooks affirms the conclusions following Loewen's exhaustive 1995 investigation (Loewen, 1995). Unfortunately, those are the same conclusions to which one must come from a careful examination of standard textbooks, especially social studies textbooks, used today in schools. Except for a few after-the-fact recently added pages (that Peggy McIntosh, 1985, refers to as "add women [and people of color and workers] and stir," whose presence is intended to quiet the criticism of multicultural educators), the glorification of Anglo-American culture as the norm prevails.

That it was so when teachers themselves were in K–12 schooling is even more obvious. Except for rare instances, it is safe to say that every paper I get from every one of my teacher education students in every semester acknowledges that in all their precollege schooling, history and literature were taught exclusively from a "white" perspective. Students from African American, Latino, Asian, and even Jewish—and even from recently arrived Italian, Polish, Portuguese, and Irish heritages—have had very sobering things to say about the lack of intersection between their home lives and the dominant culture in school. The most astonishing papers, however, have been from people who identified themselves as "WASPs," or other European Americans whose families had been here many generations. Most of them had not ever thought of themselves as having ethnicity. They were proudly "just Americans." Whereas some of them acknowledged that they felt bereft of connection to their original cultures, once we paid attention to the omissions and distortions in textbooks, others were fiercely protective of the dominant culture. Some reflected on their defensiveness:

> I guess it isn't easy to look at how our own culture has trampled on other cultures, so it is sometimes easier to simply cover up the unpleasantries.

Many said, "I never had to think about it," and several implied or stated outright, "And I don't want to." Often, teacher education classes, approached from a multicultural perspective, were the first places where they were ever confronted with alternative views, unless the required undergraduate U.S. history course happened to be taught by someone with a perspective outside the norm. But the evidence in the schools suggests that most teachers have not had such courses, or that such courses, like others lecturing rapidly through heaps of disconnected factoids to memorize, were mere blips on their screens.

Moving from Right Answers to Multiple Perspectives

My goal in exposing people who are about to be (or who already are) teachers to a different way of seeing is not at all to evoke guilt. Guilt paralyzes. My goal is the opposite of the paralysis and powerlessness to which most are accustomed. My goal, instead, is to invite active and conscious understanding of the complex contexts in which all our lives and histories are lodged. It is to ask preteachers and teachers to consider another way of looking at the "right answers" they had absorbed. It is to have them notice that the one side of the chair they happen to see from the position they happen to be in is only one side of the chair. To get the entire picture, it is necessary to look at it from all possible angles. Those who go allow themselves to, go through that process come out feeling not guilt but empowerment to take on the new and important responsibility of asking of every story, every text, Whose perspective has been left out here?

Initial exposure to perspectives other than the ones they have always been taught and assumed to be the only truth shocks most teacher education students. Often, that first exposure comes within my classes, even if the students are well beyond conventional college age. Most report:

> I had complete faith in every word I read. If it [were] written in
> a book, I would take it for the truth. I thought it was as black and
> white as the words on the page.

Even by the end of the semester, that student, representative of many, was not fully convinced:

> I am in struggle with this situation, almost in denial that this
> could be true. Why would the textbooks that I've learned from
> and would teach from be wrong?

Why, indeed?

> Why do our schools sugarcoat the story of the Pilgrims? Do they
> believe children cannot handle the truth? Is it because we were
> the cause of those injustices?

In almost all classes, even those other than social studies methods, I have students read and write response papers to articles of their own choosing from the excellent Rethinking Schools publication, *Rethinking Columbus* (Bigelow and Peterson, 1998). The Columbus story, told in essay, poetry, story, maps, reprints of paintings, and song from the perspectives of native peoples, becomes the arena of students' most significant cognitive dissonance:

> I never realized how much pain and suffering the Native Americans
> have experienced. Because this was never in my history books nor
> a topic of discussion in my other classes, this was an eye-opener.

The term *eye-opener* appears in almost everyone's papers in response to this set of brief readings, which I spread out over the semester to give students time to digest the disturbing implications of what they are now seeing for the first time. Many ask in their own ways what one student asked in a writeback: "Does anyone else feel as betrayed as I do for having been misled?"

But more than one becomes defensive, like the undergraduate history major who had obediently memorized right answers all the way through high school and most of college. She fought fiercely against the first articles she had chosen from *Rethinking Columbus* (Bigelow and Peterson, 1998), proud to have a knowledgeable argument against them, insisting that they were biased, unfair, wrong, and incomplete in challenging what she already knew. Our conversation through many rounds of writebacks brought her to a startling and very uncomfortable place, similar to the shocking first realization that, first, a chair seen from the opposite side of the room looks different from how it looks from this side, and second, both views are legitimate. How accurate she is in indicting the traditional processes and content of social studies teaching, even at the "excellent" elementary and secondary schools from which she had graduated:

> It somehow never occurred to me that there [are] truly two sides to every story. I don't think it's not that I didn't think of the other side before, but . . . in school we are taught to see things in a certain way.

Perhaps more frightening about the traditional teaching of the Columbus story may be this: even if "the truth" gets told in textbooks and classrooms, it seems to be told in such a way that students come out still justifying "our side":

> I knew Columbus invaded America and that he did not discover it, but what I did not know is how intrusive it was.

Students seem to have been taught that if bad things happened, at least it wasn't Columbus's own fault—it was his men, his brutal, ignorant, untamed (working-class?) men who did the awful deeds:

> Even now, as a college student, I was somewhat shocked by the outline of Columbus's actions. I think that even when I was taught

the truth, it was more [that] Columbus was the catalyst for the destruction of Native Americans. It was shocking to read that he himself had taken slaves to Spain.

Another simply states, "As a student, I was never taught to explore the history of the people who were driven from their lands." Because social studies is traditionally taught as "objective" facts to memorize, without paying attention to the feelings of the people involved, students of the dominant culture, socialized within those classes, can come out knowing all the facts but not understanding anything about what the events meant to the people involved—all the people involved:

> Even when I learned of these injustices, I never stopped to think that Thanksgiving wouldn't be a holiday enjoyed by Native Americans.

Students of color, of course, face a more difficult situation as they are taught from the same textbooks and through the same lenses as the rest of the students in their classrooms. This is certainly the case for African American children, of whose very existence the only formal recognition is usually the institution of slavery. What must they feel when slavery is taught as an economic necessity, and then dismissed? Political as well as textbook pressures almost guarantee that Puerto Rican and Chicano children will hardly ever hear their heritages and history addressed in mainland U.S. classrooms, unless they are lucky enough to be placed for a while in an active and proud bilingual program. As several pieces in *Rethinking Columbus* address, how confusing and even humiliating it must be for children of color to see themselves and people like them represented in ways that are, at the very least, inaccurate and inadequate.

From well-meaning teachers' perspectives, without a transformed textbook to guide them, it can feel overwhelming and even unfair to be faced with the expectation that they will teach with content and processes that fully include everyone. How are they to teach what they themselves never learned? As a result, if they remain confined within the boundaries of their own schooling, teachers may very likely keep doing the same thing to the next generation of students. One cooperating teacher in a high school social studies class leaves Africa totally out of his geography curriculum;

of all of Latin America, he does only Brazil. His rationale is, "They're all the same, anyway." Ralph's Twentieth-Century Writers high school English course consists entirely of Western European or American white males. We teach what we know.

In some cases, their one-right-answer habit of thinking has caused troubled preteachers to demand of me, as we discuss the Columbus story, "Then which side is true?" It feels like success to me when preteachers come to realize that both "sides" have truth, and that there is a much more complex and honest story that must be told, if necessary, of course, without the gory details, even to very young children. Though many resist that idea, they realize that they themselves had come to teacher education courses still holding onto indelible early notions.

Wondering about how things they were learning about in *Rethinking Columbus* (Bigelow and Peterson, 1998) were being taught in the schools right now, some preteachers did some investigations of their own. Now that they themselves were aware of a much more complex set of truths, how disappointed several were with what they found on display on the walls of elementary schools they visited in October: only the familiar commercially-produced heroic pictures of Columbus and his three ships, happily colored by small children. Two other university students interviewed school-age family members to find out what is being taught, and they used the interactions as an opportunity to teach as well as learn. One asked her thirteen-year-old sister on Thanksgiving vacation about what she knew about the celebration. Her sister gave her the "cookie-cutter response about generous Pilgrims and grateful Indians feasting together." As Rebecca probed, and explained what she herself had begun to learn, her sister answered, confused and distressed by the contradictory information and its implications, wanting to believe that we are the good guys: "I thought the Indians made friends with the English? What about Squanto?"

> Although ignorance is dangerous, it is far worse to teach lies. I would be infuriated if schools taught children a candy-coated bunch of lies about the Holocaust. Yet students are still being taught about the "savage Indians."

Reflecting on the interview she conducted informally in her own home, Victoria's story is a complex and fascinating exposure of how early children are trained to defend the people they are trained to consider heroes:

> What timing! My son, in the third grade, has been reading auto-biographies on Christopher Columbus. So I thought I would see what he is learning. The other day, while we were waiting for the bus, I asked him what he knew about Christopher Columbus.
>
> He said, "He was an explorer." He then went on with, "He discovered America." I asked him what he thought about the Indians who were already here. His response was that without Christopher Columbus we would never have settled in America.
>
> He knew that Christopher Columbus "whipped" the Indians. This didn't seem to bother him? I questioned him on this and he said Columbus was not at fault, he was only following the orders of the King and Queen. I was really bothered that he would think that that was justification.
>
> While I was on the phone discussing the homework with some-one from class and we were talking about Columbus, Jeff became very agitated and vocal declaring, "Christopher Columbus did discover America!" Needless to say, at dinner tonight, we had quite a conversation about what would happen if someone came down from Mars and decided to "discover" [the town we live in].
>
> Part of Jeff's assignment is that they are to dress up in the character that they have been reading about and put on a show for the class. He may now have a little different perspective. It will be interesting to hear how his teacher handles it.
>
> I must admit, until reading some of the articles in *Rethinking Columbus* I had never really given much thought about the Indians being here before us. I feel I was brainwashed in school. This book has really caused me to rethink history and to question how teach-ing can mold people.
>
> Why do the texts not question the Indians' feelings? I posed that question to my son. He was quiet. I could tell he had never thought about it from that angle before. Isn't that what we should be doing—getting the kids to think and feel, not just absorb facts?

As I write, our teacher education program still does not require a full elementary social studies methods course for certification. Because in 2003 the state regulations were expected to change, our program finally changed accordingly: it added a *one-credit* social studies methods course for elementary teaching certification. Until then, we had squeezed it into the already packed curriculum of other courses. How—and even if—it has been taught has depended on the background and interests of the individual faculty members teaching those courses. Even from such a brief exposure as some of my colleagues and I provide, students can put together for themselves the reasons why a strong social studies methods course belongs in an elementary teacher education program:

- I never once questioned the authority of the historian before I came to this class. . . . I believe that it is important for me to teach an alternative view of history because children will get the traditional view from everywhere else.
- I have learned to question from you and from this class. If I don't teach them to question what their history book tells them, who will? Will they have to wait until they get to college like I did? Even when they got there, they would more than likely graduate without ever being taught to question.

The *process* of exposing students to alternative ways of seeing must be as important as the new content. I use the quick drama of "stealing the backpack," from Bill Bigelow's article in *Rethinking Columbus* (1998), to have students experience what indigenous peoples must have felt when Columbus "discovered" America. The person whose backpack I dramatically pick up from the floor and rifle through feels violated. Most make the connection when I say, "It's mine! I discovered it!" The rest of the class characteristically feels her violation with her—and shock. However, even as they are learning for the first time to understand that fact viscerally, I learn how much more we need to do in terms of moral development in our society when I hear some students react to my violation of one student's privacy and property with, "Whew, well, at least it wasn't me."

The active, direct process of coming to understand a range of concepts here is crucial. Without a personal, intensive, but time-consuming experience of problematizing text, students hearing an efficient lecture from a professor about how inadequate textbooks are could legitimately say, "Yeah, yeah, that's just *her* bias." Wonderful cognitive dissonance can come from close hands-on analysis of a wide range of samples of texts, and from asking the key questions: Whose perspective is presented? Why? Whose is left out? Why? How can I find out more?

Finding Oneself in the Curriculum

It is hard to believe that people can get through teacher certification without having to examine the school curricula that molded them. But for generations it has been "easier to simply cover up the unpleasantries," as one student wrote about genocide and imperialism, on the one hand, and the resistance to oppression, on the other hand. Most teacher education students—and I would suspect most high school students of the dominant culture as well—automatically identify with the "we" of "We, the People." They are socialized to that identification as if many of their own ancestors had not been oppressed for language of origin or religion when they came here; as if women had ever been included in the public franchise before 1920; and if they happened to be Anglos, as if their ancestors had all been "of property." So identifying with the winners of our history, and socialized to think in zero-sum, either/or, us-or-them terms, students, not surprisingly, join the rest of our well-schooled society in fearing or resenting newer immigrants to the United States and, in fact, everyone who is not "like us" in any way.

Preteachers can come to realize much of their own narrow socialization at some point within the combination of assignments investigating bilingual education and their feelings about their own ethnicity. One student asked, "How can you fear comparison if you truly value what you have?" Exactly. So I begin there, by having each student investigate his or her own family of origin, as far back into the preimmigrant experience as they are able. This is not the standard geneology chart but an investigation of what life was like in both the old country and here when their first ancestors first came to the United States, what work people did, what stories had been handed down, what languages were spoken, and how much schooling was had, and why. The goal is to learn as much as they can about, understand more deeply, and cherish their home/ ancestral cultures on their own terms, not in comparison with any others. A month into the semester, we share those products I call *genograms,* not as full-class presentations—and not as performance—but in very small intimate groups, perhaps five going on simultaneously. Those events are particularly beautiful to observe. Everyone is involved, with intense pleasure, investment, participation, fascination, connection, and interest. It is not like any history they have ever studied, but, of course, it *is* history! Sometimes students plot their families' histories on a partial time line of world and/or U.S. history. Students report really loving the genogram activity, probably more than any other assignment. They find it significant for their own lives and also as a basis for fully valuing themselves as people with a culture before being asked to understand someone else's.

That is a crucial first step, because I do ask people planning to be teachers, and people who are already teachers, to understand and value cultures other than their own. As I indicated in Chapter Four, learning to decenter has been not only the most important but also the most difficult task of the students' semester with me. At this point, in addition to the ones I have already mentioned, I think I have found a combination of other readings and activities that help students, over time, begin to achieve that goal.

Pivotal Readings

The Street

Except for *How to Talk So Kids Will Listen, and Listen So Kids Will Talk* (Faber and Mazlish, 1980), which I use in almost all of my courses, students find Ann Petry's novel *The Street* (1946) to be the most compelling book of their semester with me. It is the story of an African American single mother working as hard as she can to make a decent life for herself and her eight-year-old son, Bub. This is the anchor book of my graduate courses on education in the inner city—one by that name, and another as a first course in a summer-to-summer program, within which students will be placed as interns and then as student teachers in one of two inner cities. In addition, in my undergraduate introductory course, I use the opening few pages of Chapter Fourteen of *The Street,* in which the reader sees Bub and his third grade classroom and classmates from the point of view of his white (and by no means culturally relevant) teacher, Miss Rinner. Needless to say, that provocative reading provides us with much back-and-forth conversation throughout the semester, unearthing lots of unexamined assumptions. At the very least, just those few pages have students ultimately realizing:

Miss Rinner serves as a reminder for us not to "write kids off" because of our perceptions of their home life. We will probably find that any preconceived notions are wrong.

Because *The Street* is such a powerful work of imagination, and because Bub's mother, Lutie Johnson, is such an admirable character, students who read the entire book are able to identify with her enough to decenter amazingly from their own comparatively much more privileged lives. Exactly because it is a work of imagination, not a research study, editorial, or sermon that they can call "biased," students can accept the conditions of the book without putting up defenses. It does not seem to attack most of them personally, as some students sometimes feel that other readings do. All the students, I have found, are completely taken in by the dramatic world of the novel; they get as close to *living* Lutie's life in Harlem as I can arrange it for them. That immersion is, importantly, free of the damage even well-meaning people of the dominant culture might do—as plenty of the white volunteers in Mississippi did in 1964, including me—if they were to go into a "Harlem" with all or most of their unexamined assumptions about race, class, and America in tact. The immersion the book initiates is the precondition, I think, for the attitude changes that have to take place if teachers are to avoid being Miss Rinners, however unconsciously.

One student's final paper represents what most white students come to think about and understand as a result of their emotional as well as cognitive experience of the book, which unearths and challenges many of their assumptions:

> Reading *The Street* has changed my life. Every chapter made me want to read more. Then the ending. The ending was so awful. I think the reason it was so awful is that I had so much hope for Lutie. She was doing things right. She was doing what we've all been told to do: follow the rules, work hard, save money, be independent—you'll get ahead by doing all this.
>
> Yes, she did do it all and it still didn't work out. All of my education and upbringing has told me all the things Lutie tried to do and yet it didn't work. How can that be? Everything tells you that if you do things right, good things will come of it for you. How could it fail?

It failed because Lutie is not like me, in that she is not white, not from a family that could give her opportunities, and not seen as being able to succeed by her teachers and society. That is the part you are never told. If you have all that and then work hard, follow the rules, and so on, then you will succeed. But first you have to have what Lutie was missing and what I have. But no one ever tells you that. Everyone tells you that you'll live happily ever after if you do what it takes to get ahead.

Throughout the book I felt myself cheering for Lutie, sure that things would work out for her and Bub, and confident that she would live happily ever after. But the book is not a fairy tale, and that is the part that I forgot when reading.

In hindsight, I can see now where I made my mistake in approaching the book. I thought of it in terms of me, not in terms of a woman of color in the 1940s, who had everything going against her even though she was smart and beautiful and worked hard.

My eyes were opened. Although I was mad at the ending, it taught me much more than it would have if everything had worked out.

Through *The Street*, white students were able to look at themselves and their position within the larger system, not only as individuals and as teachers but also as members of the dominant culture:

- It seems to me that the inner city is a world of its own and white society has the key of hope. The real estate and jobs are dominated by whites. . . . And the problem is, myself included at times, society labels the people in these environments as lazy, no good, dumb individuals.
- I thought Lutie had what it took to make it out. I realized she did have what it takes, but she did not have the opportunity. . . . It brings into focus how deep-rooted racism is.
- As individuals, what we can do is think clearly about the circumstances that others are forced to battle with daily, and how that correlates with their outcomes in society. If Lutie were born into a white family in Connecticut and had the same drive and determination, what would she have become?

Some, seeing the system in place, recognized their own oblivion as part of the problem. More than one took a hard look at herself in terms of her family, her society, and the school in which she teaches, courageous enough to face the thing she most feared. Maybe she has been like Miss Rinner. And so she resolved not to be, because of *The Street:*

> Miss Rinner seemed so entirely inhuman, and racist, that I had myself up on a pedestal, compared with her. However, I had certain assumptions that I needed to get past. . . . For instance, I didn't realize how much of a poison racism really is.
>
> I thought that some people are evil and some are good, but I never realized how much of a white superiority perspective I myself had. It was handed down to me by my family and their families, and I don't consider my family racist by any means. Yet when confronted with difficult issues, we fall back on those same assumptions because no one ever challenges us to think about them.
>
> Miss Rinner and *The Street* forced me to look inside myself and ask, "How am I behaving like her?" It was scary, because I recognized that I had already (as a new teacher!) begun to make assumptions about my students, based on what part of town they came from. I was beginning to feel that they were hopeless cases, that they [were] not going anywhere, anyway, so why bother? And if their own parents didn't care about them, how could I possibly help them?
>
> Yet Lutie was a real person with so many problems and odds stacked against her, with the same passion for wanting the best for her child that I have for my children, that I began to see things differently.

I was pleased that many students linked *The Street* with the article "Why Some Parents Don't Come to School" (Finders and Lewis, 1994), a research article whose content caused much argument, and eventually so much insight, in the class:

- I never took into consideration that parents are trying to hold jobs and support their family, and this does not translate into parents don't care. . . . *The Street* helped me really see the false assumptions that people have about black mothers. Lutie is a loving mother who works hard to make money so [that] she can give Bub a good life. Both Miss Rinner and the detectives assume that Lutie is a terrible mother who is at fault for all of Bub's problems.

- Teachers assume that parents are not helping with the education of their children because they are not involved in school conferences or programs. I know that this is something that I'm going to have to deal with on a daily basis when I begin teaching, so I need to remember to stay strong and not assume or prejudge.

Reading *The Street* so intensely may have been the catalyst for many teachers learning to see the situation through the eyes of someone other than the teacher, without guilt or defensiveness, but with a new and much more complex consciousness.

A Strong Dose of Kozol

Except for *The Street,* and especially in combination with it, nothing challenges university students' assumptions more completely than Jonathan Kozol's books. I now have students in those classes each reading at least one of the six chapters of Kozol's *Savage Inequalities* (1991). In that way, in six groups, we effectively jigsaw the entire book. With his *Rachel and Her Children* (1988), and sometimes his *Death at an Early Age* (1967), the whole book is read by several people as one of a set of jigsaw choice books. In responding to these works, students of relative privilege are forced to examine what they have been "taught" by everything in their lives about the structures of our society.

Savage Inequalities

In their reader response papers about *Savage Inequalities,* more than about any other reading, students exclaim, I never realized! and often, How can that be, in America? Most react viscerally: That is not fair! What reading Kozol releases, I think, is a genuine, innocent reaction of outrage and compassion that is innate in most students—and perhaps all of us. It forces readers back into that deepest moral place within themselves, holding up a mirror from which courageous and honest people cannot turn away:

> Reading this book has made me very angry. I almost dread having to pick it up to read it because of all the horrible things I'll find. But isn't that an easy way out? Just don't read it, close your eyes

to the truth, to what children in our country face every day. If you don't read about it, it doesn't actually exist.

Although some students say that they had already read the entire book, usually in a sociology or foundations of education course, most had not had the intense experience of it that the processes of reader response, sharing, jigsawing, and writebacks provided. Most had had no sustained emotional connection to it. My hope is that by deeply engaging with the book, instead of just reading it all through quickly, students will see it in terms of their own lives, coming to terms with how "sheltered," or even "culturally deprived," they themselves have been. Then, perhaps for the first time, they might see that position as being part of a problem for them to work on:

> I realized that I was just like one of those people in The Bluffs [the affluent white towns literally "above" East St. Louis, Illinois, described in Kozol's first chapter]. I would go into Hartford for concerts at the Meadows Theater and use it for other resources, but when it came down to it, I didn't want anything to do with what was going on there.

Many students feel shock and outrage as they engage with *Savage Inequalities,* especially in combination with other readings, such as the Miss Rinner chapter from *The Street* (Petry, 1946) and excerpts from Valerie Polokow's *Lives on the Edge* (1993). Most (though not all, which is not amazing, considering how they were taught to "read") were able to distinguish Kozol's voice from the voices he quotes, especially those from the *Wall Street Journal* and from some of the parents and students in the affluent towns. Most readers of the dominant culture, seeing so graphically the contradictions Kozol presents, had to let go of their incoming assumptions that children of color and of poverty, and their parents, are innately averse to education:

> I hate the idea that poor children see that they are viewed by their teachers, principals, and all of society as poor investments. That is an absolutely horrible thing for a child to hear. What incentive, then, does that child have to do well when it's obvious that nobody sees enough of his potential to help him?

Some students, in their outrage, try to figure it out, and they come to startlingly logical, even radical conclusions:

> Differences in almost $10,000 per student in expenditures from the rich communities to the poor ones is just outright disgusting. . . . Since it's not equally divided now, and probably won't ever be, shouldn't whoever needs the most get the most?

Others are even more personally reflective, honestly representing their own and others' ambivalence regarding the still-unfulfilled desegregation order in Connecticut (*Sheff* v. *O'Neill*, 1996), after reading the Connecticut Supreme Court judges' opinions in terms of *Savage Inequalities*. These students saw from several sides of the "chair" at once:

- It is easy to read books like *Savage Inequalities* and think, "Boy, they really should do something about their public schools," but when it's our own state, it seems much harder to find solutions.
- I can say that I am outraged at the whole situation, but if I had children and was directly affected, I honestly don't know what I would do. I don't know if I'd be wholeheartedly willing to send my children off to the Hartford schools. I feel extremely hypocritical right now, especially since I'm an educator in an inner city.
- Maybe that's where we'll need to start, with getting to know each other and breaking down the walls built up by years of fear.

Rachel and Her Children

Strong reactions to children being serviced so inadequately in what should be "public" schooling are pretty automatic for teachers. But it is to their credit, and Kozol's, that, for most students, the stories of adults who find themselves homeless are also compelling and transforming. For some, of course, as with all the readings, it takes more than just reading *Rachel and Her Children* itself (Kozol, 1988):

> While reading, I felt some compassion for the victims, but before I was finished I had also made some judgments about them, too. I

did not even realize how much I judged them until I shared my response with Mark, in our class. He was so sympathetic to the plight of these lives depicted by Kozol that I felt like a heel, which I should have, for my reactions.

Many such students write that before reading the book, they had had some pretty automatic judgments about people who are homeless. Many write or speak about their prereading views. Because of, or maybe even despite, their own life experiences, they are still somehow safely able to keep the concept of homelessness at a moral distance from themselves. Through all the recent decade of layoffs, a few never connect their family's or neighbor's bread-winner's loss of a job with this condition. They need desperately to believe that homelessness "happens to bad people, not to us":

- Before reading this book, I always thought that it was their fault and they got themselves in[to] the situation and they should get themselves out. Whenever I would see a homeless person on the street, I said (to myself), What is wrong with you? Get a job! Stop being so lazy! But now . . . I have a totally different view of homeless people. I see them as victims of the system that has failed them terribly.
- I also did not realize how easily tragedy could strike me and my family. I always remember hearing my father voice his concerns about losing his job, but I never took them to heart. You bet now though [that] I will listen to his concerns and try to comfort him. In the blink of an eye, any one of us can lose everything.

Another student acknowledged, in a very last writeback:

I grew up with the idea (from parents/media) that the homeless were lazy, had no work ethic, and would rather be on welfare than working! All of these ideas were quickly removed as I read and realized . . . I could just as easily be one of them!

This writeback came at the end of that student's series of extremely troubled, personal, moving papers, in which she faced, head-on, everyone's worst fear:

I remember when I first heard of the welfare cutbacks. I cheered. I thought, "Now people on welfare and food stamps can work for the money instead of collecting it for free." . . . I never thought about the situation fully.

I am also beginning to rethink crime. Who is really at fault, the mother stealing to feed her children or the people who took her food stamps away? I think I feel a need to be a part of the solution because I feel that I was a part of the problem with my uneducated judgments.

All the more reason to teach our children to think critically. . . . I am now going to cancel all my magazine subscriptions and stop watching so much television. . . . I am going to stop using competition in my classroom and I am going to call and write to my local politicians and send them excerpts from this book.

In some classes in which I use Kozol's books, however, there have been a few students who persist in arguing against Kozol, especially this book *Rachel and Her Children*. They insist that he is giving us only part of the picture and deliberately leaving the rest out. It is another side of the "I can't believe what he is presenting!" reaction that many have. In such a case, I first try to acknowledge both that the details and stories are indeed astonishing to read and that the student clearly has strong feelings. Then I ask, and try to get the student to examine, to what extent he or she generally applies such a standard of objectivity to all the other sources of information to which he or she is exposed. If students reject that invitation, I recognize how invested they are emotionally in needing to believe, because it has been true for them, that America must be a meritocracy for everyone. At that point, I tend to back off, hoping that the other approaches will bring them to see that there are indeed other sides of the "chair" besides their own.

Some of the time the in-depth work we do with the books, over time and from multiple angles, allows such students to begin to relax their protective stance and see that the complexity of what is being described does not require that they give up what they have. Kozol's writing is so clear and immediate, so personal and powerful, that most of the class is crying through the chapters, resolving to volunteer in soup kitchens, or write letters to governors or mayors—or to the Monsanto corporation (as several individuals, small groups, and even whole classes have chosen to do, after reading their chapters and then seeing it all put back together). They look with new eyes at many situations they had previously not considered relevant to their own lives.

The Dilemma: That's Who's in the Pipeline

But even as all of that is going on for almost everyone in the class, some remain unmoved, except for being angry at Kozol. One student, Jennifer, after reading *Rachel and Her Children* with great empathy and clarity, found herself having to deal with two others in her jigsaw group of five who resisted being moved, and who insisted on arguing. I am grateful to Jennifer for her personal insights, her obviously careful reading, and her gentle persistence. She first encouraged the other two in the group who felt as she did but were somewhat intimidated by the other two, and then, with them, she was able to urge the two debaters back to the actual stories in the book. Although those two resisted seeing beyond their positions, they at least did not sabotage the clear, respectful, and quite powerful representation of the book, upon which the rest of the group had finally decided.

Jennifer wrote of her struggle to reach those group members. Her account of how she came to her own thinking and decentering is something I wish we could institutionalize:

> I don't know how people can believe that these people *want* to be there [in miserable shelters], that they are taking advantage of "the system." It really boggles my mind.
>
> I can't help but feel the homeless people's pain. I see them almost every day. I have lived in the past eight years in Willimantic, New Britain, and Hartford. . . . In the beginning, when I was younger, I may have chosen to avoid eye contact, [would] cross the street, perhaps even snicker.
>
> As time went on, I began to see them and see them, really see them. One cannot deny the look of despair and sadness in their faces and eyes.
>
> I guess that is why I can at times get angry when [I hear] people [in her jigsaw group] want to know, Well, how did they end up here? People always want an answer. They want to be able to blame the homeless.
>
> I think it is because if we can blame them, not only do we not

have to feel any responsibility for helping them, but we also don't have to worry that it could ever happen to us.

I have gotten to the point in my life where I have stopped looking for someone to blame for everything, and [I've] begun to look for improvements, for solutions.

There may exist some teacher education programs that have figured out a way to develop a consciousness like Jennifer's within their students. Perhaps the program that Ladson-Billings describes in *Crossing Over to Canaan* (2001) is one, though students accepted for that special program at the University of Wisconsin-Madison must have declared an intention to be teachers in inner-city schools as a precondition for entry. As a result, it may be that the only ones chosen to participate are those who have already evolved on their own as far as Jennifer had on her own before the program. My own caution about even that declared intent, however, is that I have worked with some preteachers whose stated preference for working in inner-city schools has more to do with a conviction that that is where the jobs are (or, worse, with their doubt about their own ability to teach well enough for "good" students in suburban schools) than with a disposition to value the cultures of the students. Those whom Ladson-Billings describes seem, like Jennifer, different from most of the students I have encountered entering teacher education programs—even as graduate students, in terms of their experience of the world. More important, perhaps, they seem different also in terms of their awareness, receptivity to learning, and readiness to be active problem solvers—courageously facing and addressing in manageable rather than romantic ways the "savage inequalities" of our society.

To be sure, the program that Ladson-Billings describes works hard and effectively to deepen all those qualities. Such a program can provide other teacher education departments and schools with a model to consider seriously. It seems to me, however, that although careful preselection would be ideal, it cannot be the only option for preparing the culturally relevant, thoughtful, reflective, and academically excellent teachers whom children who live in inner cities deserve. Demand for teachers right now is so great that schools and districts are forced to hire whoever has a certificate—and sometimes even people without certification, or without much preparation beyond their own academic majors, in emergency situations. Beyond inner cities, as populations shift, teachers being prepared in the new century are already finding themselves in position, whether or not they have so chosen, to work (we pray, effectively) with children to whom and to whose families and communities they have grown up feeling superior.

Like all public school K–12 teachers, we as teacher educators must teach whomever we are given to teach. That means we must believe in all our students, at whatever stages they have reached, and with whatever habits and assumptions they bring. We must also believe in our own capacity to reach them in terms of all that we feel they need to learn before we send them out to teach. The people "in the pipeline," preparing to be teachers, should be able to present and maintain proper paper qualifications. Thereafter, educating them about social consciousness and cultural relevance is largely in our hands.

Chapter Seven

Reserved Seats for Musical Chairs

Those in the pipeline, nationwide, preparing to be elementary school teachers, and also, for the most part, middle and high school teachers, are overwhelmingly white, and have grown up in predominantly or entirely white neighborhoods. Most are the first in their families to go to college; they were raised by parents who were originally manual workers, but who now enjoy relative economic comfort. Many admit that their parents, or at least their grandparents, have used racially offensive language. Almost all insist, however, that they themselves are not racist. Most declare themselves to be "color blind" and are very uncomfortable with my bringing up the taboo topic of racism. They are insulted when asked to consider whether they might harbor racist stereotypes.

This is the position from which we begin. I have found a combination of activities to be necessary and useful, although not universally successful, in helping students take an introspective look at the relationship between class, culture, and student success. As I have indicated, it is important that students first come from a place of as much security as possible about their own identities. The genogram project is designed to encourage students to claim ancestors' stories, work histories, and struggles, in order to gain a less isolated, less static, less present-bound, and less decontextualized sense of themselves.

At the same time, we read about Miss Rinner in *The Street* (Petry, 1946), a miserable and terrified white teacher who does not believe the African American children entrusted to her can or even deserve to learn; therefore, she does not bother to teach them.

Through her brief story, students come to see, most for the first time this blatantly, the complex reality of both individual and institutionalized racism. Many students want very much to believe that this teacher must have had a single terrible experience with black people, or in Harlem, that caused her feelings. Otherwise, they come to realize, they might have to notice that they were brought up by the same society and therefore with the same assumptions as those Miss Rinner had been brought up with, regardless of their parents' efforts. It is difficult for students to come to terms with that, even though Miss Rinner clearly states (though many students miss it on a first reading) that the white middle-class New York City school board thinks of the children in the same way she does: "Because the school was in Harlem, she knew she was not expected to do any more" than just contain the children in the classroom (p. 330). The problem students grapple with is this: How close is what she believes and what her school board believes to what they have come into the course believing, having unconsciously and certainly not by choice (but nevertheless quite completely) absorbed what Beverly Daniel Tatum (1997) calls "the smog" of racism in America?

With the specter of Miss Rinner's perspective (Petry, 1946) and her terrible teaching as a background, and after more freewriting and plenty of conversation to help discharge their fears and assumptions about the "inner city," we visit, within a few weeks, the inner-city neighborhoods and schools, at first visiting safely from the reading of chapters in *Savage Inequalities* (Kozol, 1991). In reading that Kozol book, students seem to have the greatest difficulty gaining a concrete understanding of the economic underpinnings of our society. So I have borrowed and developed a set of primarily kinesthetic activities that approach the complexities of that issue in a more accessible way, again using chairs, as I did in the spatial and kinesthetic decentering exercise described in Chapter Four.

This time, instead of using one chair in the middle of our circle, I use several chairs. First, I re-create/adapt the powerful activity, The Ten Chairs, designed by United for a Fair Economy and used in their popular economics workshops all over the country. The whole exercise, including the most important freewriting and conversation afterwards, takes about an hour. Briefly, I line up ten chairs or desks, all facing the same way, and I ask for one volunteer to sit in each. Each chair represents 10 percent of the wealth of the country. Of course, as I explain, because our country never was characterized by that kind of equality—10 percent of the wealth for each 10 percent of the population—I ask three students to vacate their chairs and go stand behind the six who are still seated, leaving one of the original ten to "own" her or his chair and also the other three now empty chairs. Then we fast forward to the 1980s, after the Reagan administration's tax cuts. Three more people are evicted. The person (who still represents 10 percent of the population) who had four chairs now has seven, owning 70 percent of the chairs. That leaves nine people, three in chairs and six standing uncomfortably crowded together behind them, breathing down the chair owners' necks. It is a powerful but safely amusing dramatic representation of the fact that 90 percent of the population must try to live on a total of 30 percent of the wealth in our country.

I ask the nine people (three seated, six standing behind them or sitting on them) to figure out what they're going to do about this situation, and I ask the rest of the class, who have been witness to the drama, to talk in twos and threes about what they think should happen. At its most authentic, the three still occupying those last chairs would refuse to collaborate with the six, recognizing themselves as the middle class and fighting off those behind them, who are the "losers," "outsiders," "immigrants," and "unworthy." In my classes, however, by the time we do the activity, and perhaps because they are still doing as they're told rather than getting into character, students do all seem to talk together.

Figure 7.1. The Ten Chairs Activity

Usually, the nine "losers" first think of storming the province of the one with all the wealth, who is comfortably lounging over all her or his seven chairs, one arm taking up the four chairs that the top 1 percent of the U.S. population owns. Taking something by force, using "power over," is the only action the nine students usually consider, after they recognize their power in numbers. I remind them that that one person—the 10 percent of the population— probably has significant control over the army and the police. They had forgotten, or had not realized. Stunned, they usually immediately back off. Some are ready to give up. But then they'll think of trying to beg or negotiate with the person in power. Sometimes, cleverly, that person, exulting in his or her power, buys off one of the nine with the offer of one chair, thus cracking the solidarity.

Often, eventually, the nine *will* realize they can outvote the one—if they stick together. But that is usually only as far as they can imagine their own power of numbers. Knowing very little, if anything, of labor, civil rights, and women's struggles in U.S. history, no other models come to mind. It doesn't occur to them to withhold their own labor, or redesign an alternative economy by pooling their numerous skills and abilities.

Before we finish that exercise, I find it especially useful, in terms of *Savage Inequalities*, to observe, listen to, and ask the class to notice the three people left in the original chairs after all the others had been evicted for the sake of the one. During the twenty or so semesters I have done this exercise, in almost every class, those three remaining people hang on to their chairs for dear life. When we talk about it, it is clear they feel they have a "right" to those chairs—that they "earned" them. That is, of course, exactly the justification middle-class students give for their own better-funded schools in the suburbs and affluent towns. They never question "the system" or fate (in this case, me!) that allowed them, and only them, to remain there.

Only once in all of those semesters did it occur to anyone in the room that the three still occupying those last chairs should get up and let the chairs (desks, actually) be remodeled into one long bench, so everyone could have a seat. That suggestion was quickly rejected by the others: they only wanted to get back "their" original chairs. I even once had a student indicate that the person now spreading out over the seven chairs had a right to keep all seven—ownership is an absolute right, no matter how it came about. Most interesting is that this was the same student who insisted that it mattered how the homeless people in *Rachel and Her Children* (Kozol, 1988) had ended up in their situations.

Now students are invested in trying to understand how class divisions could be so marked in our society, so we move from Ten Chairs into Musical Chairs. We realign the same ten chairs into the familiar arrangement for the game everyone remembers from as early as four years old, and the whole class plays. Everyone except recently arrived foreign students knows the rules. After the first round we talk. How do "the losers" feel? Like losers. Worthless. Inadequate. Angry. Embarrassed. Usually someone says, "That was unfair!" I ask, "Would it have been fair if you had won?" That student and the rest have to think about what they mean by "fair." *When* did it become unfair? A very useful conversation!

Many of the students, surprised that others felt the same, admit to having always hated the game, even in earliest childhood. They want to lose the first round so they can go sit down.

But I have noticed that most of the people in my classes who have been (or are) athletes tend to love playing Musical Chairs. Lots of lifelong A students also love it.

The winners—those who got the chairs—are happy, satisfied with their achievement. So we problematize: What did it take to achieve a chair? Another very useful conversation follows, looking at the extent to which we assume merit and intelligence when what is really operating is chance based on systems of privilege and advantage. We look, as well, at the strategies—no risk taking, sticking close to the chairs, hurrying and slowing down—and at being aggressive. They laugh. But most of them get it: to win in such a game, and in the society for which it prepares children (as young as four years old), one needs to connive, use aggression, and sometimes violence. In this game, winning is not really about skill or hard work; at most, it is about trying to be in the right place at the right time. Consequently, players learn early to guard tightly and aggressively whatever position of advantage they find for themselves. At the very least, the game teaches children to regard all other players as rivals for scarce resources. As we talk about all of this, most students recognize the voices of some of the parents and students Kozol (1991) quotes from the affluent towns, and from *The Wall Street Journal:* "We earned this; we're entitled to it; too bad for the losers, but, hey, that's life."

Then we play again, with everyone in play—this time with an inner circle and an outer circle. I arbitrarily assign roles associated with race and culture. Those who have the role of Standard English-speaking white people get to be on the inner circle. Those with the role of people of color or newly arrived immigrants have to be in the outer circle. When the music stops, amazing things happen. There is rich content for conversation, especially about the expectation of entitlement, and about affirmative action. One white woman, whose role in the game was also "white," was stunned when a young man of color, whose role also happened to be "of color," slid like lightning from the outside track right into the seat she had been about to claim. "I thought that was mine!" she cried. What a wonderful entry for the conversation about systems of privilege: the assumption that there are—and should be—reserved seats for Musical Chairs!

Of course, I then have the class play the game collaboratively—noncompetitively with the goal being the sharing of seats. Those who thrive on competition say it is more fun to win by the loss of others. Win-win is not fun for them. But those who hated the anxiety (the feeling of adrenalin that the ones who love competition have come to identify as excitement) are grateful for the alternative way to play. A few decide to go out and try the redesigned, now collaborative game with their classes, especially if they are teaching in child-care settings. They come back to report great fun and laughter—and relief.

Even so, competitive socialization persists, despite all that students learn from the activity. It always interests me that there is still more status in having a seat to offer than in needing an invitation. By some time in elementary school, maybe by third or fourth grade, it is already considered weak in our society to need, to be without, to have to accept someone else's generosity, to have to rely even in part, even temporarily, on someone other than oneself.

But who *did* bring Emerson his meals while he was writing *Self Reliance? Who* built the railroads? Steel mills? Was it Carnegie all by himself? Lacking real knowledge of our history perpetuates the assumptions and feelings that allow a population to hate "losers," most especially people who are homeless. One semester, after we had played both games with the chairs, a jigsaw group decided to present their book, *Rachel and Her Children,* to the rest of the class by having us all engage in a variation on Musical Chairs, in which some people had permanent chairs and others were homeless. Those whose roles were "homeless" were always on the outside, shunted around from office to office, pushed out of every chair they tried for within the system. It was an incredibly effective role play. In *that* semester, everyone in the class "got it."

The Salt-and-Pepper Routine

I also use activities suggested in books and articles I have read, or classes I have witnessed. Particularly effective is the card game "With the Odds Against Them," from *Cooperative Learning, Cooperative Lives* by Nancy Schniedewind and Ellen Davidson (1987). Another activity that my closest colleague and I have made our own and do together in our classes and workshops was adapted from Peggy McIntosh's article "White Privilege: Unpacking the Invisible Knapsack" (1989). In recent semesters, in order to make the points visibly accessible to everyone in the class, we have put the items on the overhead, so we can address them one by one.

We have also added our own variation: instead of just white privilege, we are looking at all forms of privilege and advantage. We deal with one oppression at a time, leaving race for last; we allow as much conversation as there is time for. Sometimes the entire exercise takes two class periods. It is worth the time. (See Appendix.) We added the set of items dealing with sexism, heterosexism, classism, ableism, language,and religious discrimination, because it makes sense to broaden the context and see all oppressions as systems of advantage.

We did it so that people could be recognized for having to endure struggles others may not have known or thought about. People in our classes always have plenty to say. Our hope is that being heard and acknowledged will give participants the stance from which to hear and have empathy for the others. For the first time, those who saw only the areas in which they were disadvantaged begin to see that, overwhelmingly, they are advantaged. We did it also because my colleague, who is African American, finds it

very difficult emotionally to be the only one to have to hear raised—
and to have to describe, item after item—each of the daily insults
that she as a person of color must bear. Almost all of our students
are—or have been—oblivious to these insults:

- I never looked at the racism that people of color have to deal
  with in their everyday lives. I had assumed that people of color
  lived the same way I did, but people of color have to live with
  racism every day. I do not know what it is like to be followed
  by a cop because he or she thinks I am in the wrong area, even
  though I might live in that area.
- I have never had to deal with someone looking at my car or
  where I live and heard him or her say that I have that because
  of drug money. I had heard people talk briefly about these topics before, but I never really took into account how serious it is.

As we finish with each oppression/system of advantage, we ask students to locate themselves in terms of what advantages and disadvantages they have in society.

Except for members of the class who happen to be white male,
heterosexual, standard English speaking, educated, fully able-
bodied, and propertied, each person has some arena of disadvantage. For the most part, students can see, from the graphic they
create for themselves (and do not have to share), that their privilege in most areas gives them a responsibility not to condemn people who happen to be "losers" in that game of chance. It also

Figure 7.2. My Place in Terms of Privilege and Advantage

Advantaged	
Disadvantaged	

Ableism, Sexism, Heterosexism, Religion, Ethnicity, Language,
Socioeconomic Class, Race.

encourages students not just to avoid taking for granted the privilege they enjoy, as a result of that same game of chance, but also to do something positive with the clout that privilege gives them. The evidence that this can happen appears in the final papers of many of the students I have worked with:

- As a white person we [*sic*] have really put a lot of obstacles in the way for people of color. The exercise in class where we played Musical Chairs with two different tracks really helped me to see this, and the descriptions of the schools in the Bronx compared [with] the schools in Riverdale also helped me to see this.
- I was always taught growing up that the only way to prevent the holocaust from ever occurring again was to educate people about what had happened. . . . I think we need to educate the privileged white people in this country.
- A lot of [white] people often say to themselves, "I'm not the one that caused oppression to happen." That might be the case, but I think that the important fact is that people become aware and are educated about other cultures so that they do not contribute to the system of hate.
- I think that the course really provided me with a lot of strategies that I can use for when I am a teacher, so that I do not become a Miss Rinner.

The Demographic Study

I am not surprised that white middle-class students will come to the course's combination of powerful, controversial readings and experiences with their minds already made up about why the world is the way it is. I go into this work expecting there will be some students, maybe many, for whom their first explorations on foot or by car (for their small-group project in an inner-city neighborhood) will only confirm what they already "knew" about the conditions there, and will only confirm their easy, judgmental conclusions about the reasons for what they see. I have to hope the cumulative effect of all the historical research—especially research about factory relocations that left cities without manufacturing jobs—as well as the ongoing reading of Kozol, the ongoing writing, as well as the impact of other group members' insights, and the in-class and in-conference activities—might help students decenter and look again at the same landscape, but with different eyes.

In the process, of course, it is terribly painful for me to read the careless and ugly statements that appear, albeit mostly unconsciously, in many students' writings. I work very hard to be patient, to start with students where they are, no matter where that is, and to probe as gently as possible. I recognize that their innocence of other sides of the chair, like my own at their age and in their position, was socially constructed. They did not invent the stereotypes and assumptions that are deeply embedded within them. I have to trust that the whole process, as difficult for them to experience as it is for me to witness and guide, will be effective. Usually, it is. Most students at least begin to make the connections between the inequalities they see today and some solidly researched economic history of one city. Especially in combination with their genograms, most can begin to see that reality is not static. After much effort on my part as well as theirs, most are actually relieved to define racism as Beverly Daniel Tatum (1997) does: "A *system* of advantage based on race" (p. 7) rather than as individual hating or acts of meanness. Once they've got that, they can see economic inequality as a *system* of advantage based on class, not as the individual "laziness" of the "other" or of their own individual entitlement. Seeing all that, my hope is that most let go of guilt and will take on at least the responsibility to run their classrooms so everyone feels, and genuinely is, included and believed in.

Occasionally there is one who will not try to see the angle someone else might see. On the one hand, I might say, "This is a person who has the courage of her or his convictions; she or he is not just going to tell me what she or he assumes I want to hear." But, usually, such students also do a disappointingly superficial job of gathering and representing history or statistics that were chosen part of the demographic research and will not have a clue about what meaning to make from their research, even in terms of what other group members had found. I can tell from journal entries and from the group presentation that such students have merely gone through the motions, were just along for the ride, quite literally, as their group members struggled against their own stereotyping. Indeed, as I read the familiar arguments included in such students' papers and writebacks, and realize their staunchly defended and unexamined opinions are canned "right answers" from family, town, media—everywhere—I worry deeply about sending another Miss Rinner out into the schools, even if, as in one case, from her school observation reports, I can see she's genuinely charmed and delighted with young children in any school. Clearly, one semester is not enough.

Stretching Beyond What You Think You Know

I like to imagine transformed ways of teaching. Instead of studying the traditional history or literature with a focus on the same heroes of "our heritage," an alternative lesson would be a long-term jigsaw lesson within a richly heterogeneous classroom. As a result of the first stage of the jigsaw process, the students would begin increasingly to be self-confident young women and young men. They would be proud working-class as well as propertied-class students, both of whom now know some labor history. They would be students of color and of other marked or disappeared cultures (as well as white students), who have now all learned about and cherished their own previously unrepresented heritages. All would have learned about their heritages after conducting library and other research, including interviewing their own families and regularly meeting together in "expert" groups. They would all then remix into smaller heterogeneous groups. Their task would be to ask, and find, what had been left out of certain textbooks, and what that meant *for them*—not as a competition for scarce or limited space, but with the assumption that there is room for all of us, both in the textbooks and in our society.

From such intensive investigation and interaction, at least two things could occur. One, students whose lives, histories, cultures, literatures, voices, and views had been left out of the school curriculum would now begin to feel represented and genuinely heard. Two, students of the dominant culture would learn to hear from people their own age something that might help them recognize their own privilege, would accept analysis of it without defensiveness or guilt, and would resolve to work positively from it, rather than with the assumption of entitlement.

I can see this sustained jigsaw working even in a high school classroom, or even in a fifth or sixth grade classroom. Since children have to take U.S. history in the fifth, eighth, and eleventh grades anyway, why not try it this way one of those years? And what a way to cover all "the material" in just a few weeks!

I have done a similar jigsaw, with an important variation, in a graduate teacher education course, with astonishing results. Having begun the semester in my course Education for Cultural Understanding—as I do in many of my courses—with the genogram, as described earlier, I have reason to hope that, grounded in respect for themselves and the family members on whose shoulders they now realize they stand, students are ready to understand and appreciate others' cultures and realities.

The way I have students choose which cultures to research in groups of two or three does not at first seem to students to be a legitimate choice. I have each student brainstorm all his or her impressions about a range of groups about whom our society generally holds negative stereotypes—groups Sonia Nieto calls "marked cultures." Then I have students indicate which of the terms they have written down they believe to be true, and which, as they think about it, they feel are stereotypes. That way, I tap into what they believe about cultures other than their own, without their having said anything aloud yet. When I determine which culture each student has the most contempt for or ignorance about, I say, "Okay. That's the one you're going to investigate."

I provide and point the way to a rich array of materials from which students can begin to learn about peoples' lives, not through the mainstream media or through bias, but from those people's own voices and stories from the inside, from some other sides of "the chair." Although all students are reluctant at first, by the end of the two-month period of out-of-class reading and journal writing, as well as in-class conferring with their group members, most have become enthusiastic, saying, "I never realized!" For obvious reasons, it is not an easy assignment for students to be asked to replace strongly held assumptions with solid information—and in some cases, with real empathy. But by the end, most have genuinely learned, and some have been transformed.

The most remarkable changes came about for two students in the one graduate multicultural education course I mentioned. One was an insistently homophobic woman whose one group member was a straight woman who, it turned out, had gay friends. Together and alone, these women researched the discrimination gay and lesbian people in the United States face, and studied how multifaceted gay lives are. By the time they presented their findings to the class, the homophobic student had changed her mind about what had originally been her most compelling concern. After her research, she told the class she had decided gay partners would make just as good parents as heterosexual parents—and in some cases better, because they had had to put so much thought into every aspect of their choice! There would be no chance of "Oops, honey! I guess we're going to have a baby, ready or not!"

The other person whose change was dramatic was the one woman of color in that particular course—a middle-class woman from the West Indies. The topic she chose, or that chose her and her three group members, was *women of poverty*. It was a terrible struggle for the four of them to resist their inclination to judge the subjects of their study as *bad* people who *just didn't want to work or care for their children*. I cannot say that, as a result of her very difficult journey to the other side of *Lives on the Edge* (Polakow, 1993) and other readings, she now felt kinship with the mothers of the children in the day-care center she directed in an inner city, but I could tell she had a great deal more respect and empathy for them. She certainly struggled courageously to let her readings temper her assumptions.

Those deep changes did not happen so obviously for both members of the pair in that course who studied Japanese American culture. One, keeping a safe academic distance throughout, despite my regular interventions, made her part of their investigation into a "heroes and holidays" unit about Japan that she could use with her class. But her co-researcher, a woman in her fifties who had grown up hating "Japs" for Pearl Harbor, found herself moved to learn *for the first time* about the internment camps here during World War II. In another group, a middle-aged Polish American woman finally understood why Puerto Ricans wear bright colors, and that they are in fact American citizens. She made it a point to welcome her Puerto Rican neighbors' children into her doorway for Halloween treats, took proud pictures of them—a set for her presentation and a set for the children and their parents—and felt exhilarated by the first positive interaction she had ever initiated with her neighbors.

The pair of students who took on African American culture delved into it wholeheartedly once they accepted the challenge. They learned a tremendous amount of new information, and both began to face themselves and their privilege quite courageously. As a result, they committed to seeing their African American students and their families with more respect. In each expert group, at least some of the original stereotyping had been undone, and the members' journeys of understanding, which they conveyed publicly in class through presentations, gave everyone else a chance to challenge some of their own biases.

I strongly feel that this much transformation could not have happened if the students had been working as individuals. It especially could not have happened if I had lectured, the students had taken notes, and I had tested them. Having to construct all the knowledge for themselves, with each other, allowed them to construct personally transformative meaning, rather than just an accumulation of facts. The weekly opportunity to share in their in-class expert group meetings—what each member of that group had discovered—extended every other member's learning, allowing for cognitive dissonance (and occasionally heated argument). Every student was engaged, not only intellectually but also to a great extent emotionally.

What I notice happening in most schools is that there is no forum through which students get to work out their distrust of difference. When racist or other oppressive comments are overheard in a high school classroom, sometimes the offending student is given a detention or is sent to the office. However, the class never has to deal with racism. I wonder if it is possible to deal with the very complex set of feelings, attitudes, and behaviors we have about racism in the United States within traditional pedagogy, since traditional pedagogy imitates the very underlying structures from which oppressive behaviors emerge: hierarchy, individualism, right answers that a person in power owns, competition, isolation from others. In a teacher-centered classroom, how can students really learn to respect each other, and respect difference?

Chapter Eight

Reluctance of High School Teachers to Use Cooperative Learning

A disturbing pattern has been emerging in the last decade or so. Fewer elementary school teachers than in the early 1990s are using student-centered strategies, such as cooperative learning and learning centers, for even a part of their teaching in their classrooms. It seems there was a brief bright moment in time when the idea had caught on, when a few teachers, schools, and even districts embraced cooperative learning. Then, it seems, they suddenly let it go. Now, even in kindergarten in some schools and in the first grade in others, especially and most unfortunately in inner-city schools, children are expected to sit still and be quiet and do the "work" that the teacher sets before them. Even when their desks are arranged in small groups, the work is individual, and talking to each other as they work is as taboo as it would be if the desks were in rows. Standardized testing has begun to direct what teachers feel they must "cover," and also how. Because a sobering percentage of elementary teachers admit to having been conditioned to do only as they were told, the test pressure has left them feeling powerless to resist.

Note: Much of the material in this chapter comes from an unpublished study I conducted in 1988. I find its content all still startlingly relevant in this first decade of the new century.

Basis for Teachers' Decisions

Perhaps even more disturbing than teachers' reluctant acquiescence in teaching to the tests is what some elementary school teachers have been saying about cooperative learning. They say they never bought into it anyway; it was just another fad that districts had imposed on them for a while, and, like other fads, it faded away and allowed them to go back to their regular teaching. In fact, most undergraduates in our teacher education classes in the late 1990s and the first decade of the new century, who would have been in elementary school in the mid- and late 1980s, seem to know nothing about cooperative learning. When I ask who among them experienced cooperative learning in any of their K–12 schooling, maybe 5 percent answer positively. Although most are convinced that they went to "good" schools, all that they describe, and that with very little positive feeling, can be recognized as rather mediocre traditional teaching.

But even in the brief moment of time in the 1980s and early 1990s when some elementary and middle school teachers were experimenting with cooperative learning, it was still quite rare for high school classrooms to invite students regularly to solve problems together. Although traditional lesson structures are now unfortunately being reestablished, even in some previously progressive teachers' elementary classrooms, and sadly even more often by new teachers, the routine configuration of desks in rows facing the teacher for the entire high school class session seems never to have changed. The teacher's voice is still the only one that is heard through the walls or the open door. That is "the way it is," and "the way it is" is a powerful model: "It has always been that way."

Interested in understanding why in many elementary and middle school classrooms children were cheerfully and productively operating interdependently, whereas in most high school classrooms children were not given the opportunity to do so, I conducted an intensive one-year qualitative investigation, based on in-depth interviews with eleven practicing high school teachers. Some were secondary student teachers, some were their cooperating teachers, and a few were other veteran teachers. My study uncovered a range of complex and interesting patterns, suggesting that high school teachers bring into their classrooms certain assumptions, which, combined with actual or anticipated outside pressures, seem to cause the teachers to teach in traditional, teacher-centered ways. After summarizing a few basic frameworks, the rest of the chapter (and the next) will attempt to flesh out more of what I discovered about a surprising number of themes that seem to converge and form the pedagogical decisions made by teachers, especially though not exclusively by high school teachers.

Although certain structural factors must be taken into consideration, none necessarily or adequately account for high school teachers' reluctance to use cooperative learning. I have identified and will discuss in greater depth, one by one in this chapter and the next, twelve other significant factors that have emerged from the research:

1. Age-appropriate structures and expectations
2. The traditional role of the teacher
3. The assumption that there is a body of knowledge to be transmitted
4. Tests and tracking
5. Anxiety about time
6. Belief that students are not able to construct their own learning
7. Fear of being judged as not a good teacher
8. High school cultures socialized as male-identified domains
9. Internalized competitiveness and individualism as values
10. Ethnocentrism
11. Teacher uncertainty
12. Poverty of imagination

Taken together, these factors are powerful forces for holding on to traditional teaching. Fortunately, despite this accumulation of powerful forces, some secondary teachers are able to choose student-centered approaches to teaching.

Structural Differences Between Elementary and Secondary Teaching

To distinguish elementary from secondary situations, certain differences are worth considering. The most obvious is that people planning to be high school teachers characteristically indicate they are choosing teaching as a career because they love their subjects, whereas elementary preteachers generally say they choose teaching because they love children. That one difference in focus and intent can make an enormous difference in practice. In addition, because elementary school teachers have to "cover" the entire curriculum of a diverse range of academic subjects, rather than just one subject, there is more chance several factors may converge to cause teachers to use cooperative groups. In addition, K–6 teachers might be more likely than high school teachers—who are already specialists in their fields—to recognize the need for further study and find, in workshops and classes, content combined with pedagogical suggestions based on developmentally appropriate practices. In those settings, as well, elementary teachers come in contact with other teachers eager to exchange ideas.

In most cases, elementary teachers see their children all day. Even with pullouts and flexible grouping arrangements that have children switching rooms for certain subjects, elementary teachers may have a more expansive sense of time than high school teachers have, with their tight forty-three- or forty-seven-minute schedules. (Perception of time constraints will be seen later in this chapter to be a crucial variable.) Subjects are more likely to be integrated than departmentalized, lending themselves to nontraditional approaches. At least there is more possibility of that happening in self-contained classrooms. Especially in very small, mostly rural elementary schools, teachers must teach more than one grade. And they have historical ties to the one-room schoolhouse as a model for allowing or, in fact, needing children to be resources for each other. Even in larger schools, elementary teachers expect to be teaching more than one ability level. Although this does not by any means guarantee that teachers will think or decide to use collaborative rather than individualistic or competitive structures, the need, the possibility, and perhaps even the inclination for them to do so exists more than it might on the secondary levels; at the secondary level, ability grouping often sorts students to minimize that heterogeneity.

Finally, the absence of an ethic of student collaboration in a school seems to be a factor in itself. For reasons I have delineated elsewhere (Aaronsohn, 1996), if it is not part of the culture of the school, or if new teachers or those eagerly returning from an inspiring workshop do not see respected colleagues in their own school regularly and comfortably using cooperative learning in their classrooms, teachers are not likely to think of trying cooperative learning, or to persist in trying it when it inevitably does not work at first with students who are not accustomed to it.

Playing the *Role* of a Teacher

In earlier chapters, I have described and referred to traditional teaching at its worst. But even at its best, teacher-centered education appropriates to the teacher the role of expert sole resource, transmitter of knowledge, fountain of meaning, decision maker, owner of right answers, primary talker, and primary thinker. Again, it quickly feels "right" to play that role, because that has been the familiar one for us as students. Besides, according to researchers Brandes and Ginnis (1986), "many teachers say they still find didactic methods safe, natural, comfortable, and appropriate" (pp. 9–10) because that is what is expected by parents, students, and staff. To many high school teachers, as well, didactic methods seem to be required by the restrictions of time, space, and the mandated curriculum, as this chapter will show.

As earlier chapters have suggested, without examination or conscious struggle, the role that preteachers expect to fill has a well-defined and familiar script for them to follow. The role has its advantages as well. The stage-and-audience arrangement that traditional classroom arrangements set up can be seductive to any teacher. The chance to be the permanent full-time center of attention is quite a temptation, especially for people who have become very knowledgeable about a subject about which they are highly enthusiastic. The role of primary thinker and primary talker is the position from which an excellent traditional teacher feels a mission to enlighten. The light goes on in students' eyes because of something the teacher has done or said, not because of a child's own interaction with text, materials, ideas, or peers.

At best, in a traditional situation, the students are a passive if polite and even receptive audience for a brilliant lesson from a teacher such as Ralph, the English department chair and twenty-five-year veteran teacher, who described himself as a performer (in Chapter Five). The performance metaphors that teachers use about themselves often include "magician," "stand-up comedian," and "spellbinding orator-actor." Ralph's conversation is full of that kind of metaphor. In interviews, he first says, "The classroom is a stage," and then he talks seven times about "showing them" or "bringing it to their attention," and five other times about "igniting them" or "exciting them."

It is easy to enjoy the performance high that comes from traditional teaching. Nevertheless, at least one of my former students, Donna, wrote about deciding after her first year of teaching to give up "that stagestruck kind of feeling." She had realized that the kids were not themselves excited, only she was—because she was the one making all the connections, all the meaning. So she gave it back to them.

Not having come to Donna's realization, Ralph says that his lessons go well when he is "on"; everything depends on his own alertness. Although a teacher's full alertness is a requirement even when a teacher is inconspicuously facilitating learning centers or monitoring cooperative learning groups, Ralph's "on" seems to have another connotation. If he were to use a baseball metaphor, I suppose he would have to consider himself playing the role of both the pitcher and the entire infield, initiating all the ideas and fielding the students' comments, which are usually bunts—fragments of sentences. He says he cannot get students to elaborate on their ideas. But as I read his narrative of how his class goes, I do not hear on his part much patient openness to students' struggle for words.

One secondary education preteacher, working part-time as a teaching assistant in a university course, realized, after reading "Language and Secondary Schooling" (Collins and Seidman, 1980):

> What I suspect would be discovered, if my sections were taped,
> is that I do most of the meaning construction, and the students'
> input is regularly channeled and interrupted as I enthusiastically
> try to explain to them the meanings I have constructed.

An important lesson about wait time: videotape is indeed a very helpful mentor! However, from another perspective, the awkwardness this new, young teacher feels—that almost all teachers and professors feel—is not just from his side of the power dynamic. Those silences are torture for students, whose early experience has been that if teachers do not get the answer they want really fast, they may call on *them,* or may condemn the whole class for not being prepared, or for being stupid. Somebody answer, please!

My own win-win solution, developed over many semesters, has been to use that time differently, neither in silence nor in jumping in myself. As I described in an earlier chapter, I try to take the pressure off of everyone—students and teacher alike—and at the same time give everyone a chance to speak to the topic in a safe way. Students have a chance to talk to each other in pairs for about two minutes, safely and simultaneously about the concept. When I resume the full-class discussion, I have found, many people feel confident enough to speak.

The university teaching assistant who is studying to be a high school teacher concludes, "I am anxious about my responsibility to do a good job and to keep the class going." How teachers define "do a good job" and "keep the class going" makes all the difference in how they operate in the classroom. The impulse to jump in and rescue, or "help" by taking over the idea, has been an automatic one for most teacher education students, secondary as well as elementary. As we work deeply with the issues raised by the "Encouraging Autonomy" chapter of *How to Talk So Kids Will Listen* (Faber and Mazlish, 1980), students are able to recognize and gain a perspective on their own need to "fix" and "tell." They begin to see alternative ways to behave when children struggle. Restraining the impulse to rescue, fix, and tell has been one of the most difficult challenges for teachers. Part of it certainly comes from equating "struggling" with "suffering," or with being inadequate to the situation. But another part comes from the deeply embedded classroom pressure to give the right answer, and give it fast. As a survivor of traditional schooling myself, I have worked very consciously over many years to restrain my impulse to be the one with the answer.

Why the Process Makes a Difference: Missed Opportunities

Even when the content is alive, relevant, and fascinating, and even when it dares to diverge from textbooks, the process can still limit students' learning by having the teacher own and transmit the knowledge. I give the following examples, knowing that any observer of my own teaching could point out many opportunities that I miss as well. Given that, consider these:

• Each year, Ellen's cooperating teacher gives her advanced high school social studies class a special project, with "controlled" authentic primary sources about the attempted and aborted invasion of Cuba at the Bay of Pigs in 1961. The materials are contained in a comprehensive packet that she carefully put together. All the students do the same project, but individually, with no class time to work on it, even though they are to decide, after reading all the material, how they would have advised President Kennedy. A marvelous concept, but what a missed opportunity for small-group interactive thinking, perspective taking, and decision making! What if, instead, she assigned a subset of those same documents to be read and understood collaboratively, first in a jigsawing of expert "roles" from history? What if cross-group meetings were then followed by a full session of discussion, a full and passionate hearing of all the possible points of view? Such an approach might very well interest students in present-day political, economic, and social issues and help them look critically at these issues, while developing a sense of themselves as citizens. Instead, students' work with rich primary sources, as assigned, is focused on right answers, vocabulary, and "writing skills," which is as tedious as any textbook assignment about ancient history, and as disconnected from their real needs, abilities, and interests as learners.

• In another high school social studies class, arriving early one day to supervise Diana's teaching, I watched her cooperating teacher manipulate what started to be an amazing dramatic simulation of nationalism and imperialism. Before it could take hold, however, the teacher threw away the opportunity for transformed understanding and interest by saying, "Okay, enough play. This is what you need to know for the test. Let's go on to the next page."

• For another example, I think of one highly praised high school social studies teacher, who, along with boundless energy, imagination, originality, intelligence, and technical skill, has a complex perspective on the world. His method of teaching employs creative and thoughtful work with video- and audiotape, putting together history in a way I had never seen before. I was privileged to attend such a production as part of a public, mostly adult, audience, and was amazed, impressed, and enlightened about the content his presentation exposed. However, if such a high-powered presentation is the dominant mode of his high school social studies class, as I am told that it is, it seems to me that the students come out of his classes entertained, dazzled, sobered, enlightened, and maybe even questioning. But they are still basically passive, believing that only Mr. G. could have put it all together like that.

By no means am I am saying that none of this exciting teacher-prepared work should go on. On the contrary, I am very impressed with it and I wish all teachers would do some of it as part of every lesson that they teach. Clearly, Mr. G. and Ellen's cooperating teacher have created—and Diana's cooperating teacher has located—powerful resources that all of us can learn from. I just worry about how the high school students are perceiving what they are getting. I wonder if the output of so much teacher energy and care is absorbed by the students as just that much more transmission of an overwhelming body of knowledge that they will be tested on. Reworking the process of using those materials might make all the difference. It depends on how the teacher thinks of his or her role: whether it is to present important material or to have students engage with that important material. It is a different focus, and it may seem minor, but I consider it fundamental for all academic subjects that are taught.

Body of Knowledge

One history professor whose thinking and teaching I greatly admire suggests that the appropriate model for the lecture method of teaching is a scholarly presentation. At a conference of scholars, the audience members are anxious to hear an expert's interpretation of material about which they have already thought—perhaps almost as much as the expert has. In that model, teaching is secondary to scholarship and research. Accordingly, what you produce, not what your students learn or what kind of people they turn out to be, is what seems to get measured by those who judge teachers on the postsecondary level.

One problem with transferring that model—even to graduate or undergraduate teaching, and certainly to high school and most certainly to elementary teaching—is that, as my friend the historian says, "Students don't know anything." Indeed, it is frustrating not to be able to count on students coming to such lectures with at least a basic frame of reference and working familiarity with certain facts, especially in history. But what is to be done with that? Professors might mine students' lack of knowledge for clues about where and how they might begin, including examination of the very traditional processes of high school, and often college, history teaching—dry textbooks, memorization, decontextualization, oversimplification, and fragmentation. The next step for social studies methods professors, of course, is not to give more of the same, but to model—and require from preteacher lesson plans—alternative approaches to the study of history, using multiple authentic, multidimensional primary and context-rich sources, and a pedagogy of student critcal inquiry and interdependence. Apart from the issue of materials and "delivery," I question whether it is even developmentally realistic to expect late adolescents to have any real grasp of the complex and interconnected realities that make up history. Instead of interrogating all those factors, traditional teachers at all levels tend to blame both the students and the individual teachers and schools who prepared them. Samuel Betances (keynote address, Every Teacher, Every Child conference, March 30, 2001) reminds teachers that physicians do not say with contempt, "Why do they keep sending us sick people?" Feeling frustrated and under pressure to fill up the students they are responsible for with as much of the given body of knowledge as they can, as fast as they can, high school teachers feel inclined to use even more of the very same processes that did not "take" for the students in prior years.

In effect, then, there is a product—in fact, a quality-controlled product—for which we are accountable: the student, full to bursting with right answers on an enormous range of topics, ready to play an academic version of Trivial Pursuit. No wonder elementary, middle, and high school teachers have anxiety about "preparing" their students for the next level. Part of teachers' investment in that preparation is that they themselves should not be judged harshly, and, in fact, they might be praised, at the next step on the assembly line (Callahan, 1962).

This very important body of knowledge that teachers assume exists and that they have to transmit is something "they need to know." The teacher's job is "getting in everything they need." Ralph says, "Knowledge is a thing. It's a thing! It's a tangible thing!" Teachers say, "We have to make sure they grasp information," but the grasping seems to go no deeper than students getting into their notes what Alfie Kohn (1999) calls "a bunch o' facts."[1] Teachers say, "We have to help them through unfamiliar territory," which usually means the teacher lectures and pulls answers through the dry and overwhelming accumulation of "facts" in a given textbook chapter. At best, the teacher connects those facts to each other and to something the students know, which makes the information meaningful, and retells the text as story. All of this, to be sure, is with the most noble of intentions: to help students become educated. The disabling of student learning processes achieved by the teacher doing all the thinking in the best case, and the tedious answer pulling in the more usual cases, is certainly unconscious, and certainly the opposite of what teachers intend.

The language in which teachers talk about this purported body of knowledge that they feel "required" to "cover" is linear, quantifiable, and product oriented. Teachers are urgently concerned about what is coming next for their students, which is never their real lives but more school. The most frequent terminology is *covering* and *has to be covered*. The next most frequent statements are "We can't waste class time," "We can't afford to suffer through endless digressions or we'll get behind," or "They'll miss something."

I would never argue for academic class periods turning into off-the-top whatever-anyone-happens-to-feel-like informal late-night college dorm rap sessions. Nevertheless, I am concerned that the "something" that teachers are afraid their students will miss is usually What is going to be on the test? or What is the other class getting? I wish I would hear more K–12 teachers and professors say, "If I cut off this discussion too soon, the students will miss the understanding they're about to uncover. So I'd better put the rest of my agenda off until next class."

It is true, of course, that certain concepts and skills will be useful and even necessary to both children and adults in the real world. But their existence and their importance does not mean that only the traditional "banking" methods of teaching (Freire,

1968) (described on page xvi in the Introduction of this book) will work to allow children to acquire them. In fact, Robert Moses (2001), writing about his revolutionary Algebra Project, recognizes perhaps more than any other math teacher how important an understanding of and accomplishment in mathematics is for entry into the economic world of the new millennium. To achieve his goal of making sure all children achieve, understand, and operate at high levels in mathematics, especially African American children who have been systematically left out of the advanced tracks where algebra is traditionally taught, he advocates using methods that are far from the worksheet-driven teaching that most inner-city schools and remedial classes in suburban schools employ. As Moses describes it, mathematics is not about memorizing and being able to reproduce or even use formulas. What he found in his twenty years of conceiving, developing, working within, and extending this project is that (1) the more constructivist and concrete; (2) the more connected to the students' daily lives, families, cultures, and communities; (3) the more interactive and collaborative; and (4) the less rushed and tested, the greater the likelihood that the students will succeed in learning to think mathematically. In his project, they do.

In our classrooms, students can succeed, too, if we let go of the unfortunate traditional notion—at least the one that students who become teachers seem to have internalized—that knowledge is a set of decontextualized facts to be committed to short-term memory.

For example, is social studies only about names and dates in history? Is science only about identifying terminology? Is English only about grammar, vocabulary, and matching titles with authors? Is literature only about knowing who said what in which scene? One secondary education preteacher remembered:

> There were definite right and wrong answers. . . . There were no reflective or analytical questions or any that might connect the literature to one's experience.
>
> How did MacBeth or Hamlet relate to me, a white woman growing up in a small Georgia town, struggling to survive the isolation I felt and to combat the racism that permeated the town? Maybe there were no connections to be made, or maybe there were. Perhaps there were more relevant pieces of literature. Miss Jackson made no attempt to find out.

This student raises a crucial question about the standard body of knowledge, or "the canon," to be sure. Who decides what is worth teaching as literature, and on what basis is that decision made? But she also raises questions about process. The tests this student describes only monitor whether students did the most narrow kind of "reading" of the material: hunting for the obscure details that the teacher is likely to trip you on. That kind of "reading" leaves out genuine engagement with the story, individually experiencing what seems important, while still focusing on the people or the imaginative world created by an author. In focusing only on "details," students miss out on struggling to make meaning of historical events beyond the details. Tests do not extend or probe for original thinking; if they did, students well socialized to traditional structures might complain, "We didn't cover this!"

The usual student writing has one goal: to prove to the teacher that the student knows what the teacher wants him or her to know. No wonder students come to class, in middle and high schools, and in colleges and universities, acting as if they haven't read. In a real sense, they have not, because we have taught them not to. No wonder, then, that many of my undergraduates could not make meaning out of Sylvia Ashton-Warner's simple journal, *Teacher* (1963); no wonder so many miss the tone and complexity of much else they consider themselves "reading." Have we not disabled them by our processes?

Uncovering and Slowing Down the Curriculum Is Risky

It is difficult to get preteachers to question why a given topic is in a curriculum. Characteristically, they assume that the curriculum comes down as a mandate from somewhere and that it is embodied in the textbooks they expect to be handed. One student reflected about the real learning he finally was able to do, several years out of school, during a visit to the former Soviet Union:

> Slowly it dawned on me that history is people, not the names and dates which I had memorized. . . . In those two weeks, two years' worth of Russian history took on real meaning.

> Although I obviously cannot take my students to the places
> where history was made, I think that history can become alive
> through other means. Diaries and memoirs, poems, and even
> nursery rhymes, . . . letters and newspapers. . . . Without these
> resources, it will not hit home that history is people. . . . Without
> these or similar resources, history is a string of meaningless names
> and dates. It is statues covered with pigeon droppings.

Once they recognize the expansive possibilities, many eager preteachers declare an intention to go deep, to do "posthole digging"
instead of just brushing the surface of the topics they teach. But
student teachers and first-year teachers are feeling their way in a
school, and they experience anxiety about the risks they are taking, because their cooperating teachers, or the teacher next door,
or the parents, or the administrators, are watching. The preference
seems to be for neat lesson plans that "keep up" with "where" the
other classes are. Practicing teachers who are more secure about
their positions and who have ongoing outside support for the kind
of teaching they want to be doing tend to feel more confident in
following their convictions about what students need. But how
many take risks, then? In her second year of teaching in a Catholic
school, Donna wrote to me:

> That was a really successful class! Because they used something
> that they had in English, they related it to a theme that was in
> Religion, and they remembered things, and they talked about
> it, and they felt good about it. But last year, I would have felt like
> I just wasted a day! I didn't get through half of Chapter Thirteen
> like I thought I would!

Despite Donna's enthusiasm, and that of her students, for connected and genuine learning, the pressure to bring children to a
place where they "should be" is enormous for all teachers, K–12,
but especially for high school teachers, who feel responsible for
preparing students for departmental exams and college. But for
what kind of college situation are we trying to get them ready?
What Ralph remembers of college, or fantasizes for his students, is
some sort of brutal contest for the teacher's attention and narrowly
granted approval, rather than a thoughtfully facilitated haven for
intellectual discourse among students:

I have a perception of college as a very competitive place where the kids exchange what they know with others who want to hear what they know—theoretically, the professors.

Many of the practicing teachers I interviewed, even the veterans, were still like Donna was in her first year: feeling obliged to cover the full body of knowledge so that their students would be fully "prepared." They frequently said, "I have to," when they spoke of the work they do: "I have to prepare them," "I have a hard time letting go of thinking I have to be somewhere at the end," "Covering is a major pressure," "I'm behind! I'm not covering this stuff! Everybody else is there already!"

In spite of those pressures, teachers who take the risk of letting go and really allowing their students to work deeply with a few topics find out that most of the fears are all inside. My daughter's wonderful project-centered, student-centered fifth grade teacher told me about her evolution as a teacher in the early 1980s: "After a few years I threw away the workbook, and no one even noticed!"

Unfortunately, the national recent pressure toward "accountability" through more widespread and frequent standardized testing makes it even harder for teachers to take those risks. In one high school, anticipating departmental tests, a preteacher of science one day observed a goldfish breathing in each of the high school biology teachers' classrooms. In another city, elementary school teachers in the Success for All program are required to be on the same page for their grade level, doing the same thing as all other teachers of that grade in the city. Worse, the expectation is that all children of a given grade level citywide, will be on the same predetermined page in the textbook math program, regardless of what concepts the individual children are developmentally ready to understand. To be sure, the superintendent's purported goal is to accommodate students whose families move to a different neighborhood within the city during the school year. Whichever school they attended, they will just pick up where they left off with reading and math, assuming, of course, that they had been able to keep up with the whirlwind race through the curriculum in their prior school.

The real goal in that superintendent's decision, also clearly stated, is higher scores for the city's schools in standardized tests.

In that city's classrooms, therefore, creative teachers despair of having enough freedom to work in the way they know best, or even to include science or social studies, since those subjects are not yet covered by the statewide mastery tests.

High-Stakes Testing, Tracking, and Fear of Judgment

The tests. What is going on? Who is making these decisions and on what basis? At the same time that progressive ideas seemed finally to be taking hold in many schools, in the late 1980s, a simultaneous backlash occurred, in which even schools designed for the wealthy began teaching entirely from the book. The national reactionary shift to scores and "achievement" was not yet obvious, but was emerging. More than any other single aspect of our educational system, it seems to me—and to many others (including Kohn, most recently in *The Case Against Standardized Testing* (2000); see also http:/www.fairtest.org)—that standardized tests function as the external agent that paralyzes educational change. Enough has been written, although not nearly enough has been read, about how standardized tests reinforce the race, class, and linguistic bias of the dominant culture. Such hardly radical sources as *Harper's* and National Public Radio, have run pieces speaking openly about whom the tests serve. Economically, the real winners are the Educational Testing Service and the real estate agents in communities that score well. Although resistance has been growing nationwide—generally by parents—it has been hard to find educators who dare to challenge the tests' necessity.

The effect that such tests have on schooling, and therefore on the rest of our lives, is to set a standard of intelligence that focuses narrowly on what is measurable, and on only two of the now recognized multiple intelligences. These standards reward the most destructive aspects of "knowing": speed rather than reflection, a single right answer rather than multiple realities, product rather than process, and linear rather than complex reasoning. Because of how the tests are administered, they further reward isolated individualism. The result, of course, is that in our classrooms and in our lives, we use the habits we have been taught: we rush to quick decisions, seeing things only in terms of right or wrong; we are impatient with process; we judge ourselves and others as fierce competitors in a world whose rules seem arbitrary, exclusive, and permanent; we never ask why some people's options get limited early, because Why? is not a question that is encouraged in schools tyrannized by tests.

Of great concern is how the tests are used to sort and track. I notice a pattern in papers about standardized testing that my undergraduate students write. Those who had been placed in honors levels in high school report feelings of superiority, even entitlement. As with all privilege, those who enjoy the benefits of the status never have to notice what that arrangement is doing to those who by this placement lack status. Many teacher education students who had been placed in "average" or "basic" or other educational categories at an early age, however become enraged when they read articles about what is really going on behind the tests and the tracking. Nevertheless, almost all students—from opposite sets of experiences—walk into teacher education courses believing that tracking is more efficient for the teacher, and is therefore necessary.

For example, because she had been in upper-level classes in high school, Sarah had not been particularly moved by the readings, writing, or discussions about tracking in our class. As a practicing teacher, however, she was struggling. She used our interview and dialogue to explore why things were going better in her "advanced" class than in her "lower-level" class. Her first thoughts were similar to Ralph's, quoted earlier. Because she had learned in our program to reflect freely on her own thinking, however, she was able to hear the contradiction in her own claims as she talked, and she was able to bring herself to another place:

> So maybe, maybe I tend to. . . . I just thought of this: the geometry class, because someone has told me that they're advanced, right? So I give them more freedom, you know what I mean? I let them do more of the thinking. And then the other class, maybe I feel they need me to tell them more. Maybe I tell them too much, which is why they don't listen, and they don't do anything. So I'll have to think about these things.

I wish Ralph could have been so honest with himself. He spoke to me of initiating laughter when one student gave what he considered the wrong answer when he asked, "What are the connotations of "mother"? What are the images that come to mind when you think of "mother"? One girl answered honestly from her own immediate experience, saying, "Hard-nosed." That was clearly not the answer Ralph expected to hear, especially just before Mother's Day. He told me, "I sort of bridled at that. I mean, I couldn't make anything of it. I couldn't go anywhere with it." I asked, "Could *they*? Did you let *them* try?" He answered, "No! The kids—I asked them, 'Is that an image that anybody here associates with "mother"?'" And then I asked her to elaborate more on it, but by then the kids had already had their little giggle."

The girl, of course, was deeply offended. To his credit, he saw her after class and apologized. But my sense was that he was still thinking that her answer was inappropriate and wrong. Most important, the damage in the presence of the other students had been done. She had been humiliated and her experience devalued, and the others in the class had learned that they had better accept the teacher's version of "mothering"—and everything else.

A teacher's unconscious giving of permission to humiliate some children by doing it him- or herself starts in some schools in kindergarten or the first grade. Those students with high status— the teacher is pleased with them—can tease those students who are less quick to learn to read, and less sure of their answers. I have witnessed this many times. Inevitably, the children who get teased and ostracized retaliate in many ways, as we have seen in the much-publicized school shootings at this turn of the century. By high school, as students tracked initially in first grade reading groups move from year to year together, the lower-tracked children have internalized the contempt they have been shown by their "higher"-level peers, and often by their teachers as well. As a result, not surprisingly, they exhibit behaviors that express their low sense of self, which sometimes get enacted as disrespect against those still trapped with them in the lower-level classes. The fear of being laughed at by peers turns out to be one of the strongest emotions students bring with them into adulthood. Students report it to be the reason for being terrified at first of sharing their ideas, even in a university class:

> I know that I and others I have observed have been shut down to learning for fear of failing or making a mistake in front of my

peers. The few times I gave a wrong answer (when I dared to risk it), I would be humiliated in front of my classmates. Who would take a risk with the threat of public disgrace?

Another reports a very painful memory:

> I remember those elementary school days when I was constantly being drilled with grammar. I was often corrected by my teachers because I was slow in learning past-tense forms of verbs. Being constantly corrected was not a good feeling. Many of my classmates laughed and made fun of children who were constantly being corrected.

A common conclusion is drawn from such experiences: "I've felt that my peers would laugh at my thoughts, so I sat in silence."

What is most instructive for me as a teacher educator is that none of the practicing teachers mention student silence as a problem they need to address in terms of the structures and processes they set up. The teachers who do not recognize what they are seeing in that silence may have forgotten, or buried, or never felt those feelings from their own early schooling. The task of teacher educators is to bring those feelings to light, to make sure the new teachers going into classrooms are able to interpret and notice what is going on in those silences.

Time

> *We're taught to rip through any and all assigned readings in college for content, not pausing to enjoy or comment on what is being said . . . to get done on time.*

I fully accept that college and graduate courses require an enormous amount of work, including (and I am told especially) mine. I recognize that in that situation, confronted with responsibilities, such as families and at least part-time jobs, overwhelmed college students may feel they must sacrifice quality for quantity. In many cases, undergraduates are also used to a high school homework load they were able to easily complete in a study hall. College homework is quite a surprise. Nevertheless, the feeling of being rushed comes from much earlier than their time in college, and from a set of experiences that have nothing to do with time management. In traditional K–12 classrooms, students feel rushed to finish whatever task they are doing, either so that the teacher will find them ready for the next task, so that they can go out for recess, or so they can be the first one in the class to give the teacher the right answer. From the teacher's perspective, calling on the first to "know the answer" helps the teacher "keep the class going." From the child's point of view, however, once *someone* has finished and has given the answer, the game—and the trying, and therefore the thinking, and any real learning—is over.

Students come to expect this arrangement early in their education. Patricia says that even though she has totally restructured her fifth grade classroom, she still has "some kids who will rush to get the work done, and [then] not know what to do with themselves." Teachers before her, rushing to cover the curriculum or to get through that day's lesson, may have first modeled impatience, even with the highest-tracked students, as this brief dialogue from an interview with a practicing teacher indicates:

> Professor: Would it have occurred to you to do the task in groups? To divide them into groups and have them work on it together?
>
> Teacher: Well, no, not really, because we can't waste class time with it.
>
> Professor: Waste?
>
> Teacher: Well, I mean, you know, . . . you know what I mean? I mean we have so much information to cover, and this is an extra assignment. That's how they get their extra points for being a Level One, is they do an extra assignment.

In his interview, Ralph frequently mentions the issue of time, referring to both the time inside the classroom and the time he puts in outside. Of inside time, he says:

> I'm the kind of teacher that values every moment in that classroom. My time with the kids is what I call "live time."

His description of what goes on within that "live time" is certainly electric. He speaks of himself as a dramatic warrior whose enemy is time:

And then the bell. The bell started to get on us now. I was looking at the clock, and I had a minute left, and I still had two more points to make . . . and then, just quickly, we talked about. . . . I had to . . . I only had about five minutes left, because I let the kids stay over; all the time I'm fighting time.

You see, the kids like it when I fight time. 'Cause they know that I'm excited, and that's where I think your teaching really comes in, when they see the teacher's excited.

Unquestionably, that sense of drama can make a class session exciting and memorable for students. And without any doubt, if the teacher is not excited about the material, forget about student excitement. Nevertheless, it seems to me that Ralph is talking about something else here. He says of his "lower-level kids," "They just sit there and watch me entertain. They want to be entertained." But when I said,

But you wouldn't think about . . . in a class like that, where maybe they're so passive anyway, they may not be taking in as much as you give . . . that it might not be worth an experiment to train them to.

He interrupted:

Only because I haven't got the time to set them up and follow them through.
I keep going back to that. I'll be glad to try anything with [a] group, but you've got to give me time, and you've got to let me follow it through.

Plenty of preteachers accept as a given Ralph's constraints, coming as they are from as yet unexamined assumptions about a body of knowledge they are expected to prove they have poured into their students by a certain end time:

It could take longer for students to reach this point than the teacher had anticipated, which could negatively affect the established goals and objectives of the curriculum. We all know that teachers are required to cover certain material in a given amount of time.

Let me establish that of all the concerns expressed by the teachers I've interviewed, teachers I have called "traditional," the issue of scarcity of time is the most compelling to me as a teacher. No matter how carefully I think I have planned, I could always use more minutes in a class session, and more classes in a semester. Whether the content is central or the students are central, there is never enough time. The irony of Ralph's insistent refrain about never having enough time, however, is that he is speaking in the context of his teaching his "advanced" students a number of books that represent the existentialist philosophy. Not once in the interview does he acknowledge that the primary tension—the fundamental absurdity within which human beings live—is that we are caught between the immensity of possibilities and the reality that life could be cut off at any moment. When he demands, rhetorically I must assume, "You give me time!" he is either raging at me or against the external forces over which he has no control.

But we *do* have choices about how to use that forty-seven minutes, that 180 days, that moment of time we have with students, just as we have choices about how to use that moment of time that is our life on earth. I have made plenty of wrong choices about time in classrooms. Doing that part better is some of what I constantly work on in my own teaching. Perhaps the issue here is the narrow way we are trained by our own schooling to think of the classroom experience in the single dimension of talk, when we need to be thinking multidimensionally, in terms of time, space, motion, and dynamics—the way one would think of a dance. Thinking of a class multidimensionally does not give a teacher more time, but it expands the possibilities within that predetermined time. It gives genuine options, and therefore genuine control, not over the children but over one's own choices.

Clearly, in the comments given by Ralph and the preteacher earlier, I hear and sympathize with teacher ownership and protectiveness of classroom time for their (and our) tight agendas. From teacher education students recalling their own schooling, however, I hear, along with awareness of a teacher's plans and directions, a plaintive request for more generous time for children. Several examples make a powerful case:

- It was most likely from a need to keep us on the prescribed timetable that our math teachers zoomed ahead when a good portion of the class was still struggling with the material.

I remember feeling that all I needed was *enough time* to work on the problems, and to understand the material the way I needed to understand it.

- From my own experiences, I can remember quietly thinking to myself when a teacher interrupted me just as I was about to reply. It never gives the student a chance to process the information and to feel successful with it.
- As a junior in high school, I remember being asked a relatively easy question, but I did not know the answer. The teacher urged me to try to think about it. Meanwhile, every other person in the class was about falling out of their chairs, begging to give the answer. I was intimidated, so I just said to myself, "Screw it!" and didn't say a word.
- The quickest student was often rewarded. Raising a hand in the classroom at age nine has developed into spinning the wheel and shouting letters out to Vanna, *and while we might not understand the puzzle that we just solved, at least we beat the buzzer* [*emphasis added*].

Rushing through one's work to beat the buzzer seems connected to students' purported short attention spans, and students and later workers not being allowed to value the work they do. One student said, "It bothers me that I do not have time to do anything slowly and carefully." To not have the time to work at the rate one needs is not a natural, healthy, or satisfying feeling. Nor is discomfort the outcome most teachers and parents really want for our children.

"Kids Can't . . ."

How will they get it if I don't tell them?

It is not at all surprising that students act the way we have trained them to act in class: dependent on us, docile, passive, silent, unable to sustain a thought beyond a surface right answer, disconnected from their work, obedient rather than inventive, unwilling or unable to listen to peers without interrupting, fearful of sharing half-formed ideas, and not able to trust each other or even their own perceptions. In other words, we have trained them well in all the skills that inhibit cooperative learning. Ralph is right:

he would have to take time—perhaps even six weeks by the time kids are in high school—before they would work effectively in reflective, serious, and constructive collaborative problem solving in school.

Clearly he is not willing to rearrange his plans to include time. But it is not just Ralph, and it is not just the time it takes to train children to work well with each other that teachers are unwilling to accommodate:

> It is often much easier for a teacher to make meaning for the students, because it usually saves time and prevents a situation wherein the teacher may lose control of the discussion.

Most educators bring assumptions such as this: that it is their job to control a discussion into the classroom. As soon as they take a step back and look critically at their own words, of course, most preteachers and practicing teachers realize they have equated learning with tasks that someone can do for someone else. This assumption, like other deep-seated ones, has to be worked out, like all genuine learning, through direct experience and reflection on that experience:

> They had questions, and it was faster for me to answer them rather than letting them work it out for themselves. Across the room, I did notice that those students I didn't get to still finished the assignment. This proved to me that if I let the students work on their own, they can help one another and teach one another what is to be done.

This one single experience while teaching a mini-lesson to her peers, even combined with a semester's worth of reading and discussion, will not be enough to convince a preteacher to restrain her urge to "do it for them." But she will be aided by her pivotal discovery that "kids *can*" get it without the teacher's spoon-feeding it to them. If she had not directly lived it, I am sure it would be harder for her to imagine teaching in any way other than the way she had been taught.

Multiple experiences are necessary for preteachers to begin to realize the possibility of this alternative to "banking" (Freire, 1968). In many teacher education classes, professors structure into the course content a set of mini-lessons or "reflective teaching," in which each student gets a chance to teach a lesson of his or her own choosing and preparation, usually to a small group of peers. Many such professors require a cooperative learning component to lessons that each student or group of students teach to a whole class of peers. On one such occasion, the feedback was very revealing, as students had to comment on each other's teaching behaviors, which are sometimes useful mirrors of their own:

> I noticed that Ray did what I tend to do—he didn't let us figure stuff out in our groups. He didn't give us time to get out of our confusion.

They learned as well from reflection on what it felt like to try to work in a way that was counter to most of their own schooling. Three examples follow:

- It took a lot of trust to be able to do this; it was a real exercise for me not to feed you more cues!
- This was tough. The immediate thing is to jump in and say something.
- I had a tremendous urge to jump in and get the group working together, but I didn't let my anxiety get the best of me, and I let the class run its course. And to my amazement, everyone settled down and began working on the topic!

In fact, I believe that the reluctance to "let the class run its course"—once a teacher has carefully planned and given careful instructions, with careful and attentive monitoring—is less a matter of not wanting to waste time, but more a fear of giving up control. Exhibiting the all-or-nothing thinking that schooling and our society create and reinforce (see Figure 4.1 in Chapter Four), many preteachers and practicing teachers alike assume that if the children are not in rows and all doing the same thing at the same time under direct instruction by the teacher, there will be chaos. I have heard the word "chaos" used almost every time I suggest to Ralph or to a teacher education class (especially one preparing high school teachers) that they might encourage kids to talk to each other, or that furniture can be moved and moved back within seconds. I have noticed, in fact, that many high school teachers—and perhaps therefore some high school students—assume that any arrangement other than rows is not likely to produce serious academic work.

Note
1. Found in several of Kohn's works—most recently, his book *The Schools Our Children Deserve* (1999).

Chapter Nine

The Pressure of Tradition

Teachers did not first start thinking in those ways on the day they became teachers. I have witnessed young children coming to the occasional open or progressive first or second grade from traditional kindergarten (or first grade) already knowing exactly what was expected of them—that is, what limits there are around motion, talk, initiative, and what the consequences are for "getting out of line." They also come with the notion that "real" student work means completing worksheets. They do not view learning centers to offer legitimate work. Even this early, they have learned well what their teachers have taught them.

Well before most children get to high school, unless they have had an unusual series of progressive teachers along the way, they are often uncomfortable with changes in the ordering of space in the classroom, angry if someone else is in "their" chair, and uneasy when invited to engage in the taboo behavior of talking to each other. Older elementary and secondary students may remember circles and small groups from early childhood classrooms, and thus associate those arrangements with "baby stuff." At any age (though the likeliness increases with time) they may experience freedom as license, because we have not given them practice in dealing with freedom responsibly. As Ralph realizes clearly, it takes time to develop the necessary skills. High school teachers—and, increasingly, I am afraid, elementary school teachers—expect that if it doesn't go well the first time, the message is that the kids can't handle it. A student teacher in a high school classroom reported on her experience:

Professor: Did you have them in a circle for this discussion, or rows?

Student Teacher: Rows. They hated . . . they didn't work well at all in circles.

Professor: How frequently did you try it, and how much time did you give it?

Student Teacher: Just once.

Professor: So it was a disaster?

Student Teacher: It was a nightmare. And also Mrs. ___ wasn't comfortable with it. And when she wasn't comfortable with it, I wasn't comfortable with it, and obviously the students weren't comfortable with it. It wasn't something I wanted to try again. If you're not comfortable with it, and the students figure out that you're not comfortable with it, they just take the ball and run.

Ralph would agree. He said, "There's a certain kind of informality that a circle dictates, and high school students can't handle it." When I reminded him about the intimacy and informality of college seminars, and of independent college projects, Ralph said quickly what many preteachers and graduate students say: "Yes, but in college you are an adult." He explained his thinking, which many of the students in my courses shared. Mostly for the same reasons, some students remember—somewhat proudly—their own high school rebellions. But they seem not to have reflected about the causes of their own rebellion:

This theory [cooperative learning] sounds good on paper, but in practice it has its realistic shortcomings. As I have stated, discussion-oriented classes work well on the collegiate level, but to hold one at the high school or elementary level could prove disastrous.

Perhaps this view reflects my own "classic" educational upbringing, but I feel that unless kids are raised on discussion-oriented classes, they may try to use it to their advantage in a negative way and only misbehave. In a circle, they'll feel, "I can screw around if I want to."

In my high school, the student who sat quietly in class and mechanically spat back out on tests all that the teacher said got good grades and was considered an excellent student. Fortunately, I did not fit into this category. I was considered a wave-maker at times and often found myself in trouble for various crimes against the system. When I was placed in a class with a teacher I did not like or respect, I caused trouble.

To be fair to all the Ralphs and the student teachers and their cooperating teachers who are afraid that the classroom will erupt into chaos if the arrangement shifts, I have to acknowledge that even at the university level, I usually have at least a few students in each class at the beginning of a semester so completely socialized to external locus of control that they test my trust of them by taking group time as avoidance of work time until I come near, eyeing me all the time to see what I will do to them. Having students test their limits can scare some inexperienced teachers, and it can reinforce the fears of older ones.

Working in a student-centered rather than teacher-centered way certainly involves tolerating some environmental and intellectual disorder and unpredictability. It requires believing that children are basically competent, even amazing human beings, who in their real lives outside of school do important work and have meaningful relationships. It requires believing that these students could do important work and have meaningful relationships in school, as well, given the opportunity. It may not be coincidence that preteachers who have been most receptive to believing in their students have been parents who deeply respect and admire their own children, or guidance counselors who had really come to know and love children as people. These teachers believe that all children are worthy of respect. And the children they teach behave as though they are worthy of respect, precisely because their teachers believe in them, no matter what anyone else in the teacher's lounge says.

However, I watched Ralph's student teacher, whom I was supervising, try very hard to become just like Ralph as she taught one of his classes. Playing the role she had been told she should, she was intolerant of the slightest motion or sound from any of the kids, particularly from one boy of whom Ralph said to me afterwards, "Yeah. I have to be on him. It's for his own good."

Part of the difficulty for teachers who are reluctant to use cooperative learning is their mistaken assumption that the teacher's role in a student-centered classroom is to step out of the picture entirely, and leave everything up to the students. They may also believe incorrectly that student-centered teaching means having one individual student at a time act as teacher. However, student-centered teaching is not about switching roles within a traditional framework. First, it goes without saying that the teacher's complete understanding of the academic material is at least as necessary as it is within the traditional lecture-test (or "banking") model of education (Freire, 1968) (described on page xvi in the Introduction of this book). Then, the teacher's obligation is even more complex: to guide, coach, make clear, figure out, and design appropriate tasks; to tune in, diagnose needs, recognize abilities, monitor, and check for dynamics as well as check for learning.

Nor is cooperative learning "unstructured." It is highly structured in terms of task, timing, and, to some extent, product. Teachers must be alert and fully present during a cooperative learning session once they have set cooperative learning into motion. That is not a time for teachers to grade papers, talk on the phone, do errands, or read the newspaper, even though they are not students' focus of attention. However, the alertness required for "eavesdropping" from a respectful distance will be considerably more relaxed than the tense state that often characterizes a teacher-centered classroom.

Finally, trusting that kids *can* does not mean that the entire day, every day, will be given over to simultaneously operating interdependent small groups. Instead, cooperative learning is most effective when it is a carefully structured activity within a specific amount of time during a particular lesson that will probably have other components as well. Teachers still have plenty of room to know something, to make conscious choices, and to inspire the students.

Fear of Being Fired

Ralph's model of teaching is one that is often admired and expected. When Meg attempted to operate in a more student-centered, project-oriented way in her high school classroom, a disapproving colleague commented, "If she's going to work in the public school setting, she'll have to pay more attention to institutional realities." Those "institutional realities" are what many preteachers worry about: principals, school boards, even parents—the anonymous "those who hold power," who are making the "back to basics" decisions, and who will judge you if your kids leak out of the classroom. The fear of being fired, or not being certified or recommended—or not being liked or approved of by your colleagues—can paralyze new and even veteran teachers who are new to cooperative learning. Teachers sometimes confide to me that they do not dare use cooperative learning because the principal doesn't like to come by and hear noise in the classroom. These fears effectively keep teachers from the risk-taking work they instinctively feel—and now have theoretical grounding to realize—is better for kids.

In order to address these fears and help teachers realize that as professionals they have more power over their own classroom decisions than they might assume, I ask preteachers, sometimes in class but more usually in individual conferences, to role-play the terrible scenario they anticipate. I play the principal, appearing unexpectedly in the doorway of the teacher's classroom, aghast at seeing it alive with students learning busily, productively, but interactively, and therefore by no means silently. I overplay dramatically:

"Ahem! Ms.—, Exactly *what* is going on here?" The young teacher usually quavers, recognizing the tone and the look. She is ready to shrink and say, "I'm sorry." We try it until she is able to say, "I am so glad you stopped by, Mr./Ms. ____! Come in and listen to what they're finding in their groups! See what they're making!" And then she practices talking that principal through how she made her professional decisions.

Trying on a different, solidly professional role, the young teacher becomes visibly more self-confident. Although by itself this exercise cannot hope to overcome her years of having submitted in order to survive in the game of school, it allows a teacher to imagine and actually experience behaving with dignity and clarity, and that is a crucial first step.

Frequently, student teachers are apprehensive of job interviews going wrong: "I'm scared of telling principals I believe in interaction." As if it were communism or something. In fact, however, the idea of student-centered, interactive, cooperative learning *is* a dangerous idea:

- I think a classroom of critical thinkers would be stimulating for my students and me. But when those critical students go to Mr. Smith's English class and put on their critical thinking caps, there is no doubt Mr. Smith will not tolerate it. Mr. Smith might try to find the source of this critical thinker and warn the teacher that if he or she doesn't stop teaching in this manner, Principal Jones might be knocking on the door.

• Teachers might see critical thinking as a direct threat to them.

The "direct threat" to school people comes, I think, from the "one right answer" thinking to which we ourselves as teachers were conditioned. "If the other person is right, I'm wrong." The next thought is, of course, "And I don't want to lose, so I'd better not let them win." I have heard a similar fear, even terror, especially but not exclusively from elementary preteachers: "What if a child asks a question and I don't know the answer? Will the students (or their parents or my colleagues or the administrators) respect me?"

Socially Constructed Male Ways of Thinking: High School as a Male Domain

Historically, teaching in elementary schools was what women did. Because it was women's work, and because young children were not considered to be capable of original thinking or problem solving, what went on there has historically been considered less rigorous, less academic, and less important than teaching at "the higher levels." Accordingly, the number of men on faculties increases as the level gets "higher," and where teachers are tasked with accumulating and transmitting a body of knowledge, in keeping with the model of religious scholars in the Middle Ages.

And who owns and controls that body of knowledge? The teacher's right to own the space and the conversation replicates the notion "children should be seen and not heard," as well as the attitude characteristic of the traditional patriarchal family, in which the woman walks several paces behind the man. It seems to me, in fact, that traditional parenting roles really are the models that operate in classrooms. As a generalization that is full of exceptions, it seems that nurturing "mother people" are drawn to elementary and, particularly, early childhood classroom teaching. In a high school situation, a female teacher who is considered to "mother" her students is mostly judged by her male colleagues with contempt, as she is not tough, or rigorous enough. While some faculty and staff members in elementary schools refuse to "baby" students, as they see it, by nurturing them, both men and women who choose high school teaching often seem to take on, by preference or necessity, a distancing, commanding, judging, all-knowing father figure posture. Ralph's student teacher said that when she was first observing in his classes, she felt his presence to be so strongly like her father's that she was frightened of him. So our nurturing side is more likely to reveal itself in an elementary school setting, and our distancing side is more likely to be expected itself in a high school setting.

In general, ownership, control, status, toughness, and rigor are historically associated with being male rather than female in our society. This is not to say that women do not also engage in conquest, or in the competitive, *power-over* behaviors and thinking that conquest seems to require. Nor is it to say that all men do spend their time in conquest. But the paradigm of conquest is deeply embedded as the dominant belief structure in North American society. Collaboration, negotiation, compromise, and relationship building are considered "weak." Aggression is expected—and usually highly praised—in competitive sports and the military, and in business practices, although *within* these institutions there may be plenty of collaboration. Also expected are win-lose outcomes. Recently, as women's sports have been televised and discussed, I have heard girls and women being admired for being "scrappy," urged by their coaches to be more "physical," meaning "aggressive."

All of that may be appropriate for those enterprises. However, the transfer of those values to education is all the more frightening in that it has become so ingrained it has hardly been noticed by the general public, a public that also includes teachers. Goals 2000: Educate America Act (http://www.ed.gov/legislation/GOALS2000/TheAct/) established national economic hegemony so clearly and firmly as the focus for schooling in the United States that when I ask elementary education students what the goal of schooling is, most quite automatically state, "to make our country competitive." That is, of course, so our country can win—but in what contest, exactly? As Gilligan (1982) describes it, the attitude that all situations must be win-lose has traditionally been part of the socialization of boys, though recently it has also become that of girls in sports, especially since Title IX.

If winning in some sort of competition is understood to be the goal of schooling, training in its attributes is necessary. And that is what one sees valued in traditional classrooms, even if teachers are not altogether conscious of it. In "advanced"-level high school and in some university courses—especially in history, a subject still identified as a male domain—teachers and professors often encourage students to debate. Debate, a win-lose game, values and teaches the adversarial processes associated with sports, the courtroom, and the battlefield: arguing rather than understanding, impatience with relationships, dominating, interrupting, and focusing on product rather than process. In a classroom debate, students joust, posturing to show off for the professor or the teacher—or the girls.

Ralph's interviews are full of the language of conquest:

> I have been trained as a historian and I love a good debate. At times I found myself resisting what the articles had to offer and with that zeal I would tear into them. I found myself arguing with people rather than acknowledging what they had to offer.

Plenty of research confirms what I have noticed when I am teaching or observing a class that is predominantly male, at any age, even in elementary school. There is a level of aggressive energy and impatience with struggle that makes it hard to work with, because the girls or less aggressive boys have a hard time being heard (American Association of University Women, 1995; Belenky, Clinchy, Goldberger, and Tarule, 1986). Preteachers themselves can be taught to be aware and respectful of each other's thinking, regardless of gender:

> I really noticed this in my [other] education class. The men talk at least three times more than the women, and they are constantly interrupting.

This male student could also have noticed it right there in the class I was teaching, as well, even though in his particular class—I had to keep counting to be sure!—there was an equal number of men and women. But it is not just boys silencing girls, or more aggressive girls interrupting other students; it is teachers interrupting students, and teachers keeping students waiting to be called on before they can speak at all, the teachers owning the total dynamic as part of the role.

The extent to which preteachers have not yet looked at their own assumptions about the appropriateness of scrappy competition and fierce individualism was revealed to me by how casually most of my students read a letter to the editor of the *New York Times* entitled, "Only Co-ed Schooling Can Prepare Women for the Real World" (Campbell, 1988). Either the students skimmed over the language, or, worse, from my perspective, they bought into the argument:

> I strongly believe that high schools and colleges are prepara-
> tory stages before [students enter] a more competitive world.
> The kindergarten girl may play freely in the block corner without
> boys to hinder her architectural capabilities. But in later life *she
> will . . . have to elbow her way* into a computer lab or compete
> for lab space and time in her company's physics department.

Such myths about "the real world" and what it requires of people leave out the entire side of the real world, including the world of corporations and science, in which people negotiate and share, rather than compete or elbow their way. It seems to me that the myths are created, as all myths are, to sustain the dominance of those in power—traditionally, though not always, men. However, those myths do not serve men any better in the long run than they serve the women they were meant to subordinate. As Belenky, Clinchy, Goldberger, and Tarule (1986) show, the relational processes that are better for women and girls are also better for boys and men. We all need each other.

Individualism

The overarching unexamined myth that informs American education is that human beings can do just fine without each other, and that the best thing to do is "tough it out" alone, doing whatever you can and whatever you have to do to "get yours." Perhaps appropriately, this is the myth that Ralph keeps reinforcing for himself and for his "top-level" seniors each year by exposure to existentialist works of literature. The effect of his dealing with these works in passive, individualistic, and competitive ways with his students is manifested when at the end of their time with him, his

"brightest class of all" turns out to be what he describes, with surprise and regret, as materialistic, egotistical, ruthless, or, as he calls
them, "callous." But why is Ralph surprised? If they turned out that
way, who in school taught them, by either content or process, that
society values caring?

The impression of Ralph that I have as I consider his interviews
is of an embattled, misunderstood, overworked, intelligent, and
supremely dedicated but supremely lonely man. With little variation, he is the Great American Hero, battling ignorance and dullness with every ounce of his strength. In every interview with
practicing high school teachers other than Ralph, I keep hearing
the kids through the words of the speaker. Interestingly, in the
words of J.B., another veteran high school English teacher, I do not
hear any other adults. In everyone else's interview, I hear the words
of both kids and adults, although Sarah's is also very lonely: her fellow adults in her first year of teaching a second grade class are at
a distance. In Ralph's interview, his is the only voice I hear.

What political-economic and social structures the myth of individualism serves have already been named. That it is, of course, a
myth is best captured in the quip I mentioned earlier, sometimes
ascribed to Gloria Steinem: "Who brought Emerson his meals while
he was writing *Self Reliance*?" History textbooks—and politicians—
would have us believe—and therefore most students do believe—
that all of America was built by a few genius entrepreneurs. But
Carnegie himself did not *build* the railroads his money financed.
Southern plantation owners did not plant, chop, pick, or haul the
cotton that made them their fortunes, nor did northern industri-
alists stand in front of blast furnaces to shape iron into steel. Each
of those "great men" stands upon the backs of a vast but anonymous cadre of workers. Even the eccentric U.S. millionaire who
attempted several times to circumnavigate the earth "alone" in a
balloon through the late 1990s, until he finally was successful in
2002, had a ground crew of at least one hundred people making
sure every aspect of the mission worked. But the myth persists.
Maybe that is to keep the not-so-important people from realizing,
and using, their collective power.

My observation of traditional teaching is that individualism is
so deeply assumed that it never gets questioned as kids "cover the

classics" in "top-level" classes, self-consciously doing "lit. crit." Nor is it raised overtly as a problem in "lower-level" classes. In fact, as Ralph describes his work with his "noncollege" class (without reflecting on what it implies that his language uses "college" as a standard, and their suitability for it predetermined), he is pushing them to rise as individuals above their peers, to be the token working-class kids who make it out, and up.

He is not the first teacher, or the first person in students' lives, to do that. Lillian Rubin (1976) describes this tension between individual and community as she powerfully describes one of the most deeply embedded myths that I see in our society. She does not locate a basic source of (or reproduction of) the myth, as I do, in the schools, but the connection can certainly be made with students in a lower-tracked classroom:

> Such turning inward with self-blame is common among the women and men I met—a product, in part, of the individualist ethic in the American society which fixes responsibility for any failure to achieve the American dream in individual inadequacy. That same ethic—emphasizing as it does the isolated individual or, at most, the family unit—breeds a kind of isolation in American life (p. 19).

> Rooted in the individualistic ethic of American life, the rebellion does not take the form of some constructive collective action directed at changing the social system. Rather it is a personal rebellion against what are experienced as personal constraints (p. 34).

> . . . . the anger, the frustration, and the pain of being defined and defining oneself a failure. For the settled livers are, at bottom, the conformists—those who have bought into the system, who believe in the American myth that everyone can pull themselves up by their bootstraps if only they have the will and the brains (p. 36).

Sennett and Cobb (1972) come near to saying it, but still do not think of indicting traditional schooling for what they see and describe so clearly: rejection of collective action, or even of being able to imagine it, in the United States. No wonder the nine people crowded around the three last chairs in the game of "Ten

Chairs" (Chapter Seven) had so much trouble figuring out what they might do with their power, or even realizing that they had it. Readers will recognize this representation, perhaps even of themselves, when first asked to work collaboratively with a group. Sennett and Cobb say:

> Having to act in concert with others means a person has to respond to them, and those relations may so entangle men with one another that a judge could not tell whom to reward for the work, nor could the entangled individual really feel he had a chance to show what he alone could do.
>   The irony is that a man who seeks to display his talents as efficiently as possible feels held back by others, and yet it is toward establishing his worthiness to be respected by others that all this concentrated striving is directed [pp. 245–246].

Deborah Britzman (1986) makes the connection between working-class job situations and schooling as the main socializing agent for those jobs: "The ethos of individuality and privatism which pervades school culture . . . the cult of individualism [which] obscures the reality of isolation . . . and dependency." Perhaps the complex thing is that many secondary school teachers, finding themselves isolated in their classrooms, make a virtue of lack of community, mistaking "turf" for autonomy. In Diana's high school student teaching placement, and in a middle school where I was asked to do staff development, the structure and permission for team teaching had been put in place, but the teachers refused to do shared planning. Their one period of the day was all they had for themselves, to do the million things that teachers need to do in the absence of their students. More important, I think, most secondary school teachers had never had occasion to develop from their own schooling the habit or disposition toward collaborative planning. The cage door had been opened, but they refused to come out.

Not everyone I interviewed equates isolation with autonomy. Patricia, an innovative veteran fifth grade teacher in an elementary school who routinely uses cooperative groups in her classroom, wishes there was more time for teachers to visit each other's classes, and talk to each other, and plan together. Meg, a first-year high school social studies teacher, longs for the team teaching work she sees happening in another grade level. Sarah would love the contact with other teachers. Donna reported that if she had not been able to interact with other adults in her first year of teaching, she would not have come back for her second. Mona, Sam, and Mike spoke of daily, if not more frequent, conversations with their cooperating teachers, and Martha felt a tremendous loss because her cooperating teacher would not communicate with her. Susan enjoyed frequent interaction with her colleagues, and Debbie was grateful to talk in her own language once a day with a Spanish-speaking aide in the school. At least three different student teachers spoke of feeling encouraged and energized by conversations with one of their student teaching colleagues.

Nevertheless, even at a School of Education, an observer noticing people talking to each other in the parking lot at first assumes them to be wasting time. Children's unauthorized talking to each other in elementary schools is usually the thing for which they get their names on the board. "Talking" is usually the first thing, and sometimes the most serious thing, for which in-service teachers tell me they have to discipline children. I hear elementary teachers admonish children: "Do your own work!" even when the task seems to me so clearly to lend itself to collaboration. When I have occasion to ask them why they chose to structure an activity individualistically, some teachers look at me in disbelief at first, and then say, "I have to grade them on what *they* do," thinking of every learning experience as a product to be assessed.

I think that what Ralph and other traditional teachers—again, Ralph as a prototype of traditional teachers—mean by cherishing their autonomy is what people interviewed for Lillian Rubin's *Worlds of Pain* (1976) mean when they talk about not having anyone looking over your shoulder. People naturally want nonevaluative interactions with other people. But that is not usually what we get, given the belief in the myth of individualism, our almost total inexperience with cooperative structures, and our habit of judging and expecting to be judged. Many of my teacher education students, focusing on the product to be produced, try to organize their long-term collaborative group projects completely by division of labor. It may be the only model they can imagine. Group problem solving at first is inconceivable:

Professor: The tendency is to be independent individuals, even though they're next to each other?

Teacher: Right.

Professor: Do you set up tasks so they will have to decide and come to a group consensus rather than all get the same thing done?

Teacher: I don't understand what you mean.

Professor: When you set them to work in twos, what kind of task do they have to work on? Are you forcing them to cooperate rather than just to . . .

Teacher: Oh, yeah. But, again, they don't . . . okay, sometimes they say, "Okay, you do the first part and I'll do the second part."

Ethnocentrism

Distrust of the other—any other—is not a big step from male-identified, conquest-oriented thinking. Because competitive zero-sum discomfort with difference quickly slips into fear of difference, only "people like me" are to be trusted or accepted, if anyone besides oneself is to be. The rest are either "better than me and I hate them for it," or beneath contempt. Those attitudes are not conducive to successful cooperative learning, but the best cure for those attitudes *is* cooperative learning (Johnson and Johnson, 1975; Aronson, 1978). The persistence of competitive, and especially ethnocentric, attitudes in a high school classroom requires just that. The hard work of helping students work through their attitudes is going to take more creativity, more time, and more collaboration.

It must first be acknowledged that one "culture" that many teachers routinely misunderstand is "kid culture"—the reality of naturally and healthily active children of all races, ethnicities, language groups, and styles. Children's bodies were not meant to sit in chairs for six hours at a time; their fingers were not designed just to hold pencils; their minds were not meant just to absorb; they are not programmed from birth to wait, either for it to be lunchtime before they can eat or for twenty-four other children to speak before they get another turn; and their primary interest, especially but by no means exclusively once they hit puberty, is not any teacher's agenda, but each other. To be sure, society requires children to eventually learn the behaviors expected in schools. The problem often is that teachers can't wait for "eventually," or for the slow, unpredictable process of their learning. This is often, sadly, true even of some kindergarten teachers, pressured as they feel to prepare the children for the next station on the assembly line.

By high school, of course, it may be reasonable to expect that students will have accepted the norms of not interrupting, of waiting their turn, however difficult and even unnatural that kind of delayed gratification still is at that age—or any age, to be sure. But by at least the end of high school, students are expected to have adopted many of the behaviors most closely associated with productive and docile factory workers, such as arriving on time, staying through a boring day, putting off all their other needs until an official break time, and getting very little satisfaction from the whole thing (Callahan, 1962).

If racial, socioeconomic, and ethnic prejudices are deeply embedded in the teacher, the institution, and the students, the problem is considerably more acute. As Janice Hale (1982) and Gloria Ladson-Billings (1994, 2001), in particular, have pointed out, schools in the United States replicate middle-class European American culture, manners, and style. They basically value European American (especially Anglo-American) language and content. Expectations for behavior are European American expectations, and are considered sacred.

The model seems to be a Puritan one; much of our Puritan culture is represented by a strict hierarchy that enforces the silencing of children and the inappropriateness (even sinfulness) of play (or even pleasure) in a stern work environment where gratification must be delayed.

Now consider cultures other than those steeped for generations or centuries in grim Puritan ideology. As much research has described, most cultures (dominant culture in the United States aside) are strongly collaborative cultures. The sense of family and community is perhaps the strongest ethic in African-based and indigenous cultures in America. Middle Eastern and Asian cultures also have a strong ethic of connectedness. Individualism is a recent overlay on even many European cultures. Whether our fierce individualism in the United States comes from Puritanism, the economic structures and belief systems of capitalism, myths about the Wild West, or the intersection of all those forces in the United States, the result is that the institution that socializes young people is antithetical to the cultures of many of the children who present themselves in schools. Research on cooperative learning has found that even when given tasks that would be more efficient to work on collaboratively, Anglo-American students automatically turn them into competitive tasks (Aronson, 1978), whereas Latino and African American students work quite comfortably at the task as given interdependently. Anglo-American or Anglo-American-identified teachers themselves have to be resocialized, so that they value cooperative problem solving. Even so, if their students are predominantly Anglo-American or Anglo-American-identified, the time and energy it takes to resocialize the students may be, as it is for Ralph, more than they want to give.

A "mismatch" between home and school has been identified as one of the problems that children of color have in classrooms run by well-meaning but culturally bound white teachers (Hale, 1982; Ladson-Billings, 1994, 2001). In such cases, instead of taking the mismatch as an opportunity to learn more about cultures other than their own, many teachers judge the child's home to be inadequate. Research on who is referred for special education classes has much to do with teachers' mistaking for defiance or dullness some of the normal and natural behaviors of children of certain other cultures, such as the narrative rather than "correct answer" style of response to an adult's questions characteristic of African, indigenous, and some Asian societies. Predominantly European American as our teaching staff is, most teachers are especially frustrated by the interactive responses that children bring from family, community, and church—appropriate and natural to the children but disruptive to an otherwise "orderly" European American middle-class arrangement.

Unless savvy teachers respect the cultures they are faced with—both kid culture and cultures other than the dominant one—they face the kind of battle that Ralph describes, accepts as normal, and charges into, determined to win. If only he would recognize that channeling children's natural preferences and styles would be more effective.

Teacher Uncertainty

The first question for teacher change is whether adults, like most of the already socialized children we teach, are fearful that if something new appears and we don't crush it or belittle it, we may be judged inadequate when we are tested on it. One new teacher found:

> The kids treat you less seriously if you have divergent views. . . .
> They're not used to being respected or included in any decisions.

Especially, they are not used to the teacher's being uncertain:

> Teacher: I didn't know how to go over the test. I guess I didn't think about it enough. And I said, "How do you want to go over this?" When I ask things like that, they don't say anything. They just kind of sit there, if they even listen to me. . . . They don't like it when I say, "Let's do something."
>
> Professor: Of course they don't.
>
> Teacher: They hate it. They think I'm stupid. They say . . . I know, they're just twelve.

But it is not just because they are twelve. No matter what age they are, they are going to be uncomfortable with it, and decide they hate it, because a teacher is supposed to be in charge and know everything. It makes students of all ages—at least, first grade through graduate school—insecure when a teacher asks them to participate in any decisions about the process of a class; they are accustomed to the teacher making all the decisions.

Especially with regard to the academic content, it is not acceptable, from a student's perspective, for a teacher to display uncertainty, assuming, of course, that the teacher has done all his or her homework and has read and figured out and thought about everything he or she possibly could before coming to class. But the teacher is still doing some rather spontaneous and exciting rethinking within the stimulating give-and-take of the classroom discussion. I never had a framework for thinking about student discomfort with teachers' improvisation until one secondary education preteacher, a very smooth debater himself, gave me a possible way of seeing it:

As for the comments [made in our class] regarding the teacher thinking aloud and transferring confusion rather than meaning to the students, this might be true. Any person skilled in debating tactics will tell you that pausing for noticeable amounts of time and thinking aloud are seen as signs of weakness and confusion by the audience and the opposing side.

It does not occur to most traditional teachers to share their thinking process, even with their student teachers, and certainly not with their students (Sarason, 1982). Maybe the debate model is at least part of the reason why. But basically,

> In student-centered learning, the route ahead is not mapped out in advance. Preparation consists of internal readiness and willingness to explore and experiment [Brandes and Ginnis, 1986, p. 80].

A traditional teacher such as Ralph is extremely uncomfortable with that kind of stance. "Prove it to me!" he demands of me. He wants proof that it will work in his classroom before he is willing to try it.

Of course, the proof can only happen with him and his students in their classroom, and it does not happen immediately. Only a very secure person, I think, can tolerate having things go wrong in the way they went wrong for Mona, a student teacher, in her first dissection lab. It was also unusual that her cooperating teacher allowed her to make mistakes:

> So I had watched her [the cooperating teacher], and I picked up a lot, and thought she did a nice job. I thought one of the things she said was really neat, so I tried to say it today [*laughs*], and suddenly I said, "Can it! Just forget that I even said that! I have no idea what I'm talking about!" [*laughs*]

It is being real with students in that way, and not requiring a perfect performance of oneself, that allows kids to know that it is okay for them to make mistakes, too.

However, one of the unfortunate characteristics of the dominant culture of our society is that it does not tolerate mistakes. As the debater quoted earlier stated so clearly, even to be less than 100 percent sure suggests being wrong, and being wrong makes you vulnerable to attack. In our culture, important people do not apologize. They are never wrong. Many international conflicts involving the United States remind me of classroom and especially playground altercations, usually between two or more boys. They cannot afford the inevitable loss of face that would come with admitting responsibility, even shared responsibility. They have no habit of figuring out how to make amends in order to preserve the relationship. So much for the moral development of our leaders.

Probably very few students had a teacher like Mona or her cooperating teacher. If they had, probably even fewer had male teachers who could admit their own errors or display uncertainty without fear of losing face. A general on a battlefield has to give absolute orders and cannot ask, "Gee, guys, what do you think?" But outside of the combat situation, I am told, away from public scrutiny, generals, like business executives, do best when they check in with each other, figuring things out collaboratively. The most effective factory managers take worker input seriously. The most harmonious families are based on mutual respect, in which there is room for everyone to be him- or herself. It takes fully self-actualized adults, who know they are human, to allow children to be fully human as well.

Apart from the question of how teachers would look if they were exposed as wrong, or even not absolutely certain, is the very unpredictability that is characteristic of cooperative learning. Teachers cannot, and should not, control what goes on in the groups. Often, teachers cannot really even know everything that is being said, as they monitor the dynamics of the six or eight simultaneously-operating groups from a watchful but respectful distance within the classroom. That can be unnerving for teachers whose whole experience has been to own the content and the conversation about it. Considering how unwilling Ralph was to entertain the possibility that a high school girl could view her mother as being "hard-nosed"(as opposed to nurturing), it might frighten him to set the task and then have to stand outside of many different discussions into which he had no input.

J.B., a veteran high school teacher who routinely uses cooperative learning in his English classes, said of that situation that he did not feel scared or out of control, just "lonely." He wanted to know what was going on in each group because he did not want to be left out.

That is the trade-off when teachers decide to give up some of the power in the classroom, of course. But in terms of teachers' legitimate need to establish accountability and direction, there are plenty of ways to get a realistic sense of what has been taking place in the groups. If teachers have a strong enough sense of self, they can risk making mistakes in front of students, can change direction in their presence as new possibilities arise, and do not have to control everything the students think. It helps most of all if the teachers see themselves as learners along with the students (Freire, 1968; Moses, 2001). Developing such a philosophy and maintaining it is the start of a much-needed paradigm shift.

Poverty of Imagination

Not having experienced or seen anything other than desks in rows and all that that arrangement of furniture usually implies, it is hard for anyone in our society to imagine doing things differently, or encouraging others to do things differently. In fact, repeatedly, the language in reaction to cooperative groupings, or any kind of student-centered learning, exposes the absence of visual representation from prior experience. Preteachers say, "I couldn't envision," "I had never pictured," "That wasn't how I'd imagined my classes," or "It does seem rather difficult to envision how a non-teacher-dominated classroom could be accomplished."

It is easy to assume that the only way you have ever seen something is the only way it can be. A certain poverty of imagination around alternatives to traditional teaching is characteristic even of teachers who have asked very far-reaching questions about the content of their courses and have made courageous changes to their curriculum. When I have attempted to engage some of these teachers in talk about change in dynamics within their classrooms, however, the most drastic alternative to their own lecturing that they can think of is having students do oral reports. But traditional reading/presentations of reports or having one student at a time play teacher is still a one-person-centered, still an information- and product-centered method. The dynamic has not changed, only the person has; the change has the disadvantage of not working as well as the old standard way for getting the material across.[1]

When teachers are clear about that, still the most drastic alternative that teachers without prior experience can think of to standing at the head of rows of students is to sit with the students in a large circle. As Ralph recognizes, of course, even in a circle, the focus tends to be on the teacher, who still, from that position, if he or she is so inclined, can field every individual response before throwing it back to the students. So it is not just a matter of how furniture is arranged; it is more fundamental than that—although thinking visually about a different furniture arrangement is an important part of the change.

I have learned that the dynamics of a classroom are not something students are generally invited to think consciously about at any grade level. Even university teacher education students generally assume that the desks have to stay where they are. Patricia, the veteran fifth grade teacher, states what may be true for even many progressive teachers. It certainly was true of me:

> I started out as a very traditional, sit-in-rows, be quiet, worksheet-workbook kind of teacher. And I think why—I've been trying to think why, but I think why is because that's what I had seen.
>
> All through elementary school, all through junior high school, all through high school, and then even in college, there were not a lot of group discussions, there were not a lot of cooperative projects, there weren't a lot of anything but traditional stereotyped teaching.
>
> And I think that's why I did it, in the beginning. I didn't know anything else; I didn't know what to do. Even in my student teaching, that's what I saw. And that's what I did as a student teacher.
>
> So it came to the first day in the classroom; that's what I did, and did it for a few years. And I was not happy, but I didn't know how to change.

Patricia's student teacher, sixteen years later, seemed to be starting at the same place Patricia had started, and for the same reason: all she had seen were the same traditional classrooms. But at least she is going to see in this fifth grade classroom what Patricia never had the opportunity to see, but had to invent for herself. Notice the student teacher's astonishment as she witnessed student-centered teaching for the first time. Patricia recalls,

My student teacher came in, and after the first week she said to me, "I can't believe those kids!" She had sat in on one little group—she just happened to wander over and sit with them.

There were probably four students at that table, and they were reading their stories to each other, and she told me, "They were reading them, and then someone would say, 'Well, this doesn't sound right. Couldn't you make that better?' And someone would say, 'Well, I like your beginning.' And someone else would say, 'I didn't really understand that part.'"

And then she said, "They were taking criticism, and they were helping each other." And she said, "I can't believe it!"

As the previous chapter discussed, people who become teachers tend not to believe that kids can do this. Ralph insists that his high school seniors can't do this kind of peer feedback because they've never done it before. It is, of course, easy to put the blame on prior teachers, who were supposed to "prepare" kids for you. But the clear, unalterable evidence is that kids can do a great deal more than our teachers ever imagined of us, if only we believe in the kids, the processes, and ourselves.

That means we need to know about kids, know about our content, know what we are doing, and have developed sufficient skill and professional judgment. But even new teachers can begin to use pairs and threes for very brief amounts of time, if they have these basic beliefs.

Most early childhood teachers, especially since the Open Classroom and British Infant School movements, know that, at least to some extent, they need to be conscious of the multidimensionality of what they do. They need to tune-in to when kids need snacks, or stretches, or naps. Would hearing a piece of music stimulate them, or calm them? When is the right moment for a story with two or three children in my lap? Or a hug? Sylvia Ashton-Warner (1963) says that when she and her "little ones" (five-year-olds) felt like it, they "danced in the middle of sums!" With children this young, as most mothers and other primary caretakers know, the flow of a day cannot be regimented by furniture, or a clock, or by arbitrary subject areas.

Unfortunately, the strictly categorized and regimented high school arrangement of time, space, energy, and ideas that fragments the world into disintegrated pieces seems, in the recent "back-to-basics" decades, to be reaching down into elementary and even some early childhood classrooms. Without attention to developmental appropriateness, many kindergartens and even preschools—especially in inner-city schools, where the push for better test scores is becoming desperate—have lost their focus on discovery, freedom of motion, generosity of time, close nurturing contact with unrushed adults, and fluid direct interaction of children with concrete materials and with each other. Three-year-olds are soon going to be expected to learn to read, well before they are developmentally ready, to prove—*something*. The purportedly competitive and high stress "real world" of high-stakes testing has gotten that serious, and that blind, in recent years. It is taking lots of energy to resist it. That is why it helps enormously to have support through this struggle (Aaronsohn, 1996).

Note

1. AAUW, *How Schools Shortchange Girls, 1995;* Belenky et al. (1986). As I suggested in an earlier chapter, I do not leave the jigsaw expert groups entirely to their own interpretations of text. I intervene in many ways, first by my comments on their three or four reader response papers, as they read the book slowly, over many weeks, in "chunks." Through my comments to individuals on their papers, I urge more accurate, more complex, and more comprehensive reading and meaning making of the text. Then, as they come to the stage of deciding, together, what aspects of the text are important for the rest of the class to understand, I urge them to think beyond mere information giving; the idea, instead, is to figure out and convey meaning. Finally, their presentations, based on what they have decided is important to convey, cannot be mere lectures. As much as possible, each is obliged to use as many of the intelligences as possible in designing their "lessons." That way, they are forced to consider meaning, rather than decontextualized facts.

Chapter Ten

The Courage and Freedom to Color Outside the Lines

Collaboration and interdependence are much more frequent in the real world than the pressures on us to be competitive and individualistic would have us believe. Carpenters and other skilled workers rely on each other, consulting and then balancing an otherwise impossible load between them. The ideal of democracy is exactly that. A model that could be transferred to high school situations, but, surprisingly, is not, is the informal study group that undergraduate and graduate students sometimes initiate for themselves so they can get through enormous quantities of material efficiently, or so they can support each other through difficult passages.

I think J.B.'s openness to student collaboration in his high school English classes is a direct result of his own professional ongoing experience of adult writers' workshops, in which he looks to his peers as resources. I saw the same thing happen when a group called Integrated Arts got elementary teachers to use movement in their elementary classrooms by first having large numbers of ordinary classroom teachers attend a series of workshops where they danced. Before they could believe it could be a useful and important thing to do with their students, they had to experience their own bodies moving in space, to rhythm, in collaboration with others. Those teachers had to unlearn deep prohibitions and fears. Although not all of them incorporated what they had learned when they went back to their schools, before those workshops almost no one was allowing, encouraging, or teaching through movement. As one teacher commented, "It's hard to imagine what you haven't seen or practice what you haven't experienced."

Consciousness

It is therefore important to have large amounts of direct experience of interdependence within cooperative learning groups in preteachers' university courses, to help make group decision making "normal." Through the small-group work, students can begin to experience for themselves the safety of the environment in which they (many for the first time) can expose their feelings and their half-formed ideas, and really trust that they will be heard with understanding rather than ridicule. They speak of undergoing the discipline, and discovery, of authentically listening and being heard. They speak of genuinely listening to others and finding out that not everybody thinks the same way, and of seeing how knowledge gets extended rather than impeded when differing perspectives confront each other. Students are glad to experience a growing sense of a class as a community—a place to safely practice awkward new steps and get constructive feedback about what was terrific, as well as how to do it better next time. Many report being grateful to have gained strong theoretical grounding for their instincts to nurture, respect, and take their lead from children, within a process that replicates the very content that they are studying.

Willingness to speak in the full group often comes only after having been heard in small groups. Once students feel the authenticity of their own voices for perhaps the first time with peers, they can begin to trust both that voice and their peers. Within the small groups, where it is relatively safe to take risks and expose imperfection, students come to realize that it is okay not to know something: "If everyone doesn't know, you don't feel so stupid." That's a big one! The fear of being seen to be stupid, as I have suggested earlier, works more than anything else to alienate students from each other.

The problem, even so, seems to be compartmentalization between their adult lives and what they expect can and must go on in a K–12 classroom. J.B. was one high school teacher who was able to make the transfer. Most teachers tend to believe children cannot conduct themselves as collaborative learners or as participants in workshops, which are so appropriate for adults. But that limited perspective can be overcome. In order to believe, most teachers and preteachers have to regularly witness effective genuine cooperative learning in action in actual public school classrooms and in classrooms of teachers who will reflect with them about their pedagogical decisions. Unfortunately, those interactions are becoming harder and harder to find, although wonderful ones exist. Seeing student-centeredness in action is a crucial precondition for teachers to believe that it can work.

Although participating in cooperative learning and observing it in action are both necessary, even that is not enough for preteachers to be ready to transform their own traditional practices and instincts. Teacher education students must also learn to plan cooperative learning lessons or, even more valuable, must learn to include a cooperative learning component (even for two to five minutes) in each lesson they plan. Preteachers can get the most out of actually implementing those carefully designed lessons, first with peers and then with public school students. It is especially helpful if they can view a videotape of the lesson and then carefully reflect about the lesson. It is also enormously helpful to have direct knowledgeable feedback from a peer, a cooperating teacher who believes in cooperative learning, and a teacher educator. All of these strategies must happen within teacher education programs— until all undergraduates come in assuming that interdependent problem-solving group work is the normal way learning happens in a classroom. Someday.

I have been suggesting throughout this book that in my work as a teacher educator I help students discover their unconscious assumptions about teaching and learning. My intention is to have students examine their assumptions as they uncover them, in order to encourage students to choose the kind of teacher they want to be and as a corrective to automatic reproduction of their own schooling. The process is complex and difficult. After all the stimulating readings, deeply engaged personal response writings, classroom discussions in many sizes and configurations of groups, visits to excellent teachers' classrooms, opportunities to role-play, and designing, implementing, and reflecting on student-centered lessons—however, students may still not be able to overcome the powerful conditioning of so many years of schooling. Nevertheless, the work my colleagues and I do is an important start. At least one student has written, "The trick is to make the unconscious conscious."

I personally felt quite gratified when three members of a secondary education class gave these directions for small-group work in a ten-minute lesson:

> Come up with a consensus of what type of government would
> best describe your high school classroom (democracy, dictator-
> ship, monarchy, and so forth). Then describe what governmental
> system (such as aristocracy, parliamentary, or republic) *this* class-
> room works under. (e.g., for just a few examples, aristocracy,
> parliamentary, or republic.)
>   Feel free to combine any governmental systems or make
> up your own words to describe the classroom's government.
> Be prepared at the end of the time to tell the class your group's
> consensus and why you feel that way.

It was personally interesting to me to be a participant in this particular lesson, to hear what students would say. In our small group, one angry young woman wanted us to consider that high schools are oligarchies: "The beautiful and the rich are in control." So we worked with that, and we decided to name it a Monarchy, in which the teacher had all the answers—with an Aristocracy of Nobles (tracking)! Regarding our own class, the group I was in chose the designation "Divine Right of Syllabus."

Another group reported their consensus about our class: "Painfully Democratic." A spokesperson for that group said, "Sometimes we want someone else to make the decisions!" Another called us "Rule by the Masses," and another "Group Consensus," in which the whole group is equal, "but you [teacher] have the ultimate power as elected president."

Even if some of these characterizations of our class were flattery, teacher-pleasing, and designed to make me feel I was achieving what they knew I wanted to be achieving, it also had the effect of getting students to generate from concrete examples their own real-life definitions of terms they probably had to memorize in high school. What an effective lesson, if only for that!

There was even homework attached to this set of directions. As always in these exercises, it was not a real one for our university class to do, but it was a way for the lesson designers to create an individual piece to complement the cooperative lesson. In this case, it is one whose products I would have loved to read:

Write a page about whether you think this class could happen in a high school. Give your reasons. How could you make it happen?

Support

Whether a teacher can make it happen, it seems to me, depends ultimately on whether or not he or she gets support for this risky way of teaching. It is crucial for teacher confidence to have a like-minded other adult in the school with whom to work out these ideas. I have read and heard of, witnessed and written about (Aaronsohn, 1996), and experienced in my own teaching the isolation of being the only one trying to do this kind of teaching in an overwhelmingly hostile environment. Working in a hostile environment is not just discouraging for teachers. It could lead to their being fired, or to their giving up teaching, or to their choosing to accommodate "institutional realities." The last possibility is the one that shortchanges the kids the most, and undermines their own integrity. As one first-year teacher told me, "It would be okay to give in if you didn't have the consciousness of what is the better way for the kids."

That is exactly the reason why an excellent teacher education program must do its best to make sure that consciousness exists strongly. Otherwise, when teachers feel threatened, insecure, or otherwise inadequate, they will naturally tend to revert to the behaviors that are more deep-seated than the newer behaviors. One student worried about herself at the end of our course:

If you get out of the habit of questioning, you fall back into your old assumptions.

A supervisor commented about her student teachers:

They don't know where to start with groups! I can see them reverting back to lecturing!

The usual solution to feeling overwhelmed and uncertain is to resort to what is familiar to everyone, both on stage and in the audience.

People who are outside of education—the general public, politicians, parents, and even administrators—cannot imagine the support that teachers need. Not surprisingly, the same system that isolates students from each other and sends them off to struggle with harder problems than they should have to deal with individually makes a fetish out of "rugged individualism," which sees the need to be nurtured as weakness and assumes that teachers should be able to "tough it out" alone.

I prefer to describe a different pattern that has emerged during almost twenty years with student teachers, with preteachers and graduate students in my courses, and as a faculty member myself. The idea of human beings being available in a caring way for each other is supported by psychological, anthropological, and feminist scholarship, as well as by the literature on cooperative learning. The new pattern starts from an assumption of the naturalness of interdependence, as natural as any ecologically healthy environment. It points to the unnaturalness, or, at the very least, the unhealthiness, of the kind of suspicious, fearful, exclusive, rejecting, and turf-protective isolation and clique making that young children in competitive situations quickly learn to exhibit, and may never let go of. One first-year teacher experienced rejection from the other second grade teachers, to whom she was yearning to reach out. College faculty members sometimes experience it as cliques among colleagues (Fischetti and Aaronsohn, 1990).

What I have noticed, from many in-depth interviews with teachers and student teachers, from student writing in my classes, and from my own direct experience as a teacher, is that those teachers who get good solid support from other adults are then able to give to the kids in their classes the nurturing they need. In fact, I have argued in another book (Aaronsohn, 1996) that professional but (most importantly) nonevaluative on-site support for practicing teachers should be considered a legitimate part of the role of teacher educators—part of their university course load credit.

I hear myself sounding like Ralph, pointing to his twenty-five class hours a week; like all teachers, I'm lamenting, "Oh, if only we had smaller classes!" And it is true: those longings are all part of the need for fewer separate obligations and therefore more time to work well with those. However, partly because the public sees teaching in traditional lecturer-audience transmission terms, and sees twenty-five contact hours—or twelve for a college professor!—

as an easy load compared to a standard *visible* workload of forty hours, public funding usually does not provide the money for enough people to be everywhere they need to be, to do all that they need to be doing.

Without recognition of teachers' need for institutionalized support, the next-best possible arrangement, valuable for itself, of course, is to establish student teacher support groups, which many teacher education programs do. The hope is that the habit of peer support—and the confidence to organize it—will carry over once student teachers are full-time faculty members in schools.

What Is Support?

The best kind of support is not advice. It is, instead, the fully attentive presence of a person who provides a space in which teachers can listen to themselves. That is the primary gift psychologists offer. Many qualitative researchers (including myself) have found that researchers are not the only ones who learn during in-depth interviews. The person being interviewed, hearing him- or herself talk, often engages in much deeper reflection than he or she is able to do without that interested, knowledgeable, and respectful but mostly silent audience. As Ralph indicated early on, he was thrilled to be offered the opportunity to talk—and be heard with full attention— about his own teaching.

Chapter Five has described the effectiveness of one particular book *(How to Talk . . .)* in helping preteachers and practicing teachers begin to understand the process of listening with full attention, and how to practice listening. It is a process that must be learned, because most students have not had any experience, or modeling, of doing that for each other in traditional classrooms. Instead, they have learned to "pay attention" only to the teacher, who, in a traditional setting, is interested in what they have to say only if it is what he or she was "looking for" to move the class along.

Is there room for feelings in a classroom, especially a high school classroom? I have sometimes seen signs on classroom doors saying, in effect, "Your personal problems are to be left at the door." I have doubts about how realistic or healthy it is for teachers to expect that much compartmentalization and repression from children. By the time they become teachers, adults must have arrived at that self-discipline in terms of issues from outside of school, as they face children.

Many teachers are frightened by the natural, as yet unrepressed, spontaneous expression of feelings by children—feelings they themselves were not allowed to express, or even to have, as children. How much more effective in classroom management would it be to *acknowledge* children's frustration rather than silence or punish them for it? Why does a classroom have to be all business, with no room for feelings, even exultation?

And what about teachers' legitimate feelings? Even as a forty-year veteran of the classroom, I still experience discouragement, doubt, and even pain, as well as joy and satisfaction, in my daily teaching. In the heat of an unexpectedly difficult situation, I have learned to take a breath and say to myself, "Okay, what needs to happen here?" and figure out what to do differently with the structures, timing, groupings, tasks, ventilation, or words I have chosen. I have learned to name my own feelings aloud: "I feel disappointed," or "I'm confused," or "I need you to be with me here." Once I have acknowledged my own feelings, even to myself, I am usually able to relax and make necessary changes.

But on occasion I find myself in despair, especially when I return to campus from observing in a school where I saw children being treated cruelly, or just inappropriately. In the car ride back, I fretted and stewed, trying to come to terms with what I experienced. If I did not soon thereafter—either in person or on the phone—have access to the ear of my colleague and dear friend with whom I share an office, what would I do with those very strong feelings? She turns around in her chair, looks directly at me, and listens. Sometimes she offers "food for thought," but mostly she reflects back the feelings under the words she has heard me say. I am enormously grateful for her support; I try to return the gift when she needs it.

It is hard to be a teacher of any number of years of experience who is trying new ways to approach the subject matter. It is hard to reject rigid roles and instead take students' lives at least as seriously as the subject matter. It is hard as well as exhilarating to be learning along with and from one's students. It is hard to be simultaneously teacher and gatekeeper. It is hard to confront the massive forces aligned against progressive teaching. It is hard to see so clearly the structures of inequality in our society. It is hard to figure out ways to help students privileged within those structures finally see clearly their own privilege, and then decide to do what they can to work against injustice.

No one should have to do anything that hard alone.

Support also exists in the nationwide "community" of multicultural and social justice educators and activists. There is more written now about multicultural education than any conscientious teacher or professor has time to read. Reading at least some of it, and attending conferences, allows us to realize that we are working within a wide, energetic, and articulate network of people similarly committed to social and educational change. That connection is crucial. Nevertheless, it does not replace the on-site presence of a nonjudgmental person who really hears and understands. Both are necessary.

Legitimate Questions About Cooperative Learning

Chapters Eight and Nine tried to indicate that certain myths, habits, and blind spots have discouraged some teachers from trying cooperative learning. Johnson and Johnson (1975) point out another blind spot held by many preteachers and practicing teachers: assuming that the world is "dog-eat-dog," we do kids a disservice if we do not prepare them for it by making them aggressively individualistic and competitive so they can "get theirs" before someone else beats them out of it.

The logical next assumption is that training in cooperation is training in weakness. I have tried to indicate that this myth serves certain structures in our society that would have to give up or share some privilege if all classrooms became places of collaboration and genuine democracy. I have also tried to describe the complex web of expectations and assumptions that must be examined, one by one and also in terms of each other, if teachers are to throw off the myths and redefine both learning and teaching in ways that genuinely serve kids. rather than the disempowering structures of our society. This work is revolutionary, necessary, and possible (Moses, 2001; Freire, 1968).

Nevertheless, there are some legitimate questions about how cooperative learning works, and they do not have quick right answers. I will briefly address these questions in this section, since most of them have already been discussed in earlier chapters, and others will be more fully developed in the next section. But it will be useful to lay them out for discussion.

Probably the hardest question is how to get past the initial resistance of kids, other teachers, administrators, parents, and school boards. I have devised several responses to this question, none of which are totally satisfactory. It is inspiring to learn the story of other people's personal commitment. I have read and listened to Paulo Freire (1968), who spoke from direct experience about the risks of doing cooperative and student-centered teaching: he was imprisoned for it in Brazil. He advises—as do D. W. Johnson and R. T. Johnson (1975), Eliot Aronson (1978), Shlomo Sharan (1984), Bob Moses (2001), and most of the other proponents of cooperative and student-centered learning, all the way back to John Dewey—that you start where the students are. That does not mean that you look at the surface of where they are within the institution of a middle or high school. That set of characteristics is likely to be a combination of passive obedience and rigid obstructionist, tuned-out, suspicious, self-protective, impatient, and competitive behaviors. Instead, it means that you let them say, in their own voices, over time as they begin to trust that you are really hearing rather than judging them, what fears, anxieties, pressures, and feelings cause them to appear the way they appear. That will be an opening for them to tell you, and themselves, who they really are.

It does take time, and it does take work, the kind that Ralph insists he is not willing to do. Exercises for helping kids develop cooperative learning skills abound, although following some of those strictly—especially "requirements," such as that there must be clearly defined and separate "roles" in each group—could kill the spirit of collaboration. There must be awareness, skill, support, and willingness to put in the time and energy to really pay attention to kids, as well as do the patient work of having them learn the necessary social skills of collaboration as they're practicing it. Underlying all that, however, there has to be a belief that this way of teaching is better for kids than the banking of a body of knowledge, and better for the teacher than performing and transmitting.

As for the dubious adults, the approach starts with understanding that they, too, are coming from an either-or mind-set. A calm, sure confidence that comes from real commitment, combined with systematic, respectful, caring inclusion of the reluctant adults all along the way, can make the difference between their being threatened and their accepting the change. Perhaps they will even support it.

Beyond that, having twice been fired myself in my first thirty-year career, and having seen other teachers fired or not rehired, I cannot tell anyone how to stay in an oppressive system. I can only talk about working well with and for the kids who are stuck in it. I can try to be within reach for them there. And I can encourage them to find and generate a small base of like-minded people within the school and community, for mutual support.

The easier questions have to do with what goes on in the classroom—but those are not really easy, either. How can a teacher know for sure that kids are learning and that they're getting it right? What about accountability for individual kids? Will they get what they need? John Holt's advice (1967) is not satisfying, or natural, to most of us, but it provides inspiration, truth, and the only useful direction if we are to step back and let kids learn: you *can't* know, for sure. You have to let go of *needing* to know (p. 189).

I have had a very hard time letting go of needing to know. Again, however, it is not all-or-nothing. First, teachers have to let go of the myth that they can *ever* know what a kid is really thinking, even—or especially—in a traditional classroom. But there are many ways to assess, or better, let the students tell us what they know or think they know. We are not inventing this for ourselves as we go out to do this. People have gone before us.

Howard Gardner's work (1993) joins a huge body of recent (1980s–1990s) research on alternative assessment. Whether students really understand most of what they read and most of what is said can be attended to by reading what they write, hearing their questions, giving them various ways to share and practice, and to want to really read what is really there. Finally, you can notice by observing and eavesdropping. You never catch it all. But you never do, anyway—even in traditional classes, or especially in those.

It is true, of course, that the work that happens in groups is not the fast race through the syllabus that the pressure of upcoming standardized tests seems to force us to run. However, research finds that if students who work cooperatively do not do better academically than a control group of students who work individually and competitively, at least they do not do worse. One fifth grade teacher who skillfully has students use manipulatives in collaborative groups for math finds each year that his kids do better on the math sections of the mastery tests than they used to, before he began to use either manipulatives or cooperative learning. The point he makes is that by the time the test comes, although they may not *remember* formulae or functions, they can *figure out* what needs to happen to solve any problem. It is mathematical thinking, asking and talking through problem-solving questions—not memorizing content or right answers—that matters in the real world of actually *using* mathematics (Moses, 2001; Joe Bolis, fifth grade teacher, personal communication, 1994).

Ultimately, of course, the standardized test is a high-stakes one, and kids absolutely have the right to be taught to maneuver within it. Test-taking skills can, and should, be taught, but on the side, as a separate though necessary course, for a few regular, brief sessions either within or after school. Students have a right to be taught the skills as a game of *guess what the test maker had in mind here*. But those skills should not replace real learning.

Hitchhiking

From students' points of view, there is a serious set of questions: Will one student have to do all the work? (Usually me?) Will strong students waste their time and be "dragged down" by "slower" students? Mostly, these failures occur when there is a group grade. So I don't give any grades, and that seems to help significantly. Occasionally when a group grade *is* at stake, though students may put pressure on slackers to pull their weight.

With or without a grade as an external incentive, it is important to look at why some students resist contributing, and at what that might mean about their having gotten by with only doing minimal work to get by. I have found, as have other researchers (Nederhood, 1986) and classroom teachers, that much of the success of cooperative groupings depends on how the task or project is structured and monitored. Another key aspect is students' stage of development in terms of locus of control. In the most highly evolved set of circumstances, if at the beginning some students pull back from the work, in time they usually get pulled in by the pleasure of the process, and sometimes by the specific instructions of the teacher that require everyone to participate in meaningful ways.

In groups of mixed "abilities," as most successful ones are, students can begin to value the different intelligences or ways of approaching a task. Furthermore, problem solving is not the same skill as memorizing facts or "getting" something as fast as you can. As for the argument that brighter kids get slowed down by having to teach the slower ones, most teachers will admit they themselves never really knew or understood the material until they had to teach it. Nevertheless, cooperative learning is not a matter of a teacher *using* the "brighter" kids. It is mutual learning for many reasons, including the following: (1) Everyone's perspective on the content is necessary for a full understanding of it from all angles. (2) The content is not the whole agenda anyway. Learning to listen with respectful attention and disagreeing courteously are crucial life skills that every child, even "bright" children, must develop. (3) "Helping" is not best defined as "doing it for" someone; in fact, that kind of helping disables. (See Figure 10.1 below and also Chapter Four of Faber and Mazlish's *How to Talk So Kids Will Listen* [1980].) (4) The tasks set for cooperative learning groups should not be the kinds of tasks that students can do on their own. Instead, they should be tasks that require the interdependence of students whose intelligences are different enough that, for example, a very "bright" verbal linguistic child is forced to rely on the spatial, problem-solving, interpersonal, kinesthetic, or musical skills of a child whose verbal abilities may never match his or hers.

The question about whether being in groups will cause kids to be less than serious about their work comes from two assumptions: (1) that kids have no inner discipline, and no ability to develop inner discipline and (2) that the only work worth considering "serious" has to do with acquisition of some predetermined body of knowledge. Having watched kids in rows over the past forty years, first as a teacher and then as an observer, I have seen a great many kids tune-out, especially from their hiding places in the back of the room, where the teacher's broadcast frequency sometimes does not reach. I have seen sloppy, surface work in which kids have zero

Figure 10.1. The "Help" Continuum

Taking over	Support through the struggle	Abandonment
Child feels:	Child feels:	Child feels:
Inadequate	Valued	Inadequate
Frustrated	Challenged appropriately	Frustrated
Devalued	Confident	Lost
Dependent	Sense of accomplishment	Scared
Angry		Angry

Defining "helping" in terms of this continuum, again not in the either-or terms at the two poles, is useful as teachers learn to restrain their impulses to "jump in and rescue," on the one hand, or just send children off on their own without adequate scaffolding, on the other hand.

This continuum is usually generated within a teacher education class after the class has participated in a kinesthetic guided-imagery activity to redeem the word "struggle."

investment. I have seen—and been the teacher in the middle of, and survived!—kids going wild with a substitute, with all stops opened. All that was when kids were coming from rows. All the discipline was external.

Cooperative learning assumes that students have to, and can, develop internal discipline. Contrary to the military myth (upon which traditional teaching seems in too many ways to be built), internal discipline does not suddenly appear full blown as a result of years of immersion in external discipline. It happens when kids are trusted to take real responsibility for their own lives, inside the classroom and out. When teacher education students practice giving children genuine choices, rather than an ultimatum designed to force a "good choice," they are shocked to see even very young children rise to the occasion. We drastically underestimate what children can do if we trust them with our respect. As for whether kids will "just socialize," studies have shown that, contrary to what we have traditionally believed, more creative, productive work gets done when students focus on tasks while socializing than when students focus grimly on tasks. And if there are clear directions, clear time limits, small enough groups, and a manageable task, the work gets done and done well. Most important, genuine learning is taking place.

The next question is, what if it flops? What if it doesn't work? At the beginning, it probably won't work. Teachers have to expect that, for all the reasons this book addresses. But that does not have to be a negative thing, if what we are working on is process as much as product. In fact, the "failure" of a group activity, and how the people involved feel about it and what can be learned from it, can reasonably be a discussion topic and problem-solving exercise for the class. We can help students overcome their fear of mistakes and their learned impatience if we overcome our own (Sharan and Sharan, 1976), which is, to be sure, where theirs comes from. What infant or toddler, without outside pressure from an adult or older child, gives up on a task that he or she has chosen when it doesn't "go right" the first time? For how many hours will a child that young, if unpressured from the outside, struggle, explore, experiment, risk, try, and learn from his or her own errors after making many? Sharan and Sharan say, "Kids need to know that you expect them not to function well automatically, and that you will help them learn how" (Ibid. p. 26). One student teacher reflected with relief on hearing that perspective: "So I shouldn't expect so much the first time."

"It's Not My Style"

Then come the questions about choices. Is how teachers run their classes to be just a matter of teacher preference or style? Are there kids for whom cooperative learning is inappropriate? Are there lessons that are better suited to individualistic or competitive goal structures? Much has been written, particularly by the Johnson brothers and their colleagues, about when it is appropriate to use cooperative learning, and when other goal structures, such as mini-lecture, full-group discussion, role playing, or brief independent work (such as a freewrite or drawing), might be more appropriate to help the students grasp particular concepts. A mix of all of those approaches is what characterizes an effectively run classroom at every level, although the Johnsons began to say in the 1980s that there is no room for competition in a classroom; there is plenty of it outside of the classroom, but having it inside interferes with the development of a collaborative consciousness (Johnson, 1986; Kohn, 1986). I agree wholeheartedly.

What I have found is that I keep seeing teachers doing individual or competitive lessons that would go so much better cooperatively, but it has not occurred to them to do it in a nontraditional way. As for teachers' styles, which both J.B. and Ralph keep emphasizing, it makes complete sense to say that we have to be who we are in our classrooms. But that does not have to mean that how we structure lessons for our students should be determined solely by our personalities, our habits, or our own dominant intelligences. After all, it is the students' classroom, too, and they have as much right as we do to be who they are in it.

If cooperative work is better for students, as research suggests it is, even if it is only "not worse" for the development of academic competence in children whose dominant intelligences are verbal and mathematical, there is still room for a wide range of personal styles within that structure. The pattern I have observed is that some of the teachers most open to nontraditional forms in the classroom are people who have had prior-to-teaching experience, not as actors but as directors of plays, particularly those who have had experience directing improvisational theater. For obvious reasons, they are comfortable with not having to be the star, or even onstage themselves. Other teachers whom I have found to be open to sharing the decision making and the careful listening to everyone in the room are those who have had experience in feminist or Quaker-identified peace and justice groups, which almost always work by consensus, with rotating facilitators. Others are those who come to teaching from an interest in guidance or social work. Not surprisingly, I have seen that people whose other lives have been in unexamined military or law enforcement careers, or who are the children of highly authoritarian parents or teachers, are likely to have some trouble with kids who "get out of line." However, one of the secondary preteachers who was most eager to implement cooperative learning, and who seemed most comfortable with it in his mini-lessons, was a former marine, though one who had done considerable reflection on that prior life experience.

To be sure, a balanced lesson will have some individual work in it, if only frequent brief freewriting, and, of course, homework.

There is even room in a balanced lesson for some direct instruction. There is certainly a need for a time when the groups report, share, and check in with each other, as well as participate in a full-class discussion, which a teacher may facilitate and to which a teacher might also contribute insights and further probing questions, without dominating. As for kids who prefer to work alone, there must always be room for them to have their own space. But *why* they are that way—as with people who insist on being competitive—has to be examined. It may be that, socialized to winning and to seeing peers as rivals, they are exactly the ones most in need of practice in collaboration, community, and trust.

Trying It: What Problems Student-Centered Teaching and Cooperative Learning Solve

It is with great pleasure, and great care, that I write this section. The caution is that I must not oversell "groups" as a panacea for all the ills of society, or even for all the ills of schooling. To claim them as a panacea, or anything as a panacea, goes right back to the single right answer way of thinking. Given that, I must admit that I am unabashedly enthusiastic about the possibilities of cooperative problem solving in small groups. I must also admit that I am overjoyed to read so much research that confirms my experience of them. I do boldly claim, therefore, that when cooperative learning is chosen because of a deep commitment to the concept of student-centeredness, it is a potentially revolutionary process that could bring about significant democracy in our society.

Sharing the Decision Making

To begin with, just on the surface, the physical shift from passive sitting in rows can diminish student boredom and lack of energy for the work in the classroom. What I have come to understand about how students use the word *bored* suggests a range of emotions—from *uninterested* all the way to *overwhelmed,* with *left out, intimidated,* and *preoccupied* in between. In this second-year high school English teacher's reflection, several of those connotations seemed to be present:

Teacher: Every time I get scared, or I have too much work to do, I always move back into that worksheet, and into rows, and I find everyone smiles. It doesn't work.

Professor: How do you recognize that?

Teacher: Extreme boredom. On their part and on my part. You find yourself faking it. You're not having fun, and there's zero response from the kids. And they let you know. Now that they know, now that they've seen something that works for them, they say, "This is boring. Why don't we just put this in a circle?"

This teacher and I were impressed with that kind of student responsibility for decisions about the environment in which they will learn. Along with everything else they learned from this teacher's choice to take the risks she did in that year, they learned that the classroom is theirs. They learned that they have rights, but they also learned that they don't have to fight their teacher for their rights; they can negotiate with her, and she will listen.

I have witnessed that deep shift in consciousness many times in my own classes. When students come to realize that they do not have to ask permission for everything, as they are accustomed to doing, and when they realize in fact that they are consulted about their preferences, they start to be *aware* of their preferences and needs as they learn. In a very real way, then, they are thinking about the process of learning as they are engaging in it. For example, at the end of the very first semester in which I experimented with the jigsaw method in a teacher education class, most of the students were supportive rather than threatened by my uncertainty. They made themselves responsible for noticing the dynamics in their own groups, and for evaluation. They were coming close to releasing me from the power with which they had automatically invested me at the beginning of the semester.

Problem-solving small groups help students begin to see each other as resources rather than as enemies. This appears to happen with great seriousness and productivity in J.B.'s high school writers' workshop, a more free-ranging interactive experience than the kind of cooperative groups one usually thinks of. When they are ready to share their work, his writers seek advice from any person whose judgment they value. What he notices is that they do not necessarily go to their friend sitting next to them. Nor does everyone go to the same person, as I have seen in some other similarly free-ranging classes, where everyone bombards the class wizard in grammar or spelling or math facts. In J.B.'s workshop arrangement, his students are looking for deep help with their ideas rather than surface help with proper forms or right answers. What I saw in J.B.'s high school class was what Patricia's student teacher saw among fifth graders. Kids *can!*

Confidence

When university students come in at the beginning of a semester terribly shy, perhaps fearful of speaking and being exposed as wrong, as suggested in an earlier chapter they often open up in their small groups. So it does not matter if they do not talk in the full group. They have had their say, on paper and in the small group, and they have been heard in both places. That, for me, is plenty of participation. What I notice about these small groups, as I eavesdrop from a respectful distance, is that very soon, once the students get out of the habit of agreeing or disagreeing (a hard one to break), people are saying a lot of "I like" things about each other's papers and really noticing what is being said. They get better and better at it, unconsciously practicing several skills at once: showing real respect to a peer, listening for ideas rather than judging the "relative merits" of a paper or an idea, having to consider several points of view that may be different from their own, solving problems, not interrupting, and trying out divergent thinking.

I say that their practice of these skills is unconscious because the collaborative behavior seems to flow very naturally after a few ground rules are agreed upon. They do not have to think about "paying attention," at least not to the teacher. Over the years, I have learned to think through and give directions clearly enough before the students get into groups, so that I no longer have to interrupt the class to clarify something, once they have begun to concentrate with each other. And how wonderful it is to watch how the members of a group lean toward the person who is speaking, looking intently and with interest at him or her. And then the focus shifts, and everyone is fully attentive to that speaker, and then it shifts again. All around the room are sets of two, usually three, or, at most, four people—oblivious to the other groups and to me, interdependent with each other. I love it!

And so do they, as they report. Semester after semester, on their evaluation forms, some variation on these representative sentences appears:

- Talking to other people in the class was great. It was like having a support system.
- I found that people's personal experiences (life and professional) were most helpful.
- The other people in the class taught me the most next to the readings and the writing, because their sharing, opening, opinions, and experiences never failed to stimulate my reevaluation of my ideas and beliefs.

Most wonderful, Donna, the second-year teacher, got similar end-of-semester affirmations about their cooperative learning experiences from her tenth graders!

Learning from each other can work to dissolve the isolation and alienation from each other that students have become socialized to feel. At the same time, it helps empower students about their work, chipping away at deep insecurities that early schooling has helped develop. Sometimes university students can name that:

> It's funny because I was having difficulty with [the word] *empowerment* in another class. I was given a definition but couldn't comprehend what it was. I felt empowerment in here.

The student previously quoted described his feeling after doing his ten-minute mini-lesson in our teacher education class: he said he felt "ecstasy." He was overjoyed with how comfortable it felt to have no pressure to be the expert, to see and hear people in all the groups excited about what he had offered them to work on, to hear the divergent ideas, and then to get such positive feedback from the whole class. What if he had never experienced this alternative way of being a teacher?

Pride—and Joy

As the research on cooperative learning indicates, people who experience small groups find themselves proud of their own ideas and pleased with each other. How far that healthy self-esteem and respect for others can extend has also been measured by research on cooperative learning. More than in any other process yet discovered, because of the qualities associated with cooperative learning, barriers between genders, races, linguistic groups, and "ability" levels have been seen to diminish significantly (Johnson and Johnson, 1975, 1976; Aronson, 1978). The qualities associated with cooperative learning include close interaction, interdependency, guided practice in respectful listening and valuing of the ideas of others, and common goals in nonhierarchical, noncompetitive settings, in which conflict is seen as an opportunity to solve problems. The very structuring of groups makes the fundamental statement that people can learn from each other across differences. The greatest possible heterogeneity is recommended to produce the greatest diversity of ideas. J.B. describes both his intuitive and his deliberate thinking about how he will compose the groups in his high school English classes:

> I will try to identify, within each class, those people who are really the best at this. And I try to mix them in. . . . I want to mix them both academically and socially. I want this kid on this side of the room and that kid on that side of the room to meet.
>   And because I want different abilities, I want the kid who's the real academic leader to rub off on some other kids. And I want him to get some resistance from some other kids.

He does it for "academic" reasons:

> You're expected for two minutes to come up with ideas within that group. I really want them to be nonjudgmental. In my mind, the idea behind that was creativity, and that means we gotta have a lot of wacky ideas. Those are easy to kill off, especially in an institution where we're supposed to think in straight lines.

And he does it for social reasons:

> We make judgments about people all the time. Our best friends
> now are people that at first sight we didn't like, and the people
> that we couldn't wait to get to know turned out, after we knew
> them for a year, they weren't what we thought. And I think that's
> really learning!

In my own classes, I have seen hierarchy disappear as shy people
get bolder about speaking. Sometimes they even take on the people who are accustomed to dominating (who, themselves, are
learning to be aware, and to listen). They help each other extend
thinking and develop ideas. Like the children learned to do in
Patricia's fifth grade class and in J.B.'s high school classes, the
process invites people to say to each other, with respect and genuine interest, "Hmmmm. Can you show me where you see that?"
or "That's not how I read it; this is what I see." One student said,
"Groups are the only way to discuss touchy issues; no one person
dominates." That is the ideal we aim for.

Sometimes there will be contradictory perceptions of how the
group is operating. That usually occurs when the group is too
large. Then, a person whose habit is to dominate, who is either
quite sure of him- or herself or is insecure with what seems to be
the lack of a defined structure, will take it upon him- or herself to
"organize" the group. When that is the extent of the "leadership,"
and the group proceeds thereafter to operate as a fluid unit, that
is fine; perhaps it was even necessary, to get things started, without
assigning permanent roles. But sometimes that person, having
tasted leadership defined as power-over, will keep it. He or she
might report in the freewriting afterwards that the group was terrific. However, that group's dynamic will look very different from
the perspective of someone with a smaller voice in that same
group, or from the perspective of the other members, who felt they
couldn't get a word in edgewise. Their freewriting to me afterwards
has shown their anger about being left out.

It is also true that—in my own classes and in others I have witnessed or heard about—outside of the teacher's hearing, one student can say cruel things to another. Although my eavesdropping
job is partly to anticipate and prevent such a thing from occurring,
these unfortunate things sometimes get past even the most vigilant
teacher. I have observed it happen behind the teacher's back when

kids sit in rows, too, and in playgrounds and halls more times than I can count. Cooperative learning happening for the first time at the high school or university level does not transform people who have spent most of their social lives being competitive and therefore defensively hostile against others, or certain others.

The most serious apparently deliberate put-down that occurred without my noticing it was an unkind remark by a young woman who had been absent with mononucleosis made to another in the first part of the semester, so had missed almost all of the community building that we had done together. Because of the group structure, however, once I was informed about it by the victim, I was able to give the situation back to the class the following week, in a safely distanced form to protect individual identities as much as possible. On the advice of a colleague, I presented the scenario not as something that had happened in our class but as a problem these preteachers might have to confront as teachers in their own classrooms. The class discussion became both a way for the offender to begin to understand and find a way to apologize for the pain she had caused without having to be humiliated and an important consideration for everyone's teaching.

Apart from the social aspects, cooperative groups are an excellent corrective for poverty of imagination and satisfaction with quick right answers. They blur the distinction between work and play by fusing interpersonal interaction with the production of meaningful decisions and ideas, and thus expand the otherwise narrow definition of work as a job or a chore or something to get out of the way. When otherwise hard work might be intimidating for people to handle as individuals, it becomes manageable in a group, so students are much less likely to avoid it. I was thrilled to hear high school teacher J.B. say that complex issues *need* groups:

> If I really believed that I could do it better through lecture, I would lecture. Part of the reason we go to groups here is because I feel that the assignment is difficult enough to warrant group participation—that people can in fact benefit from exchanging ideas. I mean, something that's real simple I don't think we should bother with groups about.

From university student reports: knowing that their groups are counting on them to do their share increases the likelihood that they will come to class prepared. They also say that knowing they are going to have to share their work with peers is an incentive to do a more thorough job than they would do if they were just slapping it together for the sometimes preoccupied teacher to check off in his or her grade book. At the same time, cooperative learning offers the opportunity for students to internalize their own locus of control—to evaluate their own work instead of depending on whether the teacher likes it. With competition gone, and with the mode of learning changed from accumulation of knowledge the teacher owns to figuring out all the possible ways to understand what is going on in a work of art, an event in history, a person's life, or a chemical bond, or how to represent in graphic terms what they have just experienced, students become less grade conscious. When grades are given, they are given based in part on how well students cooperate, as well as on the quality and timeliness of products. With all of these factors operating, students really become much less grade conscious. Then, the work itself, both process and content, has a chance to take on real meaning. The whole arrangement, carefully thought through and carefully facilitated, spreads out the responsibility, easing the pressures and anxieties that usually accompany traditional schooling and thus usually interfere with learning and with healthy being.

A teacher who decides to try to work in a student-centered manner has to be able to find satisfaction that has nothing to do with performance highs. There is a certain amount of regret in teachers' acknowledgement of this, but I sense, as well, as I listen to them or read their reports, a wise, deep joy in their voices that means they have gotten beyond the self, and beyond the expectations of the role. It is a more frequent pleasure, I think, than this more traditional one that many high school teachers and college professors say they live for:

> I feel good in the classroom those two times a year when
> somebody lights up, and I say, "Wow! I got someplace!"

It is hard to believe that that is enough satisfaction: only two times a year? So many small wonderful things can happen in every given class period, if a teacher is open to seeing them. That is, if the focus is as much on the students as on the material, and certainly on the students rather than on the self. If teachers can redefine what can make them happy with a class, those kinds of things can happen all the time. A second-year teacher's new "high" is of a very different consciousness than the one she came home with her first year, when she was "psyched" to have all the kids looking at her, being quiet, and enjoying her dramatic presence. Now, she reports:

> He had six or seven sentences put together in one paragraph, and he had part of another paragraph developed, and this was a kid I couldn't get to write a complete sentence! And I was so psyched!

And here is the consequence of Mona's very small amount of noticing and caring about the boy the other kids and other teachers had ignored, because, they had determined, "He wants you to leave him alone":

> I was just going to have them move right into the next activity, and this fellow, Richard, that I had just started breaking the ice with, said, "Well, are we going to read these?" And I said, "Yeah! You want to be the first person to read?"
> And he said, "Yeah." And he really got into it. He loved it! And I was just like. . . . I got home that night and I was over the moon, you know, I was so excited! I couldn't wait to tell my husband, "Richard volunteered and read in class, and smiled, and talked to everybody in the class!"

As a high school teacher, I used to be proud to think I was teaching by the force of my own personality. It took me many years to realize that rather than stimulating by my own impressive performance or getting a point across, I was teaching more effectively *for the students* when I began to realize what Mona and Donna were able to recognize. Now, for me, sometimes the joy is hearing the spokesperson for a group say "We decided" rather than "In my opinion." That much success in moving away from individualism is thrilling. In addition to the light in the eye, and instead of looking for it to come from something I say, I look for and take pleasure in the comfortable sound of four, five, six, seven, eight intense small-group conversations going on at the same time around the room. I take pleasure in seeing students completely focused on each other's faces, instead of mine, and watching that light shine back and forth within that small circle of learning.

I remember that when I first started teaching (in rows, of course, because that was all I had ever experienced or seen), the best classes were always the ones in which someone would turn around in the row and address another student. My aim then was to keep that conversation between students going, without me, for as long as it could go, like New Games volleyball, in which the aim is for the two teams to keep the ball in the air as long as they can. I think lots of teachers might see the value in that—even traditional high school teachers and college professors, who, perhaps like me when I started, just don't yet know how to facilitate it.

The Process of Overcoming

The commitment to student-centered teaching and the confidence to practice it will require that teachers engage in all of the following steps to recover from the compulsion to teach traditionally:

1. Seeing it in action, from enough distance that you can get a sense of the shape of how it works so the structure within the "disorder" appears, but close enough to hear how focused and respectful the conversational energy is.
2. Reading and talking and writing about alternatives to traditional structures. Theory! Research!
3. Direct and repeated positive adult experience of learning through collaboration.
4. Practice at undoing assumptions programmed into us by the dominant culture.
5. Letting go of a focus on subject matter as a body of knowledge, replacing it with two things: first, a recognition that learning, at all ages, is about constructing one's own understanding and not about absorbing information; and second, a focus on what in the subject matter might be meaningful for the present and future lives of these kids who are in your life right now.
6. Being dissatisfied with doing it the way it has always been done, even if, as Ralph says, "It works for me," because you recognize that in lots of ways it does not "work" for kids, even if some of

them go on to get high grades in your class, and then even next year.

7. Regular brainstorming support sessions with teachers who are themselves struggling to do teaching differently.
8. Direct "help" in your classroom: close observation and unrushed, nonevaluative feedback by a knowledgeable person who will provide a mirror and a sounding board.
9. Writing in a reflective journal.
10. Deep breathing—and laughter.
11. Forgiving yourself for mistakes and using them as information.
12. Having courage.

Can all of these qualities, including courage, be developed within a teacher education program? I have to believe that they can, and must, for the sake of the children our graduates will teach.

Note

1. This is shown in Chapter Four of Faber and Mazlish's *How to Talk So Kids Will Listen . . .* (1980).

Chapter Eleven

What Would Success Look Like?

I have learned to see children as people, which I had never considered doing prior to this class.

My goal is to have teacher education students enlarge their range of options as they *think* about what they had previously only taken for granted. In terms of learning how to learn, this means not mistaking fragmented facts for knowledge, but aiming to understand concepts. It means not exchanging one set of "right answers" for another, but instead looking for and genuinely considering all possible perspectives. It means letting go of having to "know," sometimes even holding in balance contradictory realities. In terms of developing a sociopolitical consciousness, it means working to understand, from within, the complex contextual factors in which all "facts," and all lives, including their own, are embedded. All of that, it seems to me, is involved in what it means to be "educated," and especially what it means to be well enough educated to be a teacher.

However, socialization into the traditional paradigms is incredibly powerful. It's so powerful that, indeed, it's not easy for students to sustain the new ways of thinking and behaving beyond one semester of a nontraditional course. That's the "failure" that opponents of nontraditional "experiments" point to: What happens when students leave the open, nurturing, empowering structures of such a classroom, or even such a whole school, and return to traditionally structured teaching, as they surely will? Aren't we doing them more damage by confusing them? Shouldn't we just prepare them for the "real world"?

In terms of their further schooling, I have certainly seen plenty of students revert to traditional ways of writing, studying, reading, and thinking about their coursework when they leave my class. They are adjusting back into the familiar expectations that characterize their next courses, probably much more easily than they initially adjusted to the unfamiliar expectations of mine. The question is, as Sonia Nieto (1992) asks in terms of whose cultures are valued in schools, "Who should do the accommodating?" This is also the key question to ask when, as I have suggested, rigidly traditional structures limit students' natural learning processes. Clearly, since teachers and schools as institutions have the power, it has been students who have had to do the accommodating. However, a model exists in young children and adolescents who come from "open" alternative schools or classrooms, and it may also exist in those who have been "deschooled" at home (Holt, 1967).[1]

Despite outsiders' grave doubts, most children from those nontraditional situations do surprisingly well when they decide to, or are required to, engage in formal or traditional schooling. In fact, more resilient than children whose only schooling experience has been in traditional classrooms, they seem to adjust comfortably to new situations. More important, by their very presence and ways of seeing, thinking, and operating, they have been known to help other students and even teachers call into question certain assumptions and structures. Nevertheless, even if they have had to adapt completely to more restrictive ways of thinking and being, a seed of resistance has been planted. I am confident—because I have witnessed it—that once people have stood outside the dominant paradigm, they are more conscious that "the way things are" is just one possible way things can be.

Because I have had those experiences and have witnessed them over and over again in my own students, I have reason to believe that having the experience of operating in an academic setting for even one brief time outside traditional structures makes a difference for students. In our teacher education programs, such an experience can put students in position to observe systems and structures as if from the outside, while reflecting deeply and critically on the persistence of traditional "instincts" within themselves.

As a result, it is possible that teachers may choose to design their own classroom structures to respect emergent original thinking, encourage collaboration and caring, give themselves and their students permission to challenge text of any kind, support taking intellectual risks, and consider alternative ways of being in the world. I cannot predict who will have been permanently affected by any of the reflection they engage in within the structures I provide, but this kind of student insight frequently occurs, and I consider it a success. One student speaks for many in saying:

> I no longer think in terms of "making" students behave or of "pouring" knowledge into them.

There is only one sure way to assess the full impact of a course whose goal is to have preteachers and teachers challenge all their incoming assumptions about learning, teaching, diversity, and the systems of our society. That is for teacher educators to observe teachers, over time, in their own classrooms. As a vital and legitimate part of our teaching load credit, teacher educators must be a presence in school classrooms, not to assess or judge teachers, but to observe and support teachers on-site in their own classrooms, if we—and the teachers themselves—want to sustain the learning, especially within the context of traditional schools (Aaronsohn, 1996). Some students themselves understand that:

> I thought about all of the ways that I would want to say "thank you" and I realized that it wasn't the words you would want to hear, but my actions to keep that promise of always looking ahead and striving for a "healthy" classroom.

Changed Consciousness

Students routinely write, "That never occurred to me," or "I never thought about that," or "I never gave much thought to . . . ," or "I just assumed . . . but now I realize." Those seemingly small successes carry weight, as far as I am concerned. More dramatically, I have witnessed enough transformation on the part of students within a course to say with certainty that, for some, significant shifts have taken place, boundaries have been stretched. Students, of course, have said all of that better than I could:

- I realize what a great challenge to [my] assumptions this course has been, and that nothing could have prepared me for the change I would have undergone by the end. Not only are things in my mind so totally different now, [but] I would even like to think that assumptions don't really have to occur anymore. I would like now to be able to find things out and not just accept what I am told.
- I have a tendency to disqualify information that is different from what I am accustomed to, or that goes against my views. . . . However, through my struggles in this course, I learned that many of my own ideas were truly just one perspective and not the *only* perspective.
- I just always assumed that my opinions were fact.

I count as success the very fact that students can recognize their own socialization. Most do—around the entire range of issues I invite them to consider:

> It is very hard to undo thoughts you've had for years. If you reinforce those feelings every day and only see things around that reinforce those feelings, it can be very hard to change them.

The Pivotal Process: Reflection

As I write, I'm starting to see . . .

Through reader response, freewrites, shared perspectives in class, and writebacks with me, it is the constant reflection, I believe, that is the most important process of the courses I teach. By the time they write their end-of-semester papers, in fact, some students will notice that they have internalized the process of reflection. They watch themselves continue to do it:

> I'm intrigued that I'm making new connections as I write this self-evaluation. I didn't assume that I wouldn't, or maybe I did. I thought of this as a vehicle for looking backward and summarizing. It's not. It's still part of the growth/learning process.

Another student, using her writing as a way to think things through rather than persuade or report allowed herself to recognize, as a

math teacher in a school system almost exclusively focused on raising test scores, that the automatic powerlessness she was used to
feeling did not have to be all that was true about her:

> Unfortunately, teaching my students to problem-solve is a time-
> consuming project. Although I wholeheartedly believe in this
> approach, I know I do not have the time to teach this necessary
> skill because our curriculum is driven by CMT (Connecticut
> Mastery Test). I know I am not courageous enough to say "No"
> to . . . [the focus on standardized tests] so I will have to "fit it
> [problem solving] in" whenever possible. As you can see from
> the above example, I am still struggling to find the courage to
> speak up and say "No" when I disagree with something.

Some students quickly get into the habit of catching themselves in
their own statements and soon begin doing the rethinking on their
own, confident they will not be "graded down" for changing their
minds or not having a "coherent position." This student's response
to a reading about multiple intelligences is especially thrilling to me
for her willingness and capacity to rethink on her own:

> In my own experience in school, I did not so much see that teach-
> ers stifled children's creativity, as is suggested [in the reading].
> Obviously, simply because of the way a classroom is managed,
> children whose creativity manifested itself in a noisy or disruptive
> manner were told to "behave." However, I remember countless
> times when we were asked to do a creative craft or music project
> (which I always dreaded, simply because I am not good at such
> things).
>   As I've just written that line, though, it has occurred to me
> that as school progressed, the creative projects lessened and the
> academic ones increased. And just as I always hated the creative
> ones, children who struggle with reading, writing, or arithmetic
> must have disliked school more and more as time went on.

The student quoted here, like several others, essentially came to
the course already able to work with the readings thoughtfully and
deeply. Most others needed at least some prodding from me
through writebacks. In many cases, at some point during the
semester, if only to avoid having to do so many rounds of write-

backs, students begin to have with themselves the kind of dialogue that they have practiced with me in writebacks. Of course, that is my goal: not to have students censor themselves, by any means, but to read back to themselves what they thought they thought, off the top, and then do some more thinking, deeper and critical thinking:

> I am very proud of this one. I started catching myself in my writing by the end of the class. I started to comment on my own writing before handing it in to the teacher. I tried to cut down on the assumptions and dig to deeper levels as I was writing things. I tried to question my responses before the teacher had a chance to. I tried to think of what your response would be before you responded, and in so doing, I would ultimately be responding to myself.

Another student began to allow this to happen to him in his reader response on an article about standardized testing. He thought his way through for himself:

> My view has long been that tests were a measure of intelligence and ability. Throughout the semester, this attitude has changed a little, but I still believed in testing. What else can give us measures if there are no achievement tests?
>
> The teacher test at the beginning of the section made me rethink my position almost immediately. I could understand that schools want their teachers to be competent, but what is competence? As I have expressed before, I think that intelligence is only one of a myriad of factors that mark a good teacher.
>
> I felt sort of stupid taking the exam, and I normally don't feel like a stupid person. I felt that these facts were either never taught to me or I had forgotten them long ago. Also, the multiple choice format is so cut and dried. It is regurgitation. A talentless teacher who studied items for this exam might get the job over a much better teacher who missed some questions. Part of teaching is working with your students to obtain answers together. I came to the conclusion that testing the teachers like this is not a very good measure of their ability.
>
> Hold on. Click! Testing teachers to see if they know general things related to school is no good in my book. What makes it so different for the students? I had to digest this for a while. It is not easy to give up old ways of thinking, but I slowly started to change my opinion.

One student did her rethinking as she proofread her paper, as if doing her own writing back to herself, processing the idea in her own terms, for herself. Clearly, she trusted that in this one class at least she could leave that new penned-in thinking on her margin (spilling over to the back of her paper), instead of either leaving it out or typing the whole paper over before handing it in:

> [Original reader response sentence, in response to a chapter in TET (Teacher Effectiveness Training)]: A solution that is reached through mutual agreement rather than outside imposition results in commitment, not resentment.
>
> [The student writes in her own margin, with an arrow to that sentence]: This makes such complete sense to me *now!* I don't know why I couldn't figure it out before. If conflicts can be resolved through mutual agreement, they are far less likely to reoccur. In other words, they are *truly resolved*. An imposed solution (by another party) is *not* resolved; it will foster resentment and breed resistance. It will reoccur, escalate, and become a multiple conflict. Nothing is resolved and the stage is set for the battle to begin (a war of wills that is never won, by anyone).
>
> [In the margin next to that last sentence]: I never knew this before. (Wow, I've learned a lot—amazing stuff, this TET!)

In the meantime, those ongoing conversations through writebacks frequently provide, over several weeks' time, astonishingly honest insights, themselves often useful to us as teachers and teacher educators. It is important to notice that all the work, as in the next example, is really being done by students who use their writing not to impress me with their knowledge but to understand:

> [She had commented that a substitute teacher had made the children into robots.]
>
> Professor: What fearful power we have over kids, right? Why do we feel we need it?
>
> Student: Maybe because if we have power over them we have power over other aspects of our lives.
>
> Professor: Wow! Say more, okay? About yourself?

Student: Well, right now I feel very stressed between school, taking a class, trying to keep up with housecleaning, and spending some time doing extra things that *I want* to do—quilting, reading magazines, which I haven't done either in a month and a half, since school started. I don't have to clean and cook; my husband really helps out. But I like to and I guess part of me still feels it is my job. (I know it's not.)

I get so stressed and I can't let that show at school, so I try to keep control in school so things don't fall apart and I lose it—emotionally. My poor husband gets it when I get home. I cried for no reason last Saturday—I mean hysterical crying, because I was so overwhelmed. I can't do that at school. I shouldn't do it at home, but gosh, it felt good.

So I keep control by having control over the kids.

I think now that I am aware of *me,* I can work on it. My students can adjust—slowly—with me.

Another example of a breakthrough that occurred as a result of the back-and-forth process again took several weeks, but it was worth it. The original paper had been a reader response to Chapter Ten of Labinowitz's *Piaget Primer* (1980). Within the process, the student recognized two important things: something real about herself and what Piaget means about a teacher's taking direction from the student:

Student (on reader response paper): First of all, the book says, "Following the direction of the children's spontaneous activity, the teacher may have only a vague plan." This made me think of myself as a person. I am a very organized person, many times overly organized. For example, the day before my wedding, I gave my husband-to-be, my brothers, and the Best Man schedules to follow on the day of the wedding, down to the last minute, what they had to do. They all looked at me as if I were crazy, but they followed their schedules and everything went smoothly. I know I have work to do in this area. Just having a vague plan, not a step-by-step procedure, will take some getting used to, even though I would have a long-term plan.

Professor: Well, let's think this through. You *need* to know things will go smoothly for the most formal, important single day in your life, of course. How invested in the smooth running of every *other* event in your life do you need to be?

Student: I need to be very organized and plan ahead.

Professor: How about the *actual* reception, beyond the details of food, timing, arrangements, and so on? Did the *guests* pretty much run things without a schedule, within the framework you set up?

Student: Yes, I never thought of it in that way. They did. I set up the framework, like in my classroom, and my students or guests will run things. *I MADE A CONNECTION!!! Hooray!!*

Vehicles for Reflection

Before taking this class, I have never had the opportunity to reflect on my own thinking.

I think the preceding sobering statement about K–12 schooling, and even some college and university schooling, suggests how necessary it is for people who plan to be teachers—and also for practicing teachers—to take courses in which they are invited, or obliged, to learn to reflect. Statements in students' papers reveal the extent to which certain processes, activities, and readings are particularly helpful as they grew in their capacity to reflect within the course, most of the students for the first time. Reader response is one important process:

> Whew! Reading this article and typing this paper helped me to work this all out in my mind, and now I feel that I can make an educated stand on this issue.

In addition, the requirement to write down the dialogues they had with people as they attempted to use *How to Talk . . .* (1980) gives many students an opportunity to reflect deeply on their own "normal" behaviors. One reported, "It was not until I had written this down that I realized I have a habit of doing the same thing." Another wrote:

> Through my dialogues, I learned about my fear of confrontation. It was a very difficult thing for me to do, but I have recognized the need to be more confident and [have] applied this to everyday life situations. . . . I still get very nervous about it but it is hard for me to describe the awesome feeling I get when I climb over one of those walls [that had been] in my way.

The writebacks are another, more complicated story, because they involve not just the student's interaction with a reading or with another person, but with me. One student described what many experienced:

> I was so afraid to get stuff wrong in the beginning. Later I realized [that] this was the thing stopping me. The thing that matters is what I think, not what is right or wrong and not what the teacher wants to hear. What she wants to hear is what I think.

Another expressed it a little bit differently, with an intent to use the capacity to reflect and be clear about her own thinking that the writebacks, more than anything else, helped her develop:

> Now I sit here and look at all the writebacks that I used to dread and worry about, [worried] that I was doing something wrong and that I wasn't making the teacher happy. I look at them now and wonder why all my professors don't do this.
>
> I have grown to understand the writebacks and that they are not to make the teacher happy. They are to make us open our eyes, hearts, and minds and see that there is more to it than that. It's about what we feel, and if we can't say what we feel, we're worrying too much about what others think.
>
> There has been a great deal of change in my writing, not just in this class but in all of my classes. . . . I am more specific and clear as to what I want to say and what I mean. . . . I am able to express myself better the first time. . . . I am proud of myself for this and I hope—no, I know—that it is an ability that I will never let go of.

Another student indicated that the complete process of reflection had become a habit in her own life:

> With this constant examining, digging, reflecting . . . this way of thinking and analyzing quickly became a part of my life . . . and everywhere I go now I find myself stopping and asking myself why, and then begins the excavation.

And another, in spite of her original resistance, began to see the usefulness of writebacks and freewrites, and began to use them in her own teaching, using them for exactly the same reason I use them:

> I admit I thought the freewrites and writebacks were a nuisance.
> It did remind me, however, that students need to reflect. . . .
> Even through my simple writings, I've been able to locate and/
> or reexamine some feelings and beliefs I might not have had the
> opportunity to reveal.
>
> I've had my students do more "quick-write" journal entries,
> just so they can process and internalize what we've just done or
> learned.

Although many students at the beginning of a semester may feel defensive about the writebacks, most of them are able to say—as two of the students quoted earlier say—that what had distressed them was their own fear of being wrong. The old, deep-seated assumption was that if the teacher questioned what they had said, then what they had said must have been wrong. Getting beyond that to what they could learn from my questions takes various amounts of time.

Not everyone is able to achieve full awareness within the structures of writing and class activities. For some, especially around issues associated with diversity and with the practice of Faber and Mazlish's *How to Talk* . . . (1980), an individual conference in my office is helpful. For *How to Talk* . . . , I usually engage them in a role play based on one of their dialogues, having them literally switch chairs with me as I play them and they play the person whose perspective they were having trouble understanding. That is often just what it takes. When they come with strong prior opinions, defensiveness, or blind spots about readings that ask them to see from the point of view of a person whose life experience is different from theirs, it is a harder task for both of us. I have to be wary, of course, not to be giving an individual student the lecture and explanation most are accustomed to from their prior schooling. I also have to be careful not to give the lecture I was tempted to give out of my need for them to "get it." However, recognizing that some of these students, who are either about to be or are already teachers, have gotten all the way through school and college without having to become proficient readers, I have to figure out how to help them understand what the readings are saying in a way that they can take it in, because the stakes are so high in terms of the children and communities in which they teach. In those cases, sometimes having them switch chairs with me and role-play works the best, again, although it is by no means as successful as with *How to Talk . . .* , even though the process is the same: seeing from someone else's perspective.

Blind Spots

There are two particular issues about which a large percentage of the predominantly white, middle-class suburban students, both graduate and undergraduate, seemed most adamant. One is their insistence that all parents have an obligation to show up at school. They usually have in mind, of course, low-income parents or parents of color. I know this because most students are quick to accept, without any irony or reflection, the reasons why parents of the dominant culture and of higher income cannot always get to school. The dominant all-or-nothing position many students hold is that when "those parents" are not showing up, it means they do not care about their children's education, or about their children.

The other blind spot is some students' resentment that bilingual education programs are, as they contend, using "our" taxpayer money to "give special treatment to and cater to Puerto Ricans." Even with all that we do in class to help people overcome their blocks on those two issues, some students will not really read the articles I give, because their own preconceptions are already so strongly set. The immediacy of a conference allows for a more personal conversation. It also allows me to work with story, to be concrete, and to work harder to locate the exact blocked place. For example, the most useful tactic for the bilingual issue, if the compelling points of the article itself do not take hold, is to remove the context from students' sole focus on Puerto Ricans and Spanish. I ask students to imagine themselves suddenly transported to China. (I will pay.) What would it take to succeed in a teacher education program in a Chinese university? What would they need?

Students who do come through on those issues—though not all do—later write about what it took for them. It was different for each. One said:

> One of the hardest things for me to overcome was my view of
> bilingual education. I was so stuck in the "learn English before
> you get here" mentality. My brain just refused to let any other

alternative in. It took over a month, [with] a lot of writebacks and two meetings with you, in order for my head to open up.

I think the words that finally got me were when you were telling me about how people from Cambodia or Vietnam would just flee with nothing but what they were wearing to come to the safety of the United States.

You said to me, "Now, you want them to stop and study English for an entire year before they get here? Their lives are in danger. If they don't leave now, they could lose their lives."

Those were the words that finally got me to go, "Oh." I can't say that I am completely over my assumptions about bilingual education, but I do know that if I find myself feeling the way I did before, your words will always be sitting there in my mind, repeating themselves. I know that will help.

Another had to process, in her own words, what she could understand in conference but had not gotten through reading, although it was right there in the article that had initially initiated the entire rich conversation: that the job market when her parents came here, even as late as the 1950s, was still such that they did not need to know English or to have a high school diploma to earn a living wage.

Another student had the same problem with reading for understanding. It was only in the intimacy of an unrushed conference that she began to understand that some parents' lives are structurally different from her parents' lives, although they love and care about their children and their children's education just as much as hers love and care about her and her education:

After listening to myself read this, I noticed something. Like I heard about this before. I realized that while I was in your office, this is what you were trying to get into my head. That things are not always so easy for people. I remember you telling me the possibilities [as to] why some parents cannot always be there. Just like the ones in the article.

Even for the ones who do read proficiently, but whose experience of the world, especially about race and class, has been mediated by the images and assumptions that surround us, the struggle to put themselves into the shoes of another can be helped by a conference:

I am really trying to understand the issue. I try to imagine, and I need to do a lot more checking in. I can imagine what it's like not to have choices and not to have opportunity. And I am afraid of what would happen were I in need of that type of public assistance.

As we discussed during our conference, I am on public assistance in the form of free tuition and the G.I. Bill. Now I see why we have welfare—it's a helping hand.

Now I am coming to an understanding. I don't believe anyone intends it to be a permanent means of support. Now I am definitely getting somewhere on this issue. I can see that it isn't someone's fault that they are on welfare. There's the blame issue. Even if someone made some bad choices . . . that in no way means that care and compassion go out the window. I will need to consider this issue more.

Feeling Empowered

I am a writer! *Everyone* in this class is!

The personal investment in the search for self is, I think, what causes the shift that many students gradually experience, from powerlessness to a feeling of their own efficacy. It is not without struggle, by any means—nor do I mean for it to be. The kinesthetic activity I use to redeem the word *struggle* for my students helps most of them realize, with great astonishment and even relief, that like a seed pushing its way in two directions through the earth, and then breaking through to the light, there can be no growth without struggle. That exercise, along with release from the pressure of grades and other forms of judgment, seems to encourage students—essentially to give them permission—to do passionate, honest, difficult work, and sometimes to emerge exhilarated.

Many express surprise, and pride, about the growth they recognize in themselves when they put the whole semester's work together. One student's statement about having intensively practiced the *How to Talk . . .* strategies in light of all the rest of the readings and activities in the Approaches to Discipline graduate class represents this:

This is a much different outcome than I expected when I started this course. It is a gift I gave myself and to all the others around me.

Many others set up the self-evaluation paper in terms of what they had been thinking before coming to the class, and then what they learned and how they grew during it. Many of those add statements about the action they are taking or seeing themselves empowered to take as a result of the course.

Some indicate having never really felt they understood what was going on in the course until they undertook the whole self-evaluation process. One student's statement represents this:

> When I was going through all of my papers to organize them for this portfolio, I realized how much more they really made me see about a situation. I started out with a thirty-second thought and then I reread it and realized why I felt a certain way. I realized things about myself that I may never have thought of. . . . I have learned about second chances and new starts. . . . Most of all, I think, I have learned about me.

There is an amazing amount of hope and commitment in the writings of some of the students, even after a semester of what seems to many to be unrelenting exposure to some harshly unromantic views of how our society structures inequality. Some students, however, welcome being confronted with a different reality from what they had imagined, as unpleasant as that reality is for them to face:

- I think, as young girls, many of us just say, "I want to be a teacher." I know I have been saying that since the first grade. Teaching was always at the end of the rainbow for me. I've never thought about any other career path. We have these glossed-over, perfect images of what teaching will be like. Perfect kids that will love me, never give me problems, and bring me an apple every day.
- I had a lot of experience with kids, but never in a school setting. So my knowledge of the educational system was very limited. Everything that we have read and discussed in this class has been so informative, to say the least. It's like the façade has been removed and we were shown the real image of the school system. Everything connected and painted a somewhat dim picture. I had never known of the injustices, the outright prejudices, and the uneven distribution among schools.

- Through that darkness, I see a light of hope: I see myself and a new generation of teachers breaking the old habits and instituting a new way of teaching.

Evidence of Empowerment Inside and Outside Our Class

What I look for, and am elated by, are indications in students' writing, talk, and carriage that say, "I don't feel so powerless anymore. I don't have to just go along with *the way things are*." Such conscious statements usually appear in final papers of self-evaluation. The most representative statement was this:

> The greatest thing this course did for me . . . was to make me realize how *much* change needs to occur in this world, and that there's a great deal that *I* can do to bring about such change.

Another student stated, with a clear sense of reality as well as of commitment:

> Through all of the readings and discussions I have come to the conclusion that, although I cannot take on the weight of the world, I can work toward a better world for myself and the ones I affect as a teacher.

The distance that many of them have to travel from dependency or powerlessness to empowerment is considerable. Just learning for the first time what is within their own realm to decide makes a difference for many:

> I assumed that schools gave teachers the books that they are to use in the class. I never thought that I could go out and get a book that was culturally relevant. . . . I am going to get a book like *Mufaro's Beautiful Daughters* (Steptoe, 1987) and read it to the class to add diversity into the lessons. Why should the students think (as I grew up thinking, until this class) that a princess is white and has long blonde hair? They should be aware that there are beautiful people of all races in the world.

It is not surprising when students who are already teachers or already parents begin to make significant changes in their ways of operating with and thinking about the children in their care long before the course is over. Students with children at home have more opportunity than others to practice the strategies—and the self-discipline—that they learn from our work with some of the readings I provide. Even within a five-week summer course, for some students, change can be swift—and remarkable, although never easy:

> When I first started this course, my focus was on my classroom and getting *my* needs met in the classroom, but even that has changed. My goal now includes all of the children that I come in contact with in the school. . . . I believe that I am on my way. I have found new hope and I feel really good about going back to school.

Another parent, at the end of a semester, had a concrete plan that excited her:

> I teach preschool with a friend, and we felt we were addressing diversity by looking for books at the library to cover every holiday of every different religion, for our reading time. We would talk to parents to learn about holidays, and make sure we gave the appropriate holiday greetings to their children.
>
> But now I have ideas that I'm going back with—our "baby dolls" need some African American and hopefully Indian friends, and any other culture we might find. Posters celebrating diversity would be a nice addition. Our dollhouse needs new children. If possible, we'll purchase "children of color" this time.
>
> These were not things that we purposely chose against; it just never occurred to us!

This kind of awakening on the part of white students may have helped students of color feel less need to beware of stepping on anyone's toes by speaking up. The course's permission to break the paralyzing taboo against talking honestly about race and racism in America feels, ultimately, quite empowering. One such graduate student, the only African American teacher in a white suburban elementary school and one of the only students of color in our Education in the Inner City class, wrote, in response to Beverly Daniel Tatum's *"Why Are All the Black Kids Sitting Together in the Cafeteria?"* (1997), that she was finding a bold new direction for herself that she could now manage without fear or despair. That reading, and our variously shaped discussions in class, had shown her a way:

> Just simply getting people to talk about race is a step in the right direction. I can do it in my classroom, with my friends, and with my family, [and] in my church and with my neighbors. When I think about it, I am in contact with many different groups of people on a weekly basis. What wonders I could do to just open a discussion about race in a non accusatory manner!
>
> In our discussion in class two weeks ago, people shared that they didn't know that racial tension and problems still existed in our society. It's hard for me to believe because I live it and see it often. But as Dr. Tatum described, it's more common for black people to sit around and discuss these problems than it is for white people. I've got my work cut out for me.

My reply to that student's last sentence was, "Yes! We all do, actually! *I'm* not got to let you feel you have to do it alone!"

To keep that promise, I continue to persist in helping white students struggle with the uncomfortable reality of their white privilege, and to find ways to move beyond denial, beyond guilt, to seeing their privilege as an obligation to do something with the clout that privilege implies. This is by no means easy for the students, or for me. Through a long series of writebacks with one white graduate student a semester later, I tried gently to prod her by first acknowledging her fears and feelings of isolation within her own family and community. At almost the final stage in those weeks of writebacks, she came to these conclusions, using her own writing more than my brief questions to think things through and make connections:

> I guess I do play the game by sitting back. Perhaps the wheel would not keep turning if the ones like me were more involved in the issues. Obviously, I have my opinions on matters but keep quiet about them. That's my "comfort zone." After all, it's "other people's children," so it doesn't affect me, right? But it does. It doesn't sit well in my soul, so I should speak up. That's my obligation, since I share this earth with others.
>
> I do care, and I feel very alone in this. But I shouldn't feel alone, because at the bottom of the flyer you passed out about the

event for children living in poverty [the Connecticut Coalition
to End Child Poverty], I looked at the bottom and read the list
of organizations that are striving to make a difference. I am *not*
alone, and I can align myself with a group such as the ones listed
to better direct my energy.

Frequently, students are proud of the breakthroughs they experienced during the semester. These occur especially as people
stretch beyond their familiar boundaries to immerse themselves in
communities significantly different from their own, which they do
through their demographic study projects (see guidelines in
Appendix), in both the undergraduate and graduate courses. Eat-
ing at a Puerto Rican restaurant was one surface-scratching starting place:

> I don't often try foods from other cultures, but this was delicious. . . .
> For me, though, the food itself wasn't as important as the fact that
> I was willing to try it, because my usual response would have been
> not to participate. I need to become more adventurous and less
> set in my ways.

Other students are able to go much deeper in their stretching,
especially as a result of their community service in the demographic study area:

> My view of Hartford has changed from a racist, television-skewed
> idea to reality-grounded knowledge! I learned I had been growing
> scared of the city. Now I feel a part of it and want to become even
> more involved.

This student's partner in that demographic study project was like-
wise deepened in her clarity and was inspired by both the project
and the readings that gave her direct experience a much larger
context. Her statement is particularly instructive in that it names
some of the forces that keep well-intentioned people of the dominant culture from engaging in social change:

> I now believe one person can make a difference. I was stuck on
> feeling guilt and sadness toward savage inequalities for a long time

after I read Kozol['s 1991 book by that title]. It was constantly on my mind. Reading Madeline Cartwright['s *For the Children* 1998], was like a bright light showing me the way. ACT, REACT, do something about the things that are meaningful to you! This was a revelation to me.

All of the things I knew in my heart and conscience needed to be acted upon because it was the right thing to do. Lack of confidence, not being sure of how to help, and fear of not being able to make a difference all kept me walled inside myself.

Now I feel more connected through helping people. Volunteering at the House of Bread [a soup kitchen] and inside elementary school classrooms helped me see I can make a difference. It was a start. . . . I know I can, I am no longer afraid to act or be unconventional.

My idea of community has completely changed. I used to believe my town was my community. I now see the whole area surrounding me as my home. Farmington [an affluent white town, just beyond Hartford] seems to be functioning without huge problems, but it is not enough. Hartford is also my neighborhood.

I am now active in my community. I am more connected and better informed. I have evolved from doing a class assignment to realizing this is truly a part of who I am.

I watch much less television and am more critical of what I do watch. My time is too valuable to waste on mindless garbage, now that I realize my self-worth.

Overcoming Powerlessness

Early in a semester, in response to reading a combination of Kozol's *Savage Inequalities* (1991) and two chapters from two different books (written in two different generations) about teachers who assume children of color and of poverty can't learn, students often say, "Why do *they* allow that to happen?" or "I hope *they* do something about that." Success for me is that, later in the semester, many, many students are writing, as this one wrote:

> I hope to see this situation changed in my generation. I know that I can't change the world, but I can change the way I view the world.

Many pass along to friends, family, and colleagues the books we have used, especially *How to Talk* . . . . Similarly, after naming some negative experiences with uncaring teachers and either hoping they won't see uncaring teachers when they're in the schools or bewailing how inappropriately some of their fellow teachers behave, many come to this nonjudgmental, fair, realistic, and empowered conclusion:

> I can't control what other teachers do with their classes,
> but I sure can be careful of how I interact with my students.

Some who are already teaching go further. They describe exactly what they are now prepared to do to make those interactions with children more humane and respectful—and, in the process, more effective. One K–6 physical education teacher reported:

> So now if I have to ask someone to leave the group I say, "Maybe you should find a safe place in the gym and get focused and then come back with the class." My older students usually don't have to leave, because they realize that all I want them to do is get focused, and they usually do. . . . My younger children have reacted well to finding their own time-out spot in the gym, and I don't yell at anyone.

Considering that students who choose to become elementary school teachers have been good little girls who do what they are told, for the most part, it has been especially delightful to me— and to them—when students can report being able to be more assertive with people other than children:

> While doing my yearly personal goals with my principal, I made it clear that my focus was going to be on making my curriculum multicultural. I expected support from him as well as reimbursement for any supplies that I bought. He was a little surprised by my up-front stand on the issue and so has supported my activities and has reimbursed me.

For some students, the course represents seeing in print and hearing discussed some of the perspectives they had already come to on their own but for which they had not previously had language. For others, it was ideas they had not yet dared to express or even allow themselves to consider seriously. One graduate student, writing in response to a section of Alfie Kohn's *Beyond Discipline* (1996), had come to the course having already traveled a much greater distance than most others in her own teaching. She found the readings tremendously affirming:

> I feel so comfortable with all the ideas I am reading about. To hear articulated a philosophy that has been brewing within me for the past few years is comforting. Actually, it's much more than comforting. I've been searching for a word to describe the feeling, but I haven't found it. I feel as though the ground under me is becoming firm, not sandy as it once was.

> Probably the most meaningful discovery for me is the knowledge that the feelings of uncertainty I experienced as I shared power with my students is *not* a signal that I'm on the wrong track, but rather that I'm going precisely in the direction I intended. . . . Granted, I have more questions now than ever before, but I can finally see the forest; the trees are no longer distracting.

Commitment to Transformed Practice

At the "commencement" ceremony for newly certified teachers at the end of a semester in which I had taught secondary education preteachers, Cliff, one of the new graduates, spoke:

> I want to resist the temptation to teach literature the way it was taught to me. I want to be more concerned with students' learning, less with my own teaching. . . . I want students to take responsibility for their own learning. I'm going to work on being creative, brave, and fun, instead of perfect.

I cannot claim as my personal triumph Cliff's consciousness or clarity of purpose. He was not even "my" student. It is always useful as a corrective to my own missionary zeal, and it serves as a relief from leftover feelings of isolated individualism, to see again and again that other teachers and teacher educators are also stimulating and supporting what I am trying to stimulate and support. It is also useful to consider that Cliff might have arrived there all by himself, without help from any of us at the School of Education. After all, we got there, so it must be possible. But how many years, decades, did it take us? And did we all get there?

What is at stake in this work is nothing less than the planet, but I am not going to talk about that here. Nor will I talk about how widespread replacement of traditional teaching with liberatory education is ultimately the way to stop wars of intervention and the rape of the environment, to equalize the distribution of resources in our own country and the world, and to solve all the other problems whose root is oppression. I do not think it would bring rain, but I know it would be the way we could imagine together and work together and care together, and thus figure out a better way to organize our society so that even huge events of nature are not so utterly devastating.

Although *I* am not quite ready to claim all of that, Sylvia Ashton-Warner (1963) was, and she did. She recognized that interactions in "the infant room," or kindergarten, embed habits that determine how politicians will behave in war rooms. She even went so far as to claim that, if we do it right, there will no longer need to be war rooms, just negotiation rooms, meeting rooms, collaboration rooms.

What we say as a nation that we cherish in a free country is not, in fact, what we are preparing our children to participate in. Nor were most of *us* prepared to do the problem solving, listening, interacting, exploring of multiple points of view, celebrating of difference, and questioning of illegitimate authority that are necessary for genuine democracy.

When I think of the negative images superficially associated with what we now refer to as our *democracy,* I keep seeing the traditional classroom. I see Congress debating, not really listening to each other's speeches. Their minds are already made up. I see presidents selling their programs until the vote is what they want to hear. I see most of our "leaders," and ourselves, making no connections between one issue and another, not seeing one in terms of another, not addressing systems within this country, just looking for the one right answer to the one isolated problem so they can finish their assignment, "get it over with," and go home for recess. I see silent, somewhat uncomfortable individuals waiting for their turn in voting booths once every few years, or all the adult residents of a town coming out to sit passively and hear the city council members and the finance committee and school committee tell them what they have already decided in their private meetings. I see young men and women from working-class and poverty-class families signing up for the military or ROTC at seventeen or eighteen because that is the only way they can pay for college. I see children saluting a flag in words they cannot possibly understand, and all of them, without irony, even in drastically underfunded and unequal schools and communities, reciting "liberty and justice for all," as if we had it. I also see people—"the weirdos"—marching with signs, "sending a message" and hoping the press will cover their presence, because that is the only public voice people outside of power in the United States have.

Hope

But I have also witnessed other models of interaction, of interdependent community, that look more like the kind of democracy that the word literally means (i.e., "the people speak"), with the implied inference that someone is really listening. For example, I have watched a gospel choir, in which the soloist—a different soloist for each song—is supported in his or her struggle and pain and ecstasy, wherever it takes him or her, by the voices and clapping of the rest of the singers and congregation. I have watched the dynamics of a jazz band, improvisational theater, and improvisational dance, where people and voices move around each other within an agreed-upon theme, sharing the space and time, without bumping into each other or grabbing from each other, finding beauty and meaning in the patterns their interactions form.

I invite the reader to engage with me in play with the idea of metaphors and images that might represent what truly democratic, conflict-resolving interactions might look like, as a way to envision, communicate, and then create what can happen in our schools, even in our high schools, and in our society. For myself, I especially love two metaphors for teachers' roles. One is that of a highly skilled waitress or waiter, the only server in a crowded restaurant dining room in which all the food is delicious and nutritious. The servers have to be fully available to all tables just exactly at the moment they are needed at each, but never so close as to interfere with private conversations. The second is that of teachers as choreographers, whose dances develop out of the group's improvisation, but are also solidly grounded in teachers' sure knowledge of centuries of movement vocabulary and under-standing of the human body. In those dances, men and women, or boys and girls, learn by practicing to fall and rise, by being lifted and by lifting, by trusting and being vulnerable, and by knowing their own power to support each other. In the making of those dances, the context would be shared hard work, full awareness of each other's presence and direction, and frequent stopping to communicate and examine and change. It would be exploration, self-discipline, practice, strength, laughter, crying, struggle, frus-tration, and pleasure. Each person, alone and consciously in com-munity with and in interdependence with the others, finds the time, space, and support to go all the way to the end of a movement, test-ing and finding, and then stretching the limits of his or her own energy, body, technique, and feeling. And then the dancers return, to celebrate everyone's getting there.

What principal would not applaud?

A Final Word About Courage

A new metaphor that I have been considering is that of a crossing guard, who carefully shepherds young children along their most dangerous paths to and from school.

Crossing guards bring a crucial adult perspective on the spac-ing and timing of traffic, based on a clear understanding of traffic that an eager, preoccupied young child has not yet developed, no matter how much we lecture them. Crossing guards must step boldly into traffic, armed only with the sense of responsibility for the children, the authority of their bodies, and the courage to walk into the road and stand there, arms raised, until the children have safely crossed.

Any parent or teacher, or course, could do that with more chil-dren than they have hands to hold onto. I have done it whenever I have taken young children on field trips. I wait for the right moment, having gathered and clearly established the children at the corner, and take the step. Then, when all cars have stopped, I gesture to the children, and they cross, free to run along happily to school or to their homes. Only when the children are safe does the adult leave the center of the street.

It sounds simple, obvious, natural—what any adult would or could do. The classroom parallels have to do with the teacher's strong sense of responsibility for children's cognitive and psychological safety and with the teacher's wider perspective and knowledge of the world. Above all, I think, the metaphor suggests that the teacher must have the courage to step forward for the children's sake.

As I indicated in an early chapter, courage is not often one of the characteristics that university students or practicing teachers think of when we are brainstorming what we hope our students will be like when they're adults. Most of the time, I am the one to suggest it. I have never had a student resist its inclusion in the list, but then when I ask teachers about their own courage to say what they know is so wrong about standardized tests, for example, most wince. They have never dared speak up against the tests, beyond their conversations with each other, even when they know that they are all in agreement, and could be a powerful force if they stood together with each other and with parents. As I have indicated, it seems to me that most teachers' early socialization as "good little boys and girls" has successfully inhibited their potential for courage.

I see it so clearly as students leave my classes in the special summer-to-summer session. After five intensive weeks of study, they are placed the very next week in summer school classrooms, most operating quite traditionally. When I ask if they are trying to implement some of the strategies I have taught them, most reply that they feel obliged, as guests and as absolute novices, to go along with whatever the regular teacher does, no matter what. It makes sense that they would defer to the regular teacher, who is usually a veteran of some years. Fortunately, the teacher education program maintains contact with the preteachers in these early field experiences through seminars and supervision to remind them of alternative perspectives on what they are seeing, and to help them figure out ways to cope so they become more than just clones of the cooperating teacher.

But then in the fall, the preteachers are guests again, and still novices, in someone's classroom, and again they feel obliged to go along. Perhaps the tension between what they are being taught at the university and what they are actually experiencing in these classrooms gets discussed in courses. That is the hope: we are still in contact with them. When they student-teach in the spring, again as guests in someone's classroom, still feeling like novices despite intensive coursework behind them, and this time needing a positive job recommendation, many continue to feel pressure to go along, no matter what they had come to decide they wanted to be like as teachers.

What a difficult position to be in!

By no means do we as teacher educators want to advise preteachers to challenge their cooperating teachers, to present themselves as experts after only a few courses. But what I hope we advise is that there are ways to advocate for children, for families, and for alternative possibilities that do not have to seem arrogant. Using *How to Talk* . . . seems analogous to the approach a crossing guard would take. For example, when the coast seems to be almost clear, why not offer an occasional "What if we did it this way?" or "Do you mind if I try . . . ?" For another example, when a veteran teacher speaks disrespectfully of a student in his or her class, or of that child's family or community, that teacher might hear the novice if the novice were to say, "That may be. Could it also be that . . . ?"

It does not have to be all or nothing, submit or attack. I do not know, however, if courage can be taught. I am not even sure it can be developed, but I have to hope that it can, because I see so little of it in teachers. There have been amazing teachers who seem to come to the profession with it: the courage to let go of some of their power in the classroom, the courage to take risks, the courage to advocate for children. Letting go of performance anxiety is probably the key factor—but if grades are still the currency, what real chance is there for college students to develop courage?

Maybe role models are what students need! What courage do we exhibit in our own lives?

Note

1. I refer here not to the Christian-oriented home schooling movement, but to its opposite: the home schooling movement advocated and supported by John Holt (1967) and those who continue his work.

Appendix

Genogram: An Individual Project

To claim our identities and see ourselves in the deep, rich context of our families and our cultures, we will start with each person's exploration of her or his own identity, in terms of ethnicity, race, heritage, culture, geographic history, and history of work.

Identity in terms of family. Make some phone calls, sit down with older family members. Do whatever you need to do to follow your family "tree" as far as you can, all the way back to "the old country" from which original immigrants came over to this continent (unless you are a full-blooded Native American). Name the most immediate family and geographic names you can (don't get obsessive about finding all the aunts and uncles and cousins), and cite all the family occupations you can. This does not need to be absolutely complete by the time you present; there will not be time! Get what you can! But don't leave out the occupations or the geography. This is different from the names, marriages, and dates that show up on the Internet or other usual genealogy charts. Focus on stories, connections, real lives!

Please represent this set of facts graphically in any way that pleases you and that will enable others to *see* what you have found.

Follow it with at least one page of writing that explores the meaning *you* make of what you have learned by doing this project: What do you now know, feel, understand, wonder, cherish about who you are?

Presentations of a collaborative nature (not in a lecture format) will begin on September 27.

Demographic Study and Community Service Project (fourteen hours): A Group Project

We will "jigsaw" an in-depth investigation of many different communities in which schools are located, in order to look at the range of opportunities to which people have access and from which children come. Working in collaboration with the Central Connecticut State University Volunteer Services Office, we will get you started thinking about and experiencing an inside view of certain communities and your own role within them.

You will work with at least one other person from the class. In addition, sometimes you will be invited to work along with an "escort" from an agency familiar with the area. Before you actually go out on a project, you will be expected to conference with me briefly about your plans for service. I will be available throughout the semester, as well, to consult with you as you gather and attempt to analyze information.

If you are already teaching, subbing, or working as a paraprofessional or volunteer in a school, here's your chance to get to know more about the lives of your students and their families, and to have them know you differently. If you live, work, and otherwise operate outside the inner city, you may have never before had an opportunity to go there. Here is your chance!

Research

This is to be a complete demographic study of the community in which you plan to do your project. This could be a whole town or a neighborhood. The most effective studies in past classes have done a close examination of a manageable geographical area. Do both formal (city hall or Internet for statistics) and informal investigations, checking out what is available commercially and noncommercially to serve the people. As if you were a teacher at a school in your study area, identify agencies available for kids and parents. Find out where people live, whether they probably rent or probably own, what jobs are around for them to work at, and so forth.

In order to understand how things got the way they are, you must learn what is *relevant* to the history of the city in terms of the issues it faces today. However, this is not a history project, as interesting as that might be on its own. Every historical fact you choose to focus on must somehow connect to what you are learning about the area, as it is now for the people who live there.

Your task will be to get *all* possible perspectives. That means, as well as hearing from the representatives of the Housing Authority, the mayor's office, or the police department, you will find community "leaders" other than those formally "in charge." Look for nongovernment and nonprofit agencies, such as soup kitchens, and look for coalitions of residents organized to bring about change from the grassroots. Talk to a range of residents (not just store owners). If one person's perceptions contradict someone else's, so much the better—you'll be getting in touch with the full complexity of a whole community!

Get a feel for what's there for the people and what life may be like for the people who live there. Be a genuine customer in stores, both enjoying and at the same time checking out how prices and quality might be different from what you're accustomed to, and analyzing why. Go to public events! Count the churches, laundromats, liquor stores, and so forth, within a certain radius. Figure out what those data mean, perhaps by comparison with your own neighborhood. Attend a church service. Ride a city bus. Do your own laundry at a laundromat and talk to the people there. Wait in a line (or stand near it) in the post office, noticing everything about the other people there. Imagine that you live in that community, and really, for a while, *do!*

It may be very useful to do a parallel visit or count in your own home community, for comparison and contrast.

Follow up on your informal data collection by doing what you can to gather a few relevant and significant official statistics about tax base, and about who lives there, who owns and who rents, and so forth. Analyze your data: figure out what it all means. If there are many rental properties, for example, see if you can find out who owns them. Who owns the businesses? What can you find out about the history of the place? What relevance does that history have to the economic situation now? See it from this perspective: What would a teacher need to know about the area in which his or her students live, in order to understand, literally, *where they might be coming from?*

In order to find an even deeper understanding of the culture of the community, see if you can research, *respectfully and as much from the inside as possible,* an aspect or combination of aspects that interests you about the music, art, dance, religion, festivals, foods, history, language, style, and so forth, that might be representative of the neighborhood or area you have chosen. Attending community cultural events, or visiting the Arts Collective (Hartford) or some other agency, would be a start.

To share your findings with the class, *you will be expected to represent what you have learned in whatever form is appropriate. However, lecturing or reading a report will not be considered appropriate. (See Presentations, later in this Appendix.)*

Service

As part of the fourteen hours, you are expected to give a minimum of six hours of service to the community you're studying. Choose a soup kitchen, a homeless shelter, a health-providing agency, a Habitat for Humanity project, a food cooperative, Foodshare, a community garden, an oral history project, or any other program you can find that needs very short-term volunteers. The assignment will be *first* to *find out* what noncommercial community service exists, and then to give your service as needed to one of those agencies, as an in-depth way of understanding it from the inside, and giving back. *In choosing where to serve, remember that one main purpose is for you to stretch yourself beyond your familiar and comfortable boundaries.*

Journal

Throughout the entire process, keep a reflective journal:

- *Describe.* Record, with no editorializing, in as much rich detail as possible, what you discover about what's available and what's not, and what's going on. Try not to assume what you cannot verify.

- *Record all of your questions and comments about what you are trying, expecting, seeing, hearing, learning, thinking, and feeling.* This is where you reflect about what meaning you are getting out of the experience as you go along. Don't censor yourself here. *This may be the most important part.* It is only by putting everything out there that you can examine your ideas and feelings.
- *Connect all that you are directly experiencing with the readings, writings, and discussions we are doing in class.* Integrate the learning for yourself!

Presentations

The presentation is *not* to be a list of facts. Information is useful only in terms of the meaning you have made of it. As the syllabus indicates, while you are turning in your journal regularly and getting feedback from me about it, you and your group will have a small amount of time inside of class, *first* to make meaning of what you are learning and, *finally,* when you understand it all, to figure out how to represent it most effectively to the rest of us. *Presentations will begin November 8.*

Remember. This is a collaborative project, not an individual one. Each of you is expected to contribute equally in terms of ideas, energy, time, and effort; no one hitchhikes. But even if you decide as a group to divide up certain tasks outside of class, you will be expected to make important decisions as a group. It may be an opportunity to use your conflict-resolution skills—as you develop them!

In Public School Classrooms (sixteen hours)

For the most part, visitors are not welcome in the schools before the middle of October, when children have finished with the Connecticut Mastery Tests. We need to respect the schools' decisions about visitors.

Depending on your prior experience, you will be moving from careful observation to active involvement in public school classrooms in both elementary and middle schools. You may spend eight hours in each of two school settings to learn as much as you can about each school as a community for learning, or to divide your three observations into three different schools: urban, suburban, and rural. Although one hour in each school is not a fulfillment of this assignment, apportioning the time will be up to you. These visits to schools are beyond the community service component of the course, but if the teacher is willing to allow you to tutor one child, or to work with a very small group of children while you are there, and if you feel ready, that would be some wonderful learning.

I will recommend some particular classrooms that model what research considers to be best practices, as well as a range of schools that would be appropriate to visit. You may check with me about possible choices, but you are also invited to make inquiries on your own. One restriction: you may not spend more than two of the required hours in the school you went to as a child. Most of your time should be in your area of demographic study. You will be expected to document your visits honestly and reflectively, thinking of your visits in terms of our readings and discussions.

In addition to your own visits, I have arranged for us to take "field trips" as a class to certain schools during the semester. These visits can serve as introductions to buildings, principals, neighborhoods, teachers, and children in the process of learning. You are welcome to make your own follow-up arrangements thereafter with those particular schools. There may be an opportunity to work with children even while we are there.

Observing in a Classroom

Make arrangements with the school secretary. Don't try to work through the principal. If possible, however, you might try to have a very brief conversation with the principal, to introduce yourself and your goals, and to see how you can fit in with, contribute to, and learn from what is going on. Many principals are not available to talk with you, but all would appreciate the courtesy of your attempt. Spend most of your time in the classroom!

Remember. You are in a classroom *not* to learn the lesson the teacher is teaching, but to notice everything you can about what is going on, and to pay attention to and reflect on your own reactions in terms of your own early experience of school, and in terms of everything we are learning in class.

Each time you observe a lesson, notice what intelligences, points of view, and so on, the teacher has chosen, and exactly how you can tell. Be very specific there. (*Note:* writing, coloring, and workbook drills are *not* "kinesthetic" tasks.) Then, increasingly as the semester goes along, beginning to imagine yourself the teacher, reflect on what you might do differently, and why. In addition to noticing the number of computers available to children, try to observe what tasks they do on the computers.

Participating

The nature of your active involvement will depend on what you feel ready to do, and what the host teacher needs to have you do: tutor, work with a small group, try the class opening, or a class meeting, or a full-class lesson—whatever you and the teacher decide on together. Your report on such an experience should, again, include both description and reflection.

You are there not to judge but to figure out what this complex job of teaching is about for you. *Reflect!*

Observing Beyond the Classroom

Go to school committee and Parent Teacher Organization meetings in the two districts, as well as to special evening events put on by the school. If invited, go to other meetings teachers participate in: middle school cluster meetings, lunch or other joint planning periods, union meetings, faculty meetings, and so forth. *If they can spare the time, interview a custodian and a secretary.* Volunteer to help supervise at recess or the lunchroom. See the school from the inside and from every possible perspective. *Reflect!*

In terms of your demographic study, it will be useful both to find out the "day jobs" held by the members of the school board and to attend a school board meeting.

Reporting

As you observe in a classroom, draw a fast (thirty-second) *diagram* of the way the room is laid out. Then take enough *notes* to process everything you are seeing, hearing, and feeling, especially but not exclusively in terms of all the reading, writing, and dialoguing we have been doing so far. Ask all the *questions* you would have asked the teacher if she or he had had time to sit down with you for two hours (which they will probably not!). Look from many approaches. The observation report should include *both description and reflection*. One without the other will not be enough.

Note: Interpret *only* in terms of what you actually see and hear. Try not to make *any* inferences that you can't back up with your own direct observations—but don't censor your questions. If you find yourself assuming, write down your assumption and then reflect on where it might be coming from. You are to be learning about schools, kids, teachers, learning, and teaching—but mostly about yourself as you think about all of these things. Let all of that be involved in what you write.

The Reader Response Paper

You are asked to respond to the assigned readings with a reader response paper—two to three pages typed double-spaced, with two photocopies to share in class, including a list of questions described below.

Reader response is different from other writing. Its intent is to allow you to become a more active reader. It captures your own thoughts as you read, encouraging you to explore your own insights into the reading. Instead of waiting for class discussion to "pull answers," reader response invites *you* to ask the questions that take you deeper into the text.

What a Reader Response Isn't

It is *not* the traditional summary or "book report" of the reading. The only functions of a summary are (1) to inform or to refresh the teacher's memory of the book or (2) to prove to the teacher that you have done the assignment. But I will have reread all the texts, and I fully expect and trust you will have done the assignments.

It is *not* the traditional judgment of the reading, persuading, or arguing a position. Agree or disagree statements are inappropriate here, because not having had the experiences that the authors have had, you cannot judge whether they're describing those experiences accurately. All you can say is: (1) whether what they describe speaks to experiences you have had or not; (2) how you relate to what they describe; (3) whether their conclusions make sense to you, given the evidence they provide; and (4) what questions and feelings they raise for you.

But this is not about censoring your reactions. If the writer's viewpoint makes you uncomfortable, *say that, and say exactly why!* You're not in debate with the writer, not out to win or defend your position; you are in the process of figuring out why *you* think what you think. Being in collision over ways of seeing is a good way to examine that. Be open—not to swallowing whole whatever you read but to rethinking assumptions.

It is *not* note taking on "important facts" for a test. I do not give tests.

If it's not any of that, what is it, then?

Reader response is the written record of a personal engagement with the text, of having really listened to both someone else and the self. A reader response starts from thinking about what you already know about what the writer is talking about, from your own personal direct experiences with learning and teaching, in and out of school. It is two-dimensional seeing: active reading. It is a way to discover what you think.

Step-by-Step Process for Reader Response

In doing active reading, take the following steps:

1. Even as you're reading, *right away start talking back on paper!* You will have to get used to writing in the book, another taboo. Jot down *notes on your own thinking* in the margins, or on separate paper if it is not your own book. Underline. Your job is to engage with the book or the article or story. Allow yourself to have *a conversation, a mutually respectful dialogue,* with the writer, to whom you're listening carefully. See what she or he is saying, trace interesting patterns, and find connections with what you already know or think you know.

   Don't rush to finish the text. Listen carefully to your own reactions as you read. Don't brush them aside, but take time to hear them, record them, and especially take time to sort out and record where they might be coming from. This is the stuff that will be uniquely *your* response to the text, because no one else has lived your exact life. Go back and forth between the text and your own remembering, reflecting, wondering, and so forth, including whatever else you are reading and directly experiencing in this course and any other. *Making connections* is the key. You may have to get used to reading this way, but the struggle itself may give you some useful information about how you've been taught to read and what that might mean for your teaching.

2. *While you're doing all of that,* keep an ongoing list of the questions you hope the text will have answered by the time you finish it. What are you not getting? What confuses you? What do you need more information about?

3. Keep some sort of record of compelling passages from the text that you think you will want to return to.

When you finish reading,

4. Go back and skim your own marginal notes and your underlining, trying to be sure you really understood what the writer meant and that you can differentiate the writer's voice from your own.

5. Next, capture your notes of dialogue on paper, in no particular form. At the same time, revise your list of questions to take account of the ones the text answered for you. Now think through and ask more completely those questions you are still puzzling about. Those questions will form a substantial part of the group conversation when we discuss the text in the next class session. They can come in separately from the paper itself, or be included in it, but they should not be *all* that the paper does.

6. Do a freewrite that shapes and develops the notes you've taken. *Your* thinking is what we're after here, with lots of specifics from both the text and from your own experience. As you write, let yourself discover where the new ideas have taken you. Remember, this is a new way of writing: not to prove anything, or to sum anything up, but to figure out what you think about some possibly new ideas, and why.

7. You may want to revise, based on what you find or don't find. But *do* proofread at the very end, and fix! I do not want to have to wade through a heavily corrected draft, but I appreciate seeing penned-in changes in spelling and punctuation on a typed sheet. They indicate *you* have read the final copy you want me to read. This stage is like dusting just before company comes, after you've constructed or remodeled your house.

Involving the Self While Being True to the Text

To do these writings, it is necessary that you feel free to use the word "I." At the beginning of the semester, you may have to struggle to give yourself permission to do that. I do not want you to distance yourself from these readings. You don't need to worry about *saying something intelligent* in these papers; you do need to let yourself be passionate, reflective, and thoughtful, careful of the text (which means that skimming is not enough), so that what comes through in the paper is your personal experience of reading the text.

There are no right answers. We need everyone's responses.

Grading "Rubric"

Expectations. As I try to help you "get" the complexity of the content of the course, I monitor and try to nurture your growth over time toward:

- A clear understanding of the complex material of the course
- Overcoming reading for performing, remembering, or arguing; instead, reading for meaning
- Responsibility to the group, however configured
- Examination of assumptions
- Original construction of knowledge
- Seeing patterns, making connections
- Practicing strategies taught in the course
- Developing the habit of multiple perspectives
- Achieving depth below the surface in *all* reading—in writing, observing, and reflecting

Details on this process will be given as the end of the semester approaches.

Because I understand this grading policy may be completely different from what most students have experienced before, I welcome your coming to see me or writing to me about whatever anxieties you might feel at any time.

Systems of Privilege and Advantage*

Process: Raise your hand if the statement is true for you as we disclose them on the overhead, one by one. At the end of our full discussion of each set of statements (each system of privilege and advantage), identify your place, above or below the line, indicating either advantaged or disadvantaged, before we go on to the next system (Figure 7.2, page 133). This whole exercise may take two to three hours, over several days.

1. Ableism

I can go along any sidewalk, approaching any intersection to cross a street, without having to consider whether there will be a curb cut for a wheelchair.

I can enter any building and have access to anyplace in it without having to look around for a ramp or an elevator.

I can assume that someone wanting to know what I think and how I feel will address his or her questions to me, not to my caregiver.

2. Religious Dominance

I can expect my employer to respect my major religious holidays, and especially my holy days.

When I go into a large supermarket in December, I can expect to find plenty of cards, foods, decorations, candles, and other materials to help me celebrate my religious or cultural holiday.

If people not of my religion visit my place of worship, or hear about what we believe, I can expect that they will respect my beliefs and mode of worship.

3. Sexism

I can wear whatever I want to wear, and go wherever I want to go, without being told I have provoked a sexual assault.

I can exercise, jog, or walk in a public place without having to think about being seen as a sexual object.

I can attend a class or a professional or public meeting and expect that my gender will not interfere with my views being taken seriously.

4. Heterosexism/Homophobia

If I am hospitalized, I can be assured that my life partner will be allowed to visit me as "immediate family," without being kept out because we are not married.

I can walk in public, holding hands with the person I love, without having to worry that someone will stare, say something unkind, or attack us.

When I die, my life partner can expect to collect my life insurance and keep custody of our children.

5. Classism

I can buy groceries without being subjected to stares of disapproval at the checkout counter for what foods I have chosen or what currency I use.

I can expect that my children's teacher will assume I care about my children and their education, even if I don't show up for Open House, PTO meetings, or routine conferences.

Whatever section of town I live in, I can expect teachers to assume that my home is a clean, safe, loving, and caring environment for my children.

I can assume that when I speak, people will focus on the content of what I say, not on whether my grammar is correct.

6. Ethnocentrism: Language and Culture

I can expect to enjoy a conversation in my own language at the lunch table without being accused of excluding others.

I can expect books honoring my culture and family structure to be available in my children's classroom and library.

7. Racism (These are taken almost verbatim from the McIntosh article, pp. 10–11.)

If I should decide to move, I can be pretty sure of being shown housing and feeling welcome wherever I'd be able to afford and be interested in moving to.

I can be pretty sure that my neighbors in such a location will be neutral or pleasant to me.

I can choose "nude" stockings, and more or less have them match my skin.

I can go into any hairdresser's shop and find someone who can comfortably and expertly deal with my hair.

I can choose taxis or restaurants, or any other public accommodations, without fearing that people of my race will not be allowed in, or will be mistreated or ignored.

Whether I use checks, credit cards, or cash, I can count on my skin color not to work against the appearance of financial reliability.

I can remain oblivious of the language and customs of persons of color (who constitute the world's majority), and still do fine in school, business, and everyday life.

I am never asked to speak for all the people of my racial group.

I can swear, or dress in old or secondhand clothes, or not answer letters, without having people attribute these choices to the "bad morals," "poverty," or "illiteracy" thought to be characteristic of my race.

I can go shopping, pretty well assured that I will not be monitored within the store because of my race.

I can be sure that if I need legal or medical help, my race will not be held against me.

I can do well in a challenging situation without being called "a credit to my race."

If a traffic cop pulls me over, or if the IRS audits my tax return, I can be sure I haven't been singled out because of my race.

I can be sure that my children will be given curricular materials that testify to the existence of their race.

When I am told about our national heritage or about "civilization," I am shown that people of my color made it what it is.

I can easily buy posters, postcards, picture books, greeting cards, dolls, toys, books, and magazines featuring people of my race.

I can turn on the TV or open the newspaper and see people of my race widely and respectfully represented.

I can take a job with an affirmative action employer without having coworkers on the job suspect that I got it because of race.

If my day, week, or year is going badly, I need not ask of each negative episode or situation whether it has racial overtones.

* This exercise uses the concept of white privilege, as developed by Peggy McIntosh ("White Privilege: Unpacking the Invisible Knapsack," Peace and Freedom, *July–August 1989). The statements stimulating discussion of the other systems were invented to set a context for understanding racism in terms of white privilege, and to show that an individual person can be both advantaged and disadvantaged within our society.*

References

Aaronsohn, E. *Going Against the Grain: Supporting the Student-Centered Teacher.* Thousand Oaks, Calif.: Corwin Press, 1996.

Aaronsohn, E., Holmes, J. H., Foley, T., and Wallowitz, J. "Teacher Pleasing, Traditional Grading—and Learning?" Study of extrinsic vs. intrinsic motivation in elementary, secondary, and post-secondary students. Presented at AACTE, Chicago, 1994.

American Association of University Women. *How Schools Shortchange Girls: The AAUW Report: A Study of Major Findings on Girls and Education.* New York: Marlowe and Company, 1995.

Anderson, G. L., and Herr, K. "The New Paradigm Wars: Is There Room for Rigorous Practitioner Knowledge in Schools and Universities?" *Educational Researcher,* 1999, *28*(5), 12–20.

Aronson, E. *The Jigsaw Classroom.* Thousand Oaks, Calif.: Sage, 1978.

Ashton-Warner, S. *Teacher.* New York: Simon & Schuster, 1963.

Belenky, M. F., Clinchy, B. M., Goldberger, N. R., and Tarule, J. M. *Women's Ways of Knowing: The Development of Self, Voice, and Mind.* New York: Basic Books, 1986.

Betances, S. Keynote address to the Every Teacher, Every Child conference. Meriden, Conn., March 30, 2001.

Bigelow, B. "Discovering Columbus: Rereading the Past." In B. Bigelow and B. Peterson (eds.), *Rethinking Columbus.* Milwaukee, Wisc.: Rethinking Schools, 1998.

Bigelow, B. *Rethinking Our Classrooms: Teaching for Equity and Justice.* Vol. 2. Milwaukee, Wisc.: Rethinking Schools, 2001.

Boulding, E. *Cultures of Peace: The Hidden Side of History.* Syracuse, N.Y.: Syracuse University Press, 2000.

Brandes, D., and Ginnis, P. *A Guide to Student-Centered Learning.* Oxford, UK: Basil Blackwell, Ltd., 1986.

Britzman, D. "Cultural Myths in the Making of a Teacher." *Harvard Education Review,* Nov. 1986, pp. 85–94.

Callahan, R. E. *Education and the Cult of Efficiency: A Study of the Social Forces That Have Shaped the Administration of the Public Schools.* Chicago: University of Chicago Press, 1962.

Campbell, E. Letter to the Editor: "Only Co-ed Schooling Can Prepare Women for the Real World." *New York Times,* March 6, 1988.

Cartwright, M., and D'Orso, M. *For the Children: Lessons from a Visionary Principal.* New York: Doubleday, 1998.

Collins, J. L., and Seidman, I. E. "Language and Secondary Schooling: The Struggle for Meaning." *English Education,* 1980, *12,* 5–9.

Committee for Children. *Second Step: Violence Prevention for Preschool Through Grade 9.* 2203 Airport Way S., Suite 500, Seattle, Wash. 98134–2035.

Elbow, P. *Writing with Power: Techniques for Mastering the Writing Process.* New York: Oxford University Press, 1981.

Faber, A., and Mazlish, E. *How to Talk So Kids Will Listen, and Listen So Kids Will Talk.* New York: Avon Books, 1980.

Faber, A., and Mazlish, E., with Nyberg, L., and Templeton, R. *How to Talk So Kids Can Learn at Home and in School.* New York: Simon & Schuster, 1995.

Finders, M., and Lewis, C. "Why Some Parents Don't Come to School." *The Best of Educational Leadership,* May 1994, pp. 15–18.

Fischetti, J. A., and Aaronsohn, E. "Collaboration Starts Inside Schools of Education: Teacher Educators as Collaborators." In H. Schwartz (ed.), *Collaboration: Building Common Agendas.* New York: Teachers College Press, 1990.

Freire, P. *Pedagogy of the Oppressed.* Translated by Myra Bergman. New York: Continuum, 1968.

Gardner, H. *Multiple Intelligences: The Theory in Practice.* New York: Basic Books, 1993.

Gilligan, C. *In a Different Voice: Psychological Theory and Women's Development.* Cambridge, Mass.: Harvard University Press, 1982.

Goals 2000: Educate America Act. [http://www.ed.gov/legislation/GOALS2000/TheAct/].

Gordon, T. *T.E.T.: Teacher Effectiveness Training.* New York: Wyden, 1974.

Haberman, M. "Should College Youth Be Prepared for Teaching?" *Educational Forum,* 1992, *57*(1), 30–36.

Haberman, M. "The Pedagogy of Poverty Versus Good Teaching." In W. Ayers and P. Ford (eds.), *City Kids, City Teachers: Reports from the Front Row.* New York: New Press, 1996.

Hale, J. *Black Children: Their Roots, Culture, and Learning Styles.* Baltimore: Johns Hopkins University Press, 1982.

Holt, J. *How Children Learn.* New York: Dell, 1967.

Johnson, V. "Anti-Democratic Attitudes of High School Students." Unpublished doctoral dissertation, Rutgers University, 1986.

Johnson, D. W, and Johnson, R. T. Learning *Together and Alone: Cooperative, Competitive, and Individualistic Learning.* 1975.

Johnson, D. W., Johnson, R. T., Holubec, E. J., and Roy, P. *Circles of Learning: Cooperation in the Classroom.* Alexandria, Va.: Association for Supervision and Curriculum Development, 1984.

Kohlberg, L., and Mayer, R. "Development as the Aim of Education." *Harvard Education Review, 42*(4), 449–496. 1972.

Kohn, A. *No Contest: The Case Against Competition.* Boston: Houghton Mifflin, 1986.

Kohn, A. *Punished by Rewards: The Trouble with Gold St*rs, Incentive Plan$, A's, Praise, and Other Bribes.* Boston: Houghton Mifflin, 1993.

Kohn, A. *Beyond Discipline: From Compliance to Community.* Alexandria, Va.: Association for Supervision and Curriculum Development, 1996.

Kohn, A. *The Schools Our Children Deserve: Moving Beyond Traditional Classrooms and "Tougher Standards."* Boston and New York: Houghton Mifflin, 1999.

Kohn, A. *The Case Against Standardized Testing.* Portsmouth, N.H.: Heinemann, 2000.

Kozol, J. *Death at an Early Age: The Destruction of the Hearts and Minds of Negro Children in the Boston Public Schools.* Boston: Houghton Mifflin, 1967.

Kozol, J. *Rachel and Her Children: Homeless Families in America.* New York: Fawcett Columbine, 1988.

Kozol, J. *Savage Inequalities: Children in America's Schools.* New York: HarperCollins, 1991.

Kozol, J. *Ordinary Resurrections: Children in the Years of Hope.* New York: Crown, 2000.

Labinowitz, E. *The Piaget Primer: Thinking, Learning, Teaching.* Menlo Park, Calif.: Addison-Wesley, 1980.

Ladson-Billings, G. *Crossing Over to Canaan: The Journey of New Teachers in Diverse Classrooms.* San Francisco: Jossey-Bass, 2001.

"Learning to Teach for Empowerment." *Radical Teacher,* 1990, no. 40, pp. 44–46.

Levin, J., and Shanken-Kaye, J. *The Self-Control Classroom: Understanding and Managing the Disruptive Behavior of All Students, Including Those with ADHD.* Dubuque, Iowa: Kendall Hunt, 1996.

Loewen, J. W. *Lies My Teacher Told Me: Everything Your American History Textbook Got Wrong.* New York: New Press, 1995.

Lorde, A. Lecture at Williams College. Williamstown, Mass., 1984.

McIntosh, P. "Interactive Phases of Curricular Development." Women's Studies Lecture, Greenfield Community College, April 11, 1985.

McIntosh, P. "White Privilege: Unpacking the Invisible Knapsack." *Peace and Freedom,* July–August 1989.

McIntosh, P. "Interactive Phases of Curricular and Personal Re-vision with Regard to Race." Working Paper no. 219. Wellesley, Mass.: Center for Research on Women, 1990.

Miller, A. *For Your Own Good: Hidden Cruelty in Child Rearing and the Roots of Violence.* New York: Farrar, Straus & Giroux, 1980).

Moses, R. *Radical Equations: Math Literacy and Civil Rights.* Boston: Beacon Press, 2001.

Nederhood B. "The Effects of Student Team Learning on Academic Achievement, Attitudes Toward Self and School, and Expansion of Friendship Bonds Among Middle School Students." Unpublished doctoral dissertation, University of Washington, Seattle, 1986.

Nieto, S. *Affirming Diversity: The Sociopolitical Context of Multicultural Education.* White Plains, N.Y.: Longman, 1992.

Nieto, S. *The Light in Their Eyes.* New York: Teachers College Press, 1999.

Oakes, J. *Keeping Track: How Schools Structure Inequality.* Birmingham, N.Y.: Vail-Ballou Press, 1985.

Petry, A. *The Street.* Boston: Beacon Press, 1946.

Polakow, V. *Lives on the Edge: Single Mothers and Their Children in the Other America.* Chicago and London: University of Chicago Press, 1993.

Rubin, L. *Worlds of Pain: Life in the Working-Class Family.* New York: Basic Books, 1976.

Sarason, S. B. *The Culture of the School and the Problem of Change.* Boston: Allyn & Bacon, 1982.

Schniedewind, N., and Davidson, E. *Cooperative Learning, Cooperative Lives: A Sourcebook of Learning Activities for Building a Peaceful World.* Dubuque, Iowa: W. C. Brown, 1987.

Sennett, R., and Cobb, J. *The Hidden Injuries of Class.* New York: Random House, 1972.

Sharan, S. *Cooperative Learning in the Classroom: Research in Desegregated Schools.* Hillsdale, N.J.: Erlbaum, 1984.

Sharan, S., and Sharan, Y. *Small Group Teaching.* Englewood Cliffs, N.J.: Educational Technology Publications, 1976.

Slavin, R. *Learning to Cooperate, Cooperating to Learn.* New York: Plenum, 1985.

Smith, F. *Insult to Intelligence: The Bureaucratic Invasion in Our Classrooms.* Westminster, Md.: Arbor House, 1986.

Steptoe, J. *Mufaro's Beautiful Daughters.* New York: Lothrop, Lee & Shepard, 1987.

Tatum, B. D. *"Why Are All the Black Kids Sitting Together in the Cafeteria?" and Other Conversations About Race.* New York: Basic Books, 1997.

Zeichner, K. M. "Key Processes in the Socialization of Student Teachers: Limitations and Consequences of Oversocialized Conceptions of Teacher Socialization." Paper presented at the annual meeting of the American Educational Research Association, Boston, Mass., April 1980.

Index

erative learning approach taken by, 193–197; uncertainty/s faced by, 182–185. *See also* Traditional teachers

"Teacher's pet" label, 84

Teaching: to create collaborative classrooms, 83–84; enlarging range of teaching options for, 216–218; final word about courage and, 240–242; multiple perspectives, 74, 75, 103–125, 136–139; overcoming poverty of imagination to improve, 185–188; performance metaphors used for, 144–145; scholarly presentation lecture method of, 148–149; structural differences between elementary/secondary, 142–144. *See also* Traditional teaching/schooling

Teaching activities: including "reflective teaching" mini-lessons in, 163–164; "Musical Chairs," 83, 130–132; My Place in Terms of Privilege and Advantage, 132–134, 133fig; reader responses, 10–13, 31–34, 33fig, 44–49, 224–226; The Ten Chairs, 127–130, 128fig, 176–177; Three–reader groups, 90–97; "With the Odds Against Them" card game, 132

The Ten Chairs activity (United for a Fair Economy), 127–130, 128fig, 176–177

Testing: high stakes, 155–158, 200; internalized pressure/anxiety over, 49–51; of knowledge, 152; negative educational impact of focus on, 188; pressures on accountability and standardized, 97–99, 154–155; reflections on standardized, 221–222; teaching reading without, 30–44; withdrawing grades as exposing problems in, 19–21

TET (Teacher Effectiveness Training), 222

Textbooks: Columbus story in traditional, 107–109, 110–111, 112; dominant culture representation in, 105–106; geography curriculum, 109–110. *See also* Curriculum

Three-reader groups: jigsaw method used in, 94–95; respectful attention element of, 93–97; successful cooperation in, 90–92

Title IX, 172

Tracking students: development of competition and, 84; high stakes testing, of judgment and, 155–158

Traditional teachers: ethos of individuality and autonomy of, 177–179; "institutional realities" concerns of, 169–170; language of combat used by, 61–62; playing the expected role, 57–61; power position of, 60–61; time concerns expressed by, 158–162; uncertainty/s faced by, 182–185. *See also* Teachers

Traditional teaching/schooling: competition as part of, 84–85; defining, 1; individualism assumption of, 175–177; influence of Puritan culture on, 180–181; "institutional realities" concerns of, 169–170; lecture–test (or banking) model of, 169; long-range social significance of, 99–102; negative outcomes of, 100, 103; poverty of imagination suffered by, 185–188; process of overcoming, 214–215; resulting in habits that interfere with learning, 6–8; students on rethinking notions of, 16–17; as teacher education outcome, 14–15; unintended but predictable outcomes of, 104–106;

Becoming Multicultural Educators
Personal Journey Toward Professional Agency

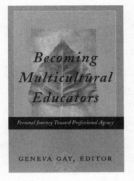

Geneva Gay
$29.00 Cloth
ISBN: 0-7879-6514-6

"Teachers won't be able to put this book down. In its personal stories, we see ourselves and our students, our visions, our uncertainties, our questions, and the sense we make of our teaching today. Multicultural teaching is a highly personal endeavor, which this book makes poignantly visible."
—**Christine Sleeter, California State University, Monterey Bay**

To help both new and seasoned teachers to become more effective with their students from diverse backgrounds, *Becoming Multicultural Educators,* edited by Geneva Gay, offers fourteen compelling stories from different regions, cultures, ethnic groups, and stages of professional and personal growth. Through these stories, we share their struggles as these educators develop their multicultural awareness, knowledge and skills by coming to understand diversity among ethnic groups and cultures, resolve conflicts between curricular and multicultural goals, and find authentic models and mentors for their students. But most important, we learn how this laudatory group of educators has come to realize that they need to know themselves if they are to truly know their students. Well-grounded in educational theory, *Becoming Multicultural Educators* is both personal and inspiring. This is the book that will help teachers, and those who prepare them, blossom as educators and human beings.

Geneva Gay is professor of education at the University of Washington, Seattle. Known for her scholarship in multicultural education, she is the author of numerous articles and books. In 2001 she received the Outstanding Writing Award from the American Association of Colleges for Teacher Education (AACTE).

(Price subject to change.)

Other Books of Interest

Intellectual Character
What It Is, Why It Matters, and How to Get It

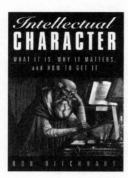

Ron Ritchhart
$24.95 Cloth
ISBN: 0-7879-5683-X

"Intellectual Character *is that rare book that successfully translates deep, complex ideas into accessible prose and illuminates key concepts with compelling examples from real classrooms. It breaks new ground by demonstrating that when skillfully guided by teachers who themselves act intelligently, students are eager to engage in meaningful, rigorous learning. Very helpful!"*
—**Tony Jackson, author,** *Turningpoints 2000: Educating Adolescents for the 21st Century*

The way we define intelligence shapes the education we provide our children. But what does it really mean to be intelligent? Ron Ritchhart presents a new and powerful view of intelligence that moves beyond ability to focus on cognitive dispositions such as curiosity, skepticism, and open-mindedness. Arguing persuasively for this new conception of intelligence, the author uses vivid classroom vignettes to explore the foundations of intellectual character and describe how teachers can enculturate productive patterns of thinking in their students. *Intellectual Character* presents illustrative, inspiring stories of exemplary teachers to help show how intellectual traits and thinking dispositions can be developed and cultivated in students to promote successful learning. This vital book provides a model of authentic and powerful teaching and offers practical strategies for creating classroom environments that support thinking.

Ron Ritchhart is a researcher at Harvard University's Project Zero, where he has worked on a number of projects focusing on the development of thinking, understanding, and creativity in schools. He spent fourteen years as a classroom teacher and received the Presidential Award for Excellence in Teaching in Mathematics. He is the author of several books, including *Making Numbers Make Sense*.

(Price subject to change.)

Other Books of Interest

Learning to Trust
Transforming Difficult Elementary Classrooms Through Developmental Discipline

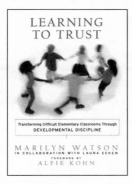

Marilyn Watson with Laura Ecken
$29.00 Cloth
ISBN: 0-7879-6650-9

In *Learning to Trust,* an educational psychologist and a classroom teacher collaborate on an in-depth case study in an inner-city classroom, told through the teacher's own voice. Using these real-life examples, they demonstrate the power and importance of caring and trusting relationships for fostering not only children's social and ethical development but also their academic growth. Based on The Child Development Project, a federally approved model for school reform and drug abuse prevention, this book will help teachers meet the challenge to care, balance their need for authority with their students' need for autonomy, and support their students' intellectual growth.

- Applies child development and attachment theory to classroom management.
- Uses research-proven methods to tackle classroom challenges and difficult children by building a positive learning environment
- Describes ways to meet the individual needs of students without sacrificing the well-being of the class as a whole
- Builds empathy through an accessible, case-study approach that involves and captivates readers.
- Offers strategies that help children understand how to develop the emotional, social, and communication skills to work collaboratively with classmates and the personal and moral understanding to be caring and responsible.

Marilyn Watson (PhD, UC-Berkeley) is a respected researcher, writer, university professor, and speaker in the areas of child development, character education, and schoolwide reform. She founded the Teacher Education Institute at the Developmental Studies Center (Oakland, CA) and was a lead architect of the Child Development Project.

Laura Ecken (MA, Spalding University) is a veteran teacher who taught second through fourth grades at Hazelwood Elementary School in Louisville, KY for thirteen years. She has done staff development for the Child Development Project, Kentucky's Ungraded Primary Program, and the Four Block Reading Model.

(Price subject to change)

Shaping School Culture
The Heart of Leadership

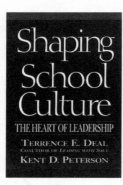

Terrence E. Deal & Kent D. Peterson
$21.00 Paperback
ISBN: 0-7879-6243-0

"No guidebook presents a better, more approachable path toward understanding and building a school culture than this one. I wish I had had Shaping School Culture *beside me during my own turbulent years as a school principal!"*
—**Roland S. Barth, educator and author of**
  Improving Schools from Within

Using real-life cases, over twenty years of research on school improvement, and their own extensive work with school leaders across the country, Deal and Peterson identify viable new strategies for effective school leadership. They reveal the key symbolic roles that leaders play in school change and identify the specific skills needed to change school culture successfully. By describing the critical elements of culture—the purposes, traditions, norms, and values that guide and glue the community together—they provide an action blueprint for school leaders committed to transforming their schools for success. Deal and Peterson also explore the harmful characteristics of toxic cultures and suggest antidotes to negativity on the part of teachers. students, principals, or parents. *Shaping School Culture* offers concrete, detailed illustrations of exemplary practice in different school cultures and is a companion to *Shaping School Culture Fieldbook* (0-7879-5680-5).

Terrence E. Deal is professor of educational leadership at Peabody College, Vanderbilt University. He is author or co-author of numerous books, including the best-selling *Leading with Soul, The Leadership Paradox,* and *Reframing Organizations* (all from Jossey-Bass).

Kent D. Peterson is professor in the Department of Educational Administration at the University of Wisconsin-Madison and founding director of the Vanderbilt Principals' Institute. He is author or coauthor of many books, including *The Leadership Paradox.*

(Price subject to change)